BENEATH THE DARK HILL

Life & Wildlife in the Scottish Lowlands

BENEATH THE DARK HILL

Life & Wildlife in the Scottish Lowlands

CHRIS FERRIS

SWAN·HILL
PRESS

First published in the UK in 1995 by Swan Hill Press
an imprint of Airlife Publishing Ltd

British Library Cataloguing in Publication Data
  A catalogue record for this book
  is available from the British Library

ISBN 1 85310 563 5

Typeset by Hewer Text Composition Services, Edinburgh
Printed in England by St. Edmundsbury Press Ltd, Bury St Edmunds, Suffolk

Swan Hill Press
an imprint of Airlife Publishing Ltd
101 Longden Road, Shrewsbury SY3 9EB

Contents

Introduction and Acknowledgements

This is a personal account of one woman's experiences in Scotland and is not intended to be an extensive survey into its history or wildlife.

I left Kent in south-east England to live in the Lowlands in 1991, first in lodgings and later as a tenant renting a small cottage. In the winter of 1992/3 I lived for four months in a shieling in the hills, hoping to observe otters in severe weather conditions.

My sincere thanks go to all the people who helped me and made this possible. Particularly to the farmers and factors who allowed me on their land, most of whom have wished to remain anonymous for the sake of privacy. Thus I have given them assumed names, together with the place names of their localities.

I would like to thank Mike Harris (and his wife Margaret) of the Grampian Badger Survey who has done so much for these animals in his region. Mike would be glad to know of any setts discovered in that area and any road traffic accident badgers seen on Grampian's roads. He can be contacted at South Skelmanae Croft, near Stricken, Fraserburgh, Aberdeenshire AB43 4QU or by telephone (01771) 653340.

Since the completion of this book in the summer of 1993 and its publication two years later, there have been some changes. The Forestry Authority has produced its *Forestry Practice Guide 9: Forest Operations and Badger Setts*. It is available from their Publication Section, Forest Research Station, Alice Holt Lodge, Farnham, Surrey GU10 4LH, telephone (01420) 22255.

Besides the Fife and Kinross group there are others now in Lanarkshire and Dumfries & Galloway. With such a small population however to its relative size, this country badly needs more of its people involved with badgers. Anyone living in Scotland who is interested can contact The Badger Conservation Officer, The National Federation of Badger Groups, 15 Cloisters Business Centre, 8 Battersea Park Road, London SW8 4BG or telephone 0171 498 3220.

My grateful thanks go also to Leigh Millward of Bristol for the use of his excellent badger photos and to my very good friend Carol Stephenson of Fordham, Essex for those of otters reproduced here.

Last, but certainly not least, I thank John Beaton of Airlife Publishing, himself a Scot, who had sufficient faith in the manuscript to want it published. I hope that faith proves justified!

Chris Ferris,
July 1995

CHAPTER ONE

A Stranger In Scotland

A nother White Settler,' remarked the lady on my being introduced as a newcomer to Scotland. Much later I heard the term again and asked the reason, this time from a Scotsman. 'Sounds as if you regard yourselves as Indians,' I said. 'That's right,' came the cheerful reply. 'We Scots are the natives and you English are the incomers, the White Settlers.'

The moment my gaze first rested on Dydor, the Dark Hill, was the moment I fell in love with the country. Though I have travelled far since, the months that I dwelt within its sight will always remain. This long, brooding hump is one of a range of hills, some steep, others gentle, that stretch for nearly sixteen miles; a wonderland for walkers and seekers of solitude except perhaps, on sunny weekends. Most times however, I shared them only with the red grouse, sheep and curlews. It was my first introduction to the startling explosion of 'go-bak, go-bak, go-bak-bak-bak' from the handsome grouse encountered on these slopes, though I never took the hint!

That first Sunday, 21 April 1991, I followed the route out of the village that led to the foot of the hills. At 7.30 a.m. it was a blustery morning with a chill in the air. A roe deer browsed in the shelter belt and two hares 'stood tall' like sentinels in a field, very brown against the verdant green of the young wheat. The air was filled with plaintive cries from the curlews and the maaing of many sheep. A light wind rippled the water of the loch that matched the blue of the sky. I crossed a bridge and looked back at the Scots pines mirrored there and the smooth, slow hump of the Dark Hill. The farther peak of sharp-etched Lytlaw had a wisp of cloud on its tip. Dew from the night sparkled on the mossy cushions of a dry-stone wall and beyond that was the moor with in the distance, what appeared to be tumbledown ruins. As I walked the track to have a closer look, the air seemed to tremble with longing – the calls of oystercatchers, lapwings and golden plover. I felt bemused by so many urgent lives.

The object of my interest turned out to be an old stone shieling, originally turf-roofed and slated only in latter years. Centuries ago, lowland areas close to the hills moved their grazing stock (mainly cows and young animals) to higher ground in summer and brought them back in the autumn; the shielings housed those who tended the animals. A bleak, inhospitable place in the winter months, but idyllic now when the weather was kind. I had no idea then how well I was to know the area of the shieling by night. Curiosity satisfied, I returned to look at an old farmhouse nearer the loch and its adjacent steadings. These were roofless now except for the house which had been renovated and was used by a local ornithologist who came whenever he could to watch and record the migratory birds and the flocks of geese and swans. Noisy black-headed gulls had gathered on the loch as a strengthening wind blew the water into deep ridges. Once children from the village had come here to skate as soon as the winter turned cold enough, but they would not know until they reached it whether the wind had caused an undulating surface of ice impossible to use.

Walking back along the lane, a small flock of lambs came hoppity-skip through the bars of their field gate, butting and scampering together in play. Fodder beets had been left inside the field on which their mothers were still feeding. As I approached, the more timorous lambs withdrew into the shadow of the stone walling. They scarcely allowed me to pass however, before they re-formed on the tarmac and continued their interrupted play. A white police car slowed to a crawl as a smiling officer saw the tiny truants ahead.

That evening I sat in the window of my room watching the dying sun touch the trees beyond the village turning them to fire. Behind them on the horizon, the light picked up the fresh shoots of heather on Dydor changing its darkness to green, as three formations of geese passed overhead into the gathering dusk. Would I ever go back to live in my home county of Kent? Somehow I doubted it.

On my walks I was continually on the look-out for signs of badgers, my abiding interest. Though there was a small sett, or badger home, in an old mound of clinker that at present seemed deserted, I was searching for something larger. In Kent these animals would have a large main sett, often consisting of many metres of underground tunnelling and perhaps eighteen to twenty-five entrances, plus variously sized other setts spaced about their territory. I was soon to find however, that Scottish badgers often failed to live up to my previous knowledge of the animal, which for me, made them all the more intriguing.

Most of the countryside belonged to old estates that had existed for centuries and the first thing that struck me about this part of Scotland was the shelter belts. A few of these were of conifer, but most near the village area were deciduous trees. The size of many fields was determined by the burns that tumbled down the steep slopes from the hills, to flow into the River Cley that meandered its way to the sea. The shelter belts had been planted with trees on either side of the burns to perhaps the width of a motorway making a narrow strip of woodland running for several miles, containing flowing water for all its length and bordered by crops or grazed fields. These connected the hills to the valleys and beauty apart, were corridors for wildlife, rather as we regard hedgerows in the south. Kent may retain remnants of its ancient woodlands, but the

Lothians have many beautiful trees of lime, sycamore, beech, oak, ash, cherry and birch.

It was in such a shelter belt beyond the village that, not entirely by chance, I saw my first badgers. There had been no obvious signs or scent of the animal, but somehow I felt that they must be about. For two nights I passed that way and loitered in hope without success. On the third I heard them well before I reached the spot – a sow and her two young cubs on the slopes below. She was urging them with much chittering to hurry on home with her, but they were tired and fearful of recrossing the fast-flowing burn. Darkness is rarely absolute except under close planted conifer, so it was easy enough to slip down by the side of the dry-stone wall to watch under cover of her fretful concern and their whimpering replies.

She trotted onto the rocks strewn about the rushing water. Halfway across her shaggy form turned and almost certainly she called them, but close as this the rushing of the surging current filled my ears. One cub came at her bidding and safely reached the mother. She bent to it briefly before continuing over as it followed close as a tiny shadow. Once across, the sow took stock of the forlorn little figure huddled unhappily on the far bank. She reared up bear-like on her hind legs and was undoubtedly calling though no sound came to me nor I suspect, to her cub. There was naught for it but to return.

Back on the bank she nosed the nervous one repeatedly, but each time she started out over the water it retreated to safety behind a great clump of primroses. Now first light was creeping into the landscape and the sow was anxious. Unceremoniously she grasped the cub by the back of its neck and carried it to midstream where she set it down on a rock. It looked around carefully from beneath its mother, then slowly they finished the journey together, she waiting patiently when the stones moved under its hesitant paws. Once over it forgot its fears and excitedly head-butted its sibling who had waited silently all this while for the family's return.

I stood on the far bank until they disappeared into a rocky overhang. What was there? Where was the sett and the rest of their clan? I was used to badgers living in social family groups, but had read that in the more rugged parts of Scotland and where food was scarce, these groups are much smaller and except for communal sleeping probably for warmth, were not the social animals I knew. The Lothian valleys are fertile however, so perhaps groups or clans interacted together more socially. There was so much to discover, so much to learn in this grand new country.

The bluebells growing on the grass verges surprised me, who knew them only as a woodland species, blooming before the leaves thickened on the trees, and I had never seen them bordering lanes before in such profusion. I walked between seas of blue to which were soon added masses of deep pink as the red campion came into bloom. The latter continued to flower intermittently throughout the summer, not only on the verges, but in the shelter belts too, but it was the bluebell that flourished so in the open spaces. The harebell is called bluebell in Scotland and the name wild hyacinth is given to what I knew as the bluebell, which at first caused me some confusion.

Early May was my first visit to the coast. It was a cold but sunny day with a choppy sea lapping the shore. I left the sand and went across to sit on the huge flat rocks nearer the seals just a few metres away watching me watching them. They had hauled themselves out and were basking on similar rocks to mine in the sea straight ahead of me. They occasionally barked and moaned to each other, individuals dropping back into the water to visit others on rocks a short distance off. These were common seals, though not so common as their name suggests. When basking they raised their tail ends and their heads to the sun making the shape of a crescent. On a later visit, a human swimmer was met by a seal that kept pace with him whilst others frolicked nearby, but that day the seals were too preoccupied sun worshipping to be interested in anyone prepared to brave the chill waters.

The cliff tops behind me were bright with flowering gorse. Some guillemots perched on the barren ledges whilst in the undisturbed water away from the seals, others dived for food. I forgot the seals in my interest in these birds that vanished and then surfaced a good distance from their dive one or two minutes later with fish in their dagger-like beaks. Guillemots I was to find, like puffins and razorbills, literally fly under water after their prey, using the wings for propulsion. When I came there a month later, crowds of guillemots jostled on the craggy ledges filling the air with cries of 'arr' that fast became a growling chorus as more and more struggled for a breeding site. With no nesting material the single egg is pear-shaped to ensure its survival. If pushed it will rotate in a small arc round its tip instead of rolling away, but in spite of this there were several smashed on the rocks far below. Standing upright, these guillemots reminded me somewhat of puffins, though with a longer, narrower head and sharper bill.

I found a sett one day well outside the village in one of the few shelter belts I knew that were planted on level, fertile ground. The tenant farmer of Clackmon gave me permission to go on his land whenever I wished to check for more setts and to watch the badgers themselves, but although he and his father before him had known this sett, he knew of only one other. That was two fields distant and dug into the open pasture where at present his sheep grazed. He owned a milking herd of cows too, so flock interchanged with herd in that field according to season and length of grass. Talking that morning I casually mentioned bovine TB to see his reaction. Oh, tuberculosis had been eradicated from cattle in Scotland years ago. In his opinion it wasn't connected with badgers in any case; that was merely hysteria speaking in parts of *my* country, he said. In the past badgers had been persecuted almost to extinction in the Lothians by gamekeepers on the lairds' estates; it was a miracle any survived. He and his wife were happy to have them on Clackmon, but I would have to go a fair distance to find any more. I often recalled his words in the following months for they had been an accurate appraisal of the situation.

Now my landlady had gone on holiday so I was walking the dogs and feeding and grooming her ponies. Moss was a gentle Exmoor, companion to Bramble a small, buxom Shetland. I noticed that Bramble had a jackdaw in attendance that stood on her back searching for parasites amongst her shedding coat. Unlike Moss, she didn't want me to brush her, but enjoyed the attentions of her avian friend. After tending the ponies, it was good to stand at the top of their field with the dogs, looking across the village to the hills. Sometimes the peaks would be shrouded in mist. At others the clarity of the air would bring them closer, clear-cut and vivid, but it was always the Dark Hill that held my attention with a great sense of wonder and joy. As the words of the psalm ran through my mind, 'I will lift up mine eyes unto the hills', I wondered if David's had drawn him as much as Dydor did me.

The first rain I had known in Scotland, gentle and persistent, fell that night. Suddenly the opening buds on the trees burst into tiny leaf that refused to stop growing. All along the Cley-side, the ramsons' white, star-like flowers appeared above their deep green leaves. Mountain and water avens, Jack-by-the-hedge, wild strawberry and pink purslane, all seemed intent on outdoing the others to prove that spring was really here. The whitebeam and wild cherry in leaf are a pretty sight as are the blackthorn and hawthorn in blossom.

One morning I walked along the burnside, the same I had seen the badgers cross, in an effort to trace its source in the hills. It was difficult going for the recent rains had swelled its waters so that they thundered and sprayed over their craggy bed. Huge clumps of primroses grew here sheltered by the rocky walls. Like a tiny spurge, opposite-leaved golden saxifrage flowered too, reminding me of my native woods. Here the burn had been dammed to form a pool deep enough for human bathing. Animal trails wound above me through the sitkas and I thought of the 'Burn Badgers' of the other night. Where did that sow and her cubs den? I could follow upstream no further as the burn rushed from a man-made cavern hung about with trailing ferns and shaggy mosses, forever weeping in the constant spray. The hillside above me was boggy. My sinking boots made walking difficult as the sphagnum relinquished them with more and more reluctance at each wrenching step.

At last the bog gave way to larch amongst outcrops of rock and the going was easier. I gained the crest of the steep slope and the end of the tree line where short, rabbit-cropped turf was firm now beneath my feet. A few metres on the ground dipped again and the loch was in view, waves slapping its rugged sides. The wind hadn't touched me in the deep ravine, but here a strong westerly blew sweeping the grey waters like an incoming tide. A pair of herons stood motionless a short distance out and over the far side mallard bobbed up and down on the choppy waves. Following the shoreline I came across badger spore in the mud, the five small pads in front of a much larger half-moon one are very distinctive. This badger had been moving slowly for the tracks of the smaller hind feet were superimposed on the front ones. A smooth, conical hole amongst the sedges and another a short distance away suggested this badger had been foraging for molluscs, most likely, the large black slug (*Arion ater*) so common here.

Now I was past the old shieling and in the shadow of the Dark Hill itself. The burn ran fast and free across the treeless moor that was dotted with black-faced sheep and their lambs. It briefly entered a small lochan then out onto steeper slopes. I came to its source unexpectedly – a spring leaping out of the ground. So this was the Dark Spring, child of Dydor. What underground caverns and tunnels did its heather-clad sides conceal? There was no way of knowing and no apparent path upwards to the top, but it wasn't difficult to scramble through bracken and heather, to the call of so many birds and stand gazing far over the lower hills to the sea. After that first hill-top encounter, I often walked the Dark Spring route to the summit. Misty or bright, it had many moods and each was a different experience. From the window of my room in the village, I had only to look up to be transported back to that long, brooding hill.

Sitting comfortably against a tree with my arms round my knees, I waited one evening in the shelter belt of Clackmon farm for its badgers to emerge. In front of me stretched the freshly dug-out earth or spoil heap from a sett entrance, covering the lush grass. The calls of crows and of ewes to their lambs seemed incredibly loud on the fields, only quietening as dusk fell. For the first time I was aware of the slight wind sighing in the branches above my head, but below there seemed to be no breeze at all either to take my scent as a warning to the badgers or to blow theirs (if I could have smelled it) to me. A white head with its startling black stripes appeared disembodied above the spoil as if looking straight at me. Knowing my sitting form would blend into the trunk to a creature with such poor eyesight, I merely waited chin on knees, completely still. The striped head turned this way and that and vanished, only to reappear complete with body, almost at once. A scratching to my left made me long to turn and see another clan member, but common sense told me that any movement on my part would be immediately noted and my watching ended.

For half an hour the first badger, a sturdy old boar with big cheek tufts, sat back exposing his chest and stomach and clawed through his belly fur with gusto. Although this undoubtedly helps remove parasites and dirt particles, watching him I had the impression that scratching was a thoroughly enjoyable occupation accompanied by grunts and huffs. The other badger, a far slighter creature, came over and helped clean him too, nibbling at his shoulders and haunches. This last turned out to be a young sow, possibly a yearling or cub from the previous year. She soon disappeared to the field and later, his grooming complete, the boar trotted off too, following the length of the shelter belt.

The sheep were much quieter and on quitting the trees I discovered the reason; they had moved over to the far side of the field. I followed a tiny burn in a dip and although now night, the stars and glittering sickle moon gave a good visibility. I passed through a stand of birches, many growing at a steep slant owing to the prevailing winds. Somewhere above me on the sloping pasture was the other sett the farmer had mentioned, its entrances dug into the open field. The lambs here were very noisy, congregating in a group of nine or ten, first lying together on the spoil heaps, then getting up to play chase and head-butting together over the sett. Sharp little hooves pounded the bare earth as the excitement mounted. A black and white head would appear, stare briefly at the nearest lamb and vanish. One lamb stuck its head down a hole and bleated after the retreating head. This did not improve matters for the badgers who wished to come out as it was late. Amidst the baas and maas could be heard sounds of grumbling and grunting from below. They didn't think much of their rowdy neighbours in the flat above! Much later I saw the badgers slip away into the birches from a farther entrance. I might not have found the Burn Badgers' sett, but I certainly enjoyed seeing the Clackmon clan at theirs.

One morning I took the dogs for a walk earlier than usual and stopped at the stables as they were on our route. Bramble peacefully grazed the field, but there was no sign of her companion. He must be in the open stable; strange for such a lovely day. Approaching quietly, I found Moss helping himself to hay from the closed stable next door. The Exmoor was on a strict diet as he was recovering from laminitis and had to lose weight. His owner stored hay in the spare stable, but had allowed the piles to get sufficiently high for the crafty pony to pull through. 'Caught in the act!' I told him and laughing, unbolted the doors to move this convenient source of food. A sound under the roof caused me to look up. There was the jackdaw rummaging amongst the articles lying on a rafter. The bright eyes had a quizzical air as it saw me, the grey neck accentuated the shiny black cap to its head. Jack continued to turn over the objects as if searching, then gave a loud 'chack' of dissatisfaction and flew off. I recalled the bright yellow plastic syringe used for worming the ponies that I had found the previous morning lying in the field. That too had been kept on the rafter, but was now safely at home. It would seem from this that Bramble's friend was the thief, but its slippery surface had caused him to drop it.

Dogs and I took the tree-lined track through the old estate. A pair of great spotted woodpeckers flew to and from a nest hole in a beech carrying insects with which to feed their young. When I first arrived in the village I had watched with great pleasure these two excavating the hole, an elongated cavity about 13 cm across. My first surprise was that local dog-walking people didn't know what these birds were; only other white settlers were familiar with them. However, great spotteds were rare here until the 1950s although they now breed in small numbers. The lesser spotted woodpecker does not occur in Scotland. The green was always scarcer to the north of the British Isles and appears to have been unknown in this part of Scotland until the middle of this century. It now breeds in the lower woodland areas and is not uncommon. Great spotted woodpeckers have a reputation for using the same tree year after year, although normally boring a new hole annually and certainly this beech had several such entrances high up in its trunk. It seemed strange to see no jays. It was so widely persecuted that by 1886 only two or three nesting pairs were reported. It is now recorded here as a rare visitor only.

Coming home we followed the River Cley and I was reminded this was a planted estate by the foreign flowers in bloom. Amongst the native ones were the drooping white heads of wood sorrel with its heart-shaped leaflets, the water forget-me-not and lungwort too. Entire rock faces were covered by shining cranesbill with its glossy leaves, a plant very localized in Kent. Bistort, ragged robin, Welsh poppy, bog pimpernel and the stitchworts were familiar enough. I found my first toothed wintergreen with its pale yellow-green flowers, but of the introductions, only a few like leopard's bane could I identify. There was a handsome perennial with long, bare flower stems that terminated in flattish heads of pink flowers well before the leaves appeared. This puzzled me until its wide leaves raised horizontally on metre-high stems, revealed it as the umbrella plant (*Peltiphyllum peltatum*). There was plenty of room for it by the river where the moist conditions encouraged it to spread freely.

It was whilst walking the dogs one early morning that I heard a sharp splashing and looked down to see a heron doing battle with a pike. Small fish they will swallow whole the head first, but this was far too large. The pike was stabbed repeatedly with that dagger-like beak as the prey thrashed about wildly in the water. Then the fisherman carried it to the far bank where it began pecking away at the flesh.

The elusive roe deer were best watched at dawn and dusk. Trees in the shelter belts had their bark frayed by the scraping and rubbing of antlers and lower branches broken, sure sign of a buck's territory. The does, I was to find, like badger sows, exhibit delayed implantation. So after a fertile mating in summer the blastocysts do not implant into the uterine wall and develop, but are delayed until December or January with the kids born between May and early June. The first time I heard a buck bark, I thought it must be a dog. The first time I witnessed the birth of a kid was one of the highlights of my life. It happened like this.

There was a badger's trail through a shelter belt that I felt was connected with the Burn Badgers a mile or so away. The old mound at the far end of the trees showed signs of recent activity with two entrances newly dugout, the pieces of coal and clinker dark against the green nettle shoots. Where the bare trail through the undergrowth passed under a barbed-wire fence, tell-tale bicoloured badger hairs were caught on its sharp prongs. First light one morning found me sitting on a rotting stump at the edge of the trees a short distance from the trail and with a good view of the surrounding field. A doe appeared amongst the ferns. She seemed restless; could she catch my scent? She turned round several times in a tight circle reminiscent of a dog before lying down. She lay and immediately rose again and stood with lowered head. Was she sick? Time passed and her flanks contracted; she was giving birth! A bag-like object dropped into the ferns and wildflowers and I watched as the afterbirth trailed behind. Now the mother bent down into the foliage. I couldn't see what she was doing. She turned and cleaned herself before settling into the ferns with only her head showing. It was well after dawn that I saw movement across the field of flowering oilseed rape; something was coming through it causing the blooms to wave at its passing. The badger gained the shelter belt leaving some more of his hairs on the barbed wire. He paused, head raised at the doe who appeared to outstare him, her large rounded eyes with their slanting pupils, fringed with dark lashes. The badger trotted along his trail rather more quickly and I continued to sit with great pleasure as the first rays of the morning sun touched the flowers of the Norway maples turning them to molten gold.

Long after the doe herself had gone I remained. The trees of this shelter belt were larch, Turkey oak, Scotch elm, beech, gean, hazel, Scots pine and rhododendron as well as the maple which was planted here both for shelter and ornament as it can tolerate harsh, climatic conditions. These maples are clothed in yellow in spring and in autumn the same colour dominates, when the foliage turns to gold or scarlet-brown. Before leaving, I approached close enough to see the fawn without allowing my shadow or scent near it. That it was a single birth rather than twins suggested its mother was under three years old. The coat was a pale reddish brown speckled with black. There were white spots on its sides with a row of these on each side of its spine; it was still damp from its mother's washing. These kids are commonly left lying alone with the mother returning to suckle them. Two nights later I found this same badger was frequenting the mound and the reason for his dingy stripes came to me one morning after an energetic burst of digging out – a clinker-based home is not one of the cleanest! I nicknamed him Spike on account of his right ear that was partly missing. Spike was a character and the dominant male of the Burn Badgers, but at that time he was just a large boar intent on renovating this outliner home on the edge of his territory.

One night a pair of tawny owls called from the village. The female's sharp 'kewick, kewick' was answered by her mate's long-drawn, quavering hoot. Their territory I found, extended to the large rambling garden where I lived together with those of adjoining properties and continued over the ponies' field as far as the Cley. There were no barn owls. I left the calling tawnies and the village behind, intent on the hills above. A white police car stopped and we stood talking. It seemed a good moment to ask if he ever saw badgers in his headlights. It was a fortunate question for not only did he and his colleagues occasionally see the Burn Badgers crossing from the shelter belt to the fields on the opposite side, but several years earlier one had been run over here. Many years ago he had been told, a badger was killed on the Wild Way. This startled me for the Wild Way was an eighteen-mile stretch of road from my village considered the bleakest of routes by some of the locals. At the back of my mind I had intended to walk it and explore, but the deadline date for finishing my next book had kept me busy, causing me to concentrate on wildlife nearer to home. The policeman promised to ask around at his station as to the approximate location of the dead badgers and I left my phone number with him. He was as good as his word. The deaths had been considered sufficiently unusual to record them he told me, adding that the Burn Badger discovery had caused quite a stir amongst the men as it was only the second to their knowledge in twenty years! 'Was the Wild Way busy at night' I asked. 'In the summer with tourists, yes,' was the answer. It was also a remarkably straight stretch of road which meant fast driving. This rather enforced the Clackmon farmer's words on the scarcity of badgers unless their setts were a long way from any roads.

The swallows were back, with their graceful flight and twittering calls. My window was high up nearly at roof level with a disused chimney to the left. I would stop typing to see the crescent shapes with their long tail streamers crossing and recrossing the tree-filled gardens to the farther dwellings. I first saw them hawking for insects over the loch, probably building up their lost food reserves after their long migration. Now they were seeking out their old nest sites not only in the village, but in the steadings or farm buildings as well. One pair seemed particularly interested in the chimney, now taken over by a pair of jackdaws. By the swallows' agitation, I felt this had probably been their nest site last year, but they finally accepted the noisy Jacks in possession and went elsewhere. The house martins appeared somewhat later and seemed to take over their breeding colonies at once. I hadn't as yet seen any swifts, but these were to come.

There were chaffinches in abundance in the village, the shelter belts and on the lower slopes of the hills; wherever I walked this attractive little bird was sure to be. Magpies were considered common which made me smile. I was used to groups of five, six or more at one sighting, whereas three in the Lothians caused grave concern. The old argument of past persecution by gamekeepers was discussed – less 'keepering, less killing and increased numbers. Whilst there is some truth in this, I suspect the British love of feeding garden birds, thus increasing their numbers, has also increased their predators too. Magpies, like the fox, are far more urban now and have learnt to exploit a good food source. This seemed to have helped the sparrowhawks too; a pair frequented the gardens especially at dusk taking tits and finches. There was a plucking post in the larch wood where their prey was defeathered before being consumed. The female was building a nest of dry larch twigs loosely put together. A flattish, rather untidy structure that she lined with leafy twigs. It proved to be far more substantial than it looked though I recorded at the time my concern for the unlaid eggs! Her mate was little interested in the affair. Only once did I see him bring twigs in offering and one of those she quietly tipped out when he was gone from sight.

Most nights I returned to Clackmon farm to badger watch too late to see them emerge from their setts. In daylight hours I had checked all the hedges, shelter belts and open fields without finding any more so concluded that the two known to myself and the farmer were the only ones the area contained. One night I followed the burn through the birches for a while and saw by the still wet paw marks on protruding rocks that the brockies had crossed over to the next meadow where the cows grazed. Close-cropped turf whether grazed or kept artificially short by man is ideal for badgers searching for worms, their main food source. Some earthworms, particularly the largest species *Lumbricus terrestris*, will rise above ground on damp nights to feed on the surface, but in long grass or vegetation, they would be very difficult to catch even for a creature like the badger that habitually forages with its snout and mouth close to the ground.

I returned to the burn and sat down on a large, flat boulder. First light came at 2.40 a.m., (earlier than in the south just as it becomes dark much later), and a heron flew down with slow-beating wings to begin fishing in the shallows. I watched until it caught one, swallowed it and moved farther downstream, then walked silently back to the sett in the field. Three badger cubs perhaps twelve weeks old, were playing in a whirl of bodies. Their favourite game seemed to be running round and round after your neighbour's tail and hanging on. In the midst of their play, four lambs appeared over the slope above doubtless lured by the considerable noise and tried to join in. Two cubs ran away into their sett, but the third could not for the lambs were in his way. For a moment he panicked then turned round to face them hissing and fluffed his fur up on end looking for all the world like a pear-shaped bottle brush and twice his real size. There was a strong smell of musk for he was really frightened under all that sham, though his black and white mask made him look quite fierce. The lambs were somewhat confused, turning back to the grazing ewes who were completely indifferent to the whole affair and the cub escaped into the sett.

I noticed that adult sheep and badgers tended to ignore each other; badgers here avoided the cows although both domesticated animals took an interest in the badgers' setts. The cows when they grazed this field would rub their necks against entrances, defecate and stamp over them and actually put their hooves and heads into the holes. Badgers hate this kind of disturbance and may vacate their homes if it becomes too great.

The Scotch or wych-elms were a glorious sight for one who remembered the beauty of elms in the English countryside before the ravages of Dutch elm disease. Their outline, like the seeds and leaves, differs slightly from the English, Dutch or smooth-leaved varieties. The branches spread more from the trunk giving the foliage an open aspect. It is the hardiest of all elms and one that reproduces itself from seed and not by suckers from the roots of parent trees. This has given it a greater resistance to the disease. There were many in the shelter belts and along the river for it likes the water courses. It is the most commonly planted park and roadside tree in Scotland's capital. I found many elm seeds encased in the round-winged membrane still green and maturing, bitten through and discarded by the grey squirrels. The Turkey oaks were splendid too. They have become naturalized in England and Wales, but I suspect were planted on the estates here.

Rhododendrons are a good indication of a once managed and keepered estate for when they were introduced to Britain two hundred years ago they were extensively planted for game cover. This evergreen is one of the few plants that can survive under the dense shade of beeches and casts an even deeper shade itself under which nothing grows. I found the home of the Wild Way badgers dug into a rhododendron-covered slope overlooking the river. It was an ideal situation for the sett, but one which would never have been allowed to occur sixty years ago when badgers, in common with most other wild animals and many birds, were systematically exterminated in Scotland on the lairds' vast lands. I had already discovered from several elderly villagers that in their youth the mound sett had been regularly gassed by the resident gamekeeper. Of recent years and then only irregularly, they had noticed that some of the shrunken down holes usually containing rabbits, had been enlarged to take a much larger animal. The shape was wrong too for rabbit or fox, more of a semicircular hole with a flat base. They hoped that some badgers at least, were recolonizing the old mound. Unfortunately it was next to a footpath and with the increase of dog-walkers, had become a very public place liable to disturbance.

The morning I took the dogs walking round the loch was bright and gusty. Many of the hill sheep were shorn with their well-grown lambs looking chunky in their woolly coats. Waves slapped the stony shore and my view of the Dark Hill was breathtaking. Light showers came and went in the sunshine with a rainbow disappearing into its summit. The young terrier chased a rabbit. After much calling, she returned only to run off again. This time I put her on the lead, but didn't need to do so with the other bitch, an old retriever who viewed rabbits with indifference. Under the pines we three walked by a leveret crouched in its form, though only I appeared to notice. Further along I tied both dogs to a gate and returned to look at it more closely. Hares as young as this are said to have no scent and if they freeze, predators usually go by unknowing. Nonetheless, I was glad the terrier had been leashed.

I left home very early one morning intending to be well on the hill range behind Dydor before dawn. I was passing the spot where the burn forms a pool when I made out badger sounds. Again it was easy to slip down under cover of the noise. Two badgers probably yearlings, were playing mock fights on the far bank. They bounded amongst the long ferns and sedges, head-butting each other with many a splash, when both stopped abruptly – there was a fox on my side, intent on crossing the burn above the pool. One badger came across the stones towards the fox who by now was halfway over. It turned tail and retreated back to the bank. Both yearlings decided this was an even better game. The fox tried several times to cross, but on each occasion, one or both bully boys came to confront him. He tried at another point, but the fast-flowing water and lack of stones made it an unpleasant venture. Now the fox disappeared into the trees on the fellside and the badgers continued to spar very noisily.

Suddenly the fox slipped out running across the stones and might have succeeded had not a badger looked up and spotted him. The two animals confronted each other over the pool; the badger tipped the fox off with its snout, but as it fell, the fox grabbed at the badger and both went in with an enormous SPLASH! Both species can swim well and at the far bank they got out, shaking themselves dog-like. As the fox went off, the other badger that had been watching made to chase it, but its very wet companion flew at it and nipped it hard on the rump. The fox made good its escape and the last I saw of the badgers was a very boisterous chase up the fellside.

Mist concealed the loch and Dydor as I continued into the hills. I hadn't been this way before, but provided I kept to the path through the bog there should be no problem. I might have been in the Lake District; indeed this place was very evocative of my Lakeland experiences. There was no one else but the sheep, larks, lapwings, grouse and the curlews' bubbling songs. I've always enjoyed walking in fog. It encloses, it mutes sounds; you are alone, yet not alone. I regretted I wouldn't see the view when I reached the peaks, but for the rest it was an exhilarating experience. The faint trail wound through areas of brilliantly red sphagnum, streams crossing and recrossing the plateau and the white tufted cotton-grass. Next a steep climb up into the greyness with rocky outcrops that sometimes materialized into sheep! These hadn't yet been clipped and I was glad for by now my anorak and hair were soaking as were their thick fleeces, but imagine being bare-skinned in this. They moved away slowly as I scrambled higher, reluctantly and it seemed with disapproval. I heard myself apologizing but my words galvanized them into life – the mist swallowed up their black faces and woolly backs.

The peak of Lytlaw was unexpected; scarcely a few metres long. It is impossible to stand upright here when the westerlies blow. There were no sheep droppings on this thin wiry grass, nor could I see what was below in the treeless landscape. The downward path seemed to dither, its wet scree treacherous, but it wasn't for long. My steps led upwards again to the next, less rugged summit. Continuing down once more, the map told me I had a choice of routes. Far away in the valley to my right there was a farm; to the left, a steep ascent following the waterfall. Straight ahead, another much larger hill top and the highest of this range. I chose the latter to the calls of geese distorted by the clinging mist. A distinct trail strewn with scree wound slowly up to the summit, but not a hard climb for already I was high. As I stood there the greyness parted, closed briefly and opened again. Mist or was it cloud, moved away and the sun's rays burst through in an unexpected warmth. There was a steading behind me; a mere collection of toy boxes far below. Sounds of the Canada geese were nearer now, the double trumpeting 'ker-honks' giving their identity away as surely as their white chin patches. They took off with slow, regular wing beats, spreading across the now bright sky in an oblique line.

The way dropped rapidly to an old 'road' once used regularly by travellers as a pass from the far village beyond these hills to the tiny hamlet in their midst. Below lay the blue edge of a loch, coloured by the sunny sky. It was here that I heard the cuckoo, my first in Scotland, calling from a circle of trees by the shepherd's house. It seems that a cuckoo calls from here year after year though none called from my village or from the surrounding shelter belts. Now I passed a waterfall created by the burns rushing off the hills I had traversed. It thundered in a plume of spray to the rocks far below. The way here was flat and twisting with Dydor on my right. This was the far side of the Dark Hill I could never see from my window, a vast barren shape rearing out of the level ground. No heather here to clothe its nakedness, only a primeval mass of scree. The stark shape seemed formidable, not the benign giant I knew so well.

A curlew glided low over the moss with wings outstretched. The bubbling song as it flew over this its breeding ground, marking its territory, was the embodiment of lonely hillsides and quiet, unpeopled places.

Now a dot in the sky came nearer and I beheld a buzzard calling and circling above me. There was another below the first also mewing and wheeling near a steep outcrop of rock. From a distance the outcrop had been a symphony of red and greens, but near to was a perfect precipice in miniature, complete with trees and vegetation clinging to it. I realized that the buzzards were unhappy at my presence; like as not they had a nest on the crag. Buzzards are not common in these hills. I walked on with pleasure nearing my homeward stretch and passing a few walkers starting out in the sunshine reminding me this was a Saturday. A truly memorable morning that I would never forget.

Chapter Two

The Burn Badgers' Sett

I spoke to the farmer who rented the area frequented by the Burn Badgers. He knew of the sett and I was welcome to go on his land. The police had informed him of the badger road casualty some years ago. Will, the shepherd from the cottage on the hill, sometimes watched the badgers, but no one had found any other setts. Mr Robertson suggested I made myself known to Will. He would tell the men I had permission to be there. On that visit the shepherd was away in the hills, so I followed the route as directed, crossing an old stone bridge that straddled the burn to the far side, and the shelter belt.

Roe twins were playing together in the speckled sunlight beneath the trees. They pranced and turned, bounding together like frolicsome puppies not far from their parents browsing on succulent buds and shoots at the field edge. Roe deer, unlike fallow with which I was more familiar, have no giveaway tails to swish. Adult roe are about the size of retriever dogs but with long, slender legs and slim bodies. The twins were losing their spots that were fading into their coats. Now they stood panting together till one went looking for its mother, stretching under her to suckle and soon its sibling was jostling for a place too. The buck's upswept antlers were tiny by comparison to fallow; very neatly set on the forehead and far less cumbersome than the larger deer. However, roe bucks are quite capable of fighting with them, locking their antlers, twisting or pushing and deaths are by no means unknown. Roe seemed to stay as a family for most of the year, although sometimes there would be two does and their kids to one buck. I was to have many pleasurable hours in the shelter belt observing this enchanting family with their pointed ears, black noses and white chins.

It was indeed a very large sett; the largest I had seen so far in Scotland with a dozen or so entrances all under sitka spruce. There was nothing growing beneath the trees of course; the ground was covered with a thick layer of pine needles which made walking silent. I sat for some while, listening to the thundering burn far below and the 'zi-zi-ziiiit' of a goldcrest above me. The pasture from which I had come with its bullocks and sheep would help sustain the badger clan, whilst the deciduous trees and bracken between burn and sitkas, gave light and air to an otherwise sombre place. I noticed old broken bottles and fertilizer bags about and felt rather sad, but obviously the farmer and his men liked badgers, so I shouldn't be. I walked on under the conifers and reached a passing place through the wire fence. To my left, the burn dashed over steep boulders and I could see, by peering through the branches, where I had watched the sow and her cubs cross that night from the far side. Then I walked through the fence and in a short space on I was out at the edge of the loch! No wonder the Burn Badgers came here so often; it was even nearer for them from this side.

It was a grey, misty day with a wind ruffling the surface of the water. Harebells were all in bloom, blowing gently in the wiry grass and the water margins were swaying masses of meadowsweet. The alders had their little green fruits; sedges and great woodrush were seeding. There were swallows too dipping for insects over the water. I returned to the sett and looked more carefully at the surrounding ground. Sometime in the past, difficult to judge when, a hole had been dug into the sett and then infilled. Time had caused the loose earth to sink slightly so that now this area was lower than the surrounding ground. Terrier-men digging for badgers call this a crowning-down hole; it was the first, though not the last I was to find in the Lothians. Returning through the farm I met Will who on my introducing myself said, 'You aren't after gassing them are you?' I felt this wasn't said as a joke as he looked so quizzical, so explained why I was interested. He seemed slightly relieved though still cautious. He mentioned that terrier-men had tried (or perhaps succeeded) in digging the badgers out some two and a half years ago; one could still see the in-filled crowning-down hole. I mentioned my first experience of the Burn Badgers, the sow and her two cubs. Will sometimes saw the cubs playing outside the sett entrance in the early morning long after the mother had returned to sleep. Walking home the wind was causing the lime trees to shed their winged seeds and the yellow iris, sneezewort, small scabious and ladies' bedstraw were in flower, together with fleabane and rosebay willowherb. The last-named seemed a favourite browsing plant of the roe deer I watched. I puzzled over our recent conversation. Never before had I been asked if I was thinking of gassing badgers. Why should Will have said that if it wasn't a possibility? He certainly hadn't meant it humorously.

One early morning I took the terrier for a walk by the Cley. Rain and hail were forecast, but it was difficult to credit in the warm sunshine. Red campion was overtaking the bluebells that were beginning to fade. The May and elder blossom hung cloying on the air and I saw that the grey squirrels were biting off bunches of oak leaves and catkins, letting them drop; the ground below was strewn with them. We stepped out onto the flat rocks and sat together, my arm round the little dog, gazing at the shoals of tiny fry, darting through the water. A mallard paddled past with her three feathered young, oblivious of us sitting above. There were thousands of fry, minnows and sticklebacks in the clear water. The sun was warm on our backs making us drowsy. A robin flew down to a fragment of driftwood wedged between stones, dipped its beak and flew into cover with a minute fish in its beak. I jerked awake as a wren took its place and did the same! Not daring to move, I glanced down at the dog who head on paws was fast asleep. The robin returned twice and finally a thrush also went fishing. Much later I came to know some of the human fishermen on the river and loch who told me this is not uncommon. Hail did arrive that afternoon, bouncing off roofs and pavements and striking my window with force. It brought down tiny still-green cherries from the geans and in places, flattened the flowering oilseed rape in the fields.

That night the Clackmon badgers were cleaning out their sett in the shelter belt. Old bedding of dried grass, bracken and leaves was dragged to the surface with the earth. Once above ground, a few strong kicks with the back legs sent it spilling over the spoil heap. A snort or two, clearing the snout of any earth particles, then down below to drag out some more. The ground beneath a spruce had been turned over by the badgers rootling for insects, beetles and grubs. It was very dry just there.

I walked at the field edge towards their other sett, but long before I reached it, a commotion from the birch stand made me veer that way. Some of these wind-tortured trunks grew almost horizontal and were covered in lichens and liverworts giving them a shaggy look. These were easy to climb and run along and the badger cubs were enjoying this new game. First one cub and then another went exploring; they were perhaps 1½–2 metres above the ground. A ewe came and rubbed herself against the rugged bole. These sheep had yet to be sheared and already their fleeces were beginning to shed; it probably irritated. Unfortunately, this attracted some well-grown lambs who easily scrambled up too and scampered along the outstretched trunk. The cubs didn't like this; their line of retreat was blocked. Gradually they backed nearly to the end, or rather the top of the tree where the trunk was very slender. The largest lamb came on so that the nearest cub fluffed up and growled menacingly. The lamb made butting movements with its head and stamped its hooves to show how grown-up it was. The cub farthest out on the trunk felt it sway, lost its nerve and successfully jumped to the ground. Relieved of the weight, the trunk bounced back and forth with the other cub and the lamb grimly keeping their balance.

The swaying finally ceased. With one of the enemy successfully vanquished, the lamb was eager to knock off the other. It rushed forward to butt, lost its balance and fell unhurt, running baaing off to find Ma. The cub felt itself slipping as the trunk bounced about and ended up sloth-like, *under* the trunk, hanging on with its paws round the birch. It looked nervously down and chittered loudly in fright. It was a drop of scarcely two metres, but must have looked far worse upside down! The other sheep came to watch the interesting sight of a badger hanging from a tree. There were lots of maas and baas that attracted the cows in the field next door. They came to look over the fence; life must get boring for them. The cub finally dropped – amongst the ewes, one of whom obligingly took the worst of his fall on her fleecy back. The badger raced off home without a backward glance and the sheep looked at one another in mild disapproval.

The beauty of following these badgers at night was that I didn't have to be particularly quiet. A wind seemed to be always rushing in the trees whilst the burn bubbled forever over the rocks. Add to this the sheep and cows that often moved about grazing at night especially if it was mild and it is clear to see how easy it was. Sometimes I would wait for the badgers in the cows' field, perhaps with my back against a tree; the bovines themselves might start the night at the burn's edge, a good distance away.

One night the waning moon was a fine crescent lying on its back. Stars pricked in a velvety sky and a slight breeze blew into my face. A badger sow appeared seeking worms rising from the pasture. She gripped one, but did not pull for its tail was still anchored for safety in its burrow. The sow merely held on carefully so not to break it, then sucked it up in the manner of spaghetti pushing out the earth particles contained in Lumbricus from the vent end as she did so. Badgers swallow a fair amount of dirt and grass with their food, but the former cannot be particularly attractive to them. Worms were consumed by this particular badger at a rate of two a minute as it moved slowly and stealthily across the pasture. Farther away another clan member had its head down doing the same. Time passed and the badgers moved from view. A fox was slowly crossing at an angle, also seeking worms. With their turn of speed and ability to pounce, foxes can catch prey such as mice and voles, that the slower foraging badger rarely captures unless it is a sick specimen or carrion.

It struck me forcibly walking home one morning that I might not know much about these badgers yet, but I was certainly learning about bovines. The noises they made were indescribable, especially when lying down chewing the cud. Given that bovines are ruminants endowed with complex, multistage digestive systems and may spend as much as a third of their twenty-four hours grinding fibrous grass into a form that their stomachs' bacteria can break down, I suppose it isn't surprising that their digestive tracts are so noisy. Three of my cows were identifiable by these sounds alone, whilst another cleared her throat from time to time as if about to make a speech. I might start my night watch with no bovines in the vicinity, but by daybreak could find myself in the midst of the herd. They were however, very tolerant of my presence, or was it that I was merely ignored?

I walked to Clackmon one morning to take photos of the setts in good light. Returning I noticed why the sheep near the farm were making so much noise; the lambs had been separated from the ewes in a field by the shepherd's cottage. I felt the adults would soon be sheared like those already fleeceless at the foot of the hills. Ragged robin's flowers lit up the sides of the burn, preferring the damp soil there. Cuckoo spit, the sticky white froth of the frog hopper nymph, lay on the leaves and stems of many plants.

When walking the dogs along the river bank, I regularly passed the village kirk. With my great interest in old places and local history, I left the dogs behind one morning to explore the churchyard. The caretaker showed me round his kirk, then outside again in the sunshine we stood talking. Until he retired and took up his job of caring for the church, he had worked in the factor's office of the laird who owned most of the land round about. This factor or manager had already given me access to parts of the estate. The caretaker, like the factor, spoke regretfully of past wildlife persecution by the laird's gamekeepers, who gassed, trapped and shot years ago, now fortunately no more. There was one keeper retained whose main job was to look after the roe and cull them which normally amounted to only six deer annually. This seemed a small cull to stop numbers building up and causing excessive damage on farmland or to trees, but the factor explained that walkers' dogs as well as roads, accounted for more. He also warned me of 'lampers' with long dogs or lurchers; a woman out on her own at night or early morning could be vulnerable. He took considerable pains to explain that these lampers were unscrupulous poachers who set their agile dogs onto the fleeing deer seen in the beam of the strong lights they carried. I was not unfamiliar with lampers myself, though Kentish poachers had been after foxes and badgers, not deer. I was warned not to approach them, but to let the local police and the factor's office know.

Recently the keeper had been out in the early morning and seen a group of lampers returning from a night's foray. In the confusion they had dropped the deer and got away. Although the keeper was armed, so too were the men and one against several could have spelt disaster. Luckily no one was hurt, apart from the deer of course. The factor was very concerned over the numbers of roe injured by dogs round the village that had to be stalked and killed. Whether lurchers or people's pets it came to the same thing and chasing dogs often injured the hindquarters or genitals. This could be bad enough for a doe. If a buck is thus castrated during the period that his antlers are in velvet, the bone never hardens and the mass of velvet will never be cast. This wig-like mass of soft bone, hair and tissue continues to build up on top of the head and may even grow down over the eyes. Such perruque heads as they are called, eventually cause blindness and death. The keeper tried to cull these at the start of the malformation, before the bucks had suffered too much. He stalked and culled in the early morning. If we should meet I would introduce myself, but in the event, we never did. Neither was I to encounter poachers. Coming home one morning however, I met a dog still worrying at the carcase of a kid it had killed. The owner was far away on the track beyond the shelter belt, blithely unconscious of her pet's activities.

The conversation turned to local history and the caretaker asked if I had noticed the ruins of a round building by the Cley? This was the remains of a hop-drying oast house. There had been a cottage nearby where the beer was sold; few pubs in those days. In my ignorance I had thought that hop growing was a perogative of the Kentish landscape; really, this white settler had a lot to learn! It was the caretaker who mentioned badgers. All my English instincts were to keep off the subject unless brought into the conversation. Did I know there was a small colony above the next village? He hadn't seen them, but he knew of another incomer and his wife who kept an eye on them and sometimes badger-watched of an evening.

Walking home I saw a dipper working its way upstream against the current; it was actually walking under water for much of the time. Its chunky, short-tailed shape seemed ideally suited to this underwater search for mayfly nymphs and other small creatures clinging to the stones beneath the clear waters. When the limits of its territory were reached, it flew downstream and started all over again. It paused, bobbing amongst the rocks, then fearlessly plunged into the fast, cold water to begin stone turning once more. There were dippers all along the river; their bobbing action together with the white throat and breast contrasting with the dark upper parts, makes them a most distinctive bird. I managed to get close to one that day and saw they also have a chestnut waistband below the white breast. Actually, they were not particularly shy. Back in my room I looked up dippers and found that the young can dive and swim before they can fly!

The Burn Badgers spent a great deal of the dark hours by their fast-flowing waters; in some places it was deep though in others quite shallow. They played by it and in it, swum about and then came ashore to groom themselves, as well as to drink. On three successive nights I watched Spike completely motionless on a flat rock apparently peering into the water, but it was only on the final night that I saw him fishing; that is putting his right paw into the water and flipping a fish out. Two were merely tossed into the water near the bank. The next dropped onto the bank under the nose of a juvenile badger who needed no second invitation, but two more were secured by Spike for himself. None of the fish were large, about 15 cm long I thought and at the time I had no idea what kind they were. There were plenty of native fish here; at times the burn seemed full of shoals of smaller ones. As I came to know Spike and his clan better however, I found they favoured the brown and rainbow trout that came down from the well-stocked loch above. All the years I have watched badgers, this was the first time I had seen them fishing, though admittedly my part of Kent had only one shallow river and the decreasing badger population no longer frequented its banks.

These Scottish badgers were finding many different foods to eat now. The thick, knobbly roots of the pignuts, that dainty white shade-loving flower related to hedge parsley and wild parsnip, was a particular favourite. Early attempts to cultivate this food source failed because it was difficult to grow on ploughed land. Medieval peasants dug for the tuber to stave off starvation and certainly for the badgers, pignuts are nutritious and satisfying. The cubs would still poke under their mother hopefully, but by the sow's brusque reaction I believed them weaned. The youngsters made snuffle holes with their snouts and clawed away the old rotten bark of fallen trees in their search for food.

The rocky overhang where the sow and her cubs had disappeared from my view that first early morning proved to have an entrance, a mere crevice, between rocks some seven metres above the burn that connected with the sett beneath the sitkas. On close inspection I found the stone was worn away in a smooth curve by the constant passing of the badgers' bodies. This could only have occurred over many years for the rock was volcanic in origin and very hard. In 1981 I stayed in Cumbria and watched a pair of badgers on a moor, high up on the fellside. An entrance to their sett was similar, but the rocks were in the entrance of a long disused wad mine. Wad or graphite, a kind of hardened glittering stone, also called black lead, had many uses, the most famous being for the making of lead pencils. Foraging ground for the badgers was very poor and clans or families were small. They travelled miles at night down the fellsides in search of food in the more fertile valleys and most especially in the village and farm areas. Why they should choose to live so far from their feeding grounds when suitable habitat could be found much nearer puzzled me at the time. It was in Scotland that I was to find the probable answer.

The oystercatchers were nesting. What immaculate black and white birds they are with those pink legs and orange chisel-like beaks. The moorland air resounded to the shrill 'kleep kleep' of their flight calls as the sharp-eyed parents kept watchful guard over their precocial broods. The downy chicks were very attractive and could follow the parents within two days of birth, picking up their own food as they went. There was danger a-plenty with foxes, stoats, weasels and gulls looking for a choice morsel; their only defence was to remain crouching motionless in the wiry grass. They are single-brooded and soon would be gone for another year.

A friend in Galloway in the southwest of Scotland invited me to stay with her. That first evening we sat in the dormer windows of Melanie's cottage waiting for the pipistrelle bats to emerge from beneath a slightly raised tile and the barn owl's arrival over the meadow in front of us. The bats were stirring, their high-pitched squeakings from the tiles to my right suggested they were soon to appear. Suddenly I forgot bats in the delight of beholding the buoyant shape of the white owl. It was 9.35 p.m. and excellent light as one would expect from a fine June evening. The barn owl apparently roosted in nearby steadings. It floated, lost height and rose again to float once more. As it quartered the field, one could clearly see it was mottled gold on white rather than pure white. It treated us to a sustained preview of its hunting abilities, then finally crossed the road to the grassland there. We went to the back windows and continued to watch, opening a window the better to observe it through the binoculars. It perched on a post then dropped below the drystane dyke (as stone walls are known here) and so flew low to a little wood. Later it returned and dropped on something in the grass. A long period elapsed before it rose again and continued hunting out of our sight.

By now it was 10 p.m. but still light as we walked up the lane behind the cottage to the moor. Wild roses bloomed in the hedgerows, white, pale and deeply pink. We noticed the cobwebby effect of a large tree caused by moth caterpillars spinning nests of silk in which to shelter during the day. The tree was so infested that the nests covering the twig ends held them together and the tree was almost denuded of leaves that the caterpillars had eaten. There were many foxgloves in bloom, my first seen in Scotland. As in the Lothians, bluebells grew freely in the verges with red campion, although by now the former's flowering season was over.

We scrambled up the moorside past the black-faced sheep and I nearly put my hand on an adder. In the fading light there was the shimmer of a loch to my left and many tiny white moths and wolf spiders on the moss. Now we descended and walked back together through the gloaming. Three frogs and many toads were moving across the tarmac towards the burn on the far side. More and more toads appeared as the lane dropped and we trod carefully to avoid injuring any. By now the pipistrelles were in flight hawking for insects along the verges.

Dumfries and Galloway Region has an exceptionally mild climate due to the warming influence of the Gulf Stream that flows around its coast. Moreover, it is very wet and the moist warm air encourages constant growth. Paths and trails must be continually used or they will not remain amongst the lush vegetation. There were no badgers in the neighbourhood due to past persecution Melanie had been told, although in less remote areas such as the Mull of Galloway they could still be found in good numbers. That first morning I went out early on a circular walk and soon found myself amongst the curlews. Their nestlings are precocial and leave the nest as soon as their down is dry. The adult curlews were probing for worms with their long, down-curved bills and carrying them together with other small offerings to their chicks. I was interested that the youngsters had straight bills with only the barest hint of the curve to come. Their creamy-buff down was marked with blackish-brown and their dark crowns had a pale central patch as if tonsured.

For a long time I stood with glasses raised watching the roe deer as they browsed in the open fields near the sheep. Now they slowly moved towards a shelter belt, instinctively seeking cover for the day. I strolled on. The lane curved, rose, fell and curved again passing several steadings in the process. Sometimes it dropped below field level and my way was overhung with trees; a delightful lane that dithered and dawdled like an unwilling child on its way to school. Eventually I reached the rhododendrons bordering the old estate and back to the cottage. At 9 a.m. it was a beautiful morning.

Over breakfast we looked at the local paper. Unusually it contained a report of a gassed badger sett not far from Loch Ken. The location was vague but from certain details mentioned and a careful study of the map, we felt it well worth a trip even if we didn't find the sett. It was a day typical of the region; a heavy shower then sunshine so hot, that within minutes all trace of the rain had vanished. Driving along I noticed the chaffinches; they are as common in Galloway as the Lothians, as common as sparrows in Kent. Sparrowhawks and buzzards hunted in the clear air and we waited a hen pheasant with her single chick wandered across our route. There were men fishing in the loch, white water-lilies blooming on its margins and lapwings on the wetlands beyond. It was good to be alive.

We did find the sett that day and sat by it discussing the newspaper article. Evidence of the gassing had been reported by a forest ranger who discovered the entrances to the sett blocked off by grass and stones. It was not yet known whether the badgers were killed – no bodies were found when the entrances were uncovered – or whether they had escaped. When a sett is gassed it is common for some of the clan at least, to attempt to get above ground before they die. We searched along the field and wood edges and along the roadside by which we had come. Fresh badger dung was deposited in pits by the latter and some appeared to be but a few hours old. At least one of the clan if not more were still alive. I suggested there was something 'not quite right' about the apparent lack of these animals near my friend's home. Dumfries and Galloway has marvellous badger country with its verdant pastures, lush valleys and mild climate. Galloway cattle including the ancient 'belties' or Belted Galloways are famous throughout Europe. Many had been bought by German and other breeders waiting for the EC restrictions to lift before transporting them abroad. Unlike the southwest of England where bovine TB is feared, the ogre here is brucellosis. Melanie admitted that when she first came to live in the village, she had searched for setts, but after locals insisted these animals were long gone from their lands, she had given up. She knew from reading old sources however, that once badgers had been numerous. We agreed to go out by day together to see what we might find.

The next day we searched the sunlit heights above the village and recorded wildflowers on the unimproved moorland there. Marsh bedstraw's tiny white flowers carpeted the grassy ground like that under Dydor. There were marsh orchids, sundews, lousewort, kidney vetch and common butterwort or bog violet too. That lover of sphagnum and such damp places, the heath spotted orchid (*Dactylorhiza maculata*) grew in great abundance. Once all the land would have been like this, only capable of sustaining a few hardy cattle. The earliest form of cultivation was the run-rig or strip system marked by the deep furrows and broad ridges of the old plough. In parts of England these are known as ridge and furrow or strip lynchets. These run-rigs were ploughed where the ground was least rocky and the cleared stones would be used to make huts and primitive shelters; nothing was wasted. Then liming as a fertilizer together with underground drainage changed the face of the land; the age of the 'Improvements' had arrived. In modern times otherwise unprofitable moors have been extensively planted with conifers, especially the water-tolerant sitka spruce. Now there is line after line of afforestation marching across the landscape hiding the shape of the hills, so few of these unimproved moorlands remain.

We found a sett with two entrances above a steading. Both holes had been blocked with rocks, but one appeared to have been reopened by a badger. Unwithered grass blades in the entrance indicated it had recently taken grass down for bedding. There was fresh dung in a pit on the slope above. We would not have noticed the presence of the sett but for the reopening. Rocks are very much a feature of this landscape and a few more or less on the steep hillside attracted no notice. It demonstrated the considerable strength of brock however, to have moved the rock which undoubtedly had been wedged in as firmly as the other which we humans could not budge, try as we might. This finding upset Melanie who felt that local response to her past enquiries regarding badgers in the parish had been evasive. She was merely told they were once in areas that are now afforested and estate gamekeepers exterminated many, regarding them as vermin. Obviously badgers in Dumfries and Galloway have led a chequered existence as *Maxwell's Guide Book to the Stewarty of Kirkcudbright* (part of the region) published in 1902 indicates: 'Thanks to timely introductions in more than one quarter, the Badger is not yet extinct, but the evil day cannot be long postponed.' The reference to introductions was curious; why introduce what you had successfully exterminated? This was the start of my research into the chequered history of Scotland's wildlife; I was to find the answer to this and much else. We had been out all day and were tired, but would return the next morning to photograph the badger signs and have a closer look at other parts of the slope.

Once we knew what to lookout for, our eyes were far more critical. Standing there the following day, we regarded any slight depression on that hill as suspect, as well we might. A few such inclines were natural contours, but a sharp tug at the grass on most, resulted in a great clump of turf coming away to reveal a hole – either rabbit, fox or badger. When a hole was gassed, if it was plugged with a sod, this quickly rerooted and grew in the humid climate. This entire hillside had been planted with young sitka. It is common practice when farms are sold, for the steadings to be retained by the incomers, often white settlers like ourselves and the land to be rented out to local contractors to plant up or for the incomers to do this themselves. The government granted a subsidy to owners who did this, thus encouraging these plantations. Roe deer were regularly shot to prevent them fraying the young trees and rabbits would be gassed to stop them nibbling the bark. Why were foxes and badgers also gassed? Was it the widely held belief that they take lambs and moreover, that badgers carry bovine TB? Foxes and badgers undoubtedly take carrion, but the proven cases of either killing healthy lambs are few and far between. Badgers in common with other mammals can have TB and the Ministry of Agriculture Fisheries and Food (MAFF) has encouraged landowners to believe that badgers are responsible for transmitting the disease to bovines. Since Scotland is free of bovine TB, might exterminating badgers, however illegal, be a 'better safe than sorry' attitude?

There seemed to be few foxes in the neighbourhood and fewer rabbits, in marked contrast to the myriads of the latter seen grazing the verges of the main roads. We were to find that the bad old days of keepering may have gone on the whole, but the instinct to destroy anything wild as vermin was too deeply ingrained to disappear – landowners were merely more discreet. There seemed to be a policy of 'If there is a hole, stop it – if it moves, shoot it.'

I spent many hours on that moor. This landscape was a contrast to the Lothians, yet both were beautiful. Here were rolling moors, lochs and afforestation with many deciduous trees too. There were incredible oaks lichened and moss-covered, their trunks made shaggy by these hanging plants. There was an old dried-out fungi (*Bovista nigrescens*) on the pasture that had freed itself from the grass and was moving slowly along on the breeze. Its fruiting season is late summer to autumn, but it persists in this dehydrated state for many months. Jackdaws probed the mounds of sheep droppings for beetles and the warm air was filled with an exultation of skylarks. Farther over a lochan nestled, blue against the verdant moor, whilst a short space distant lay the ruins of a small steading. All its roof and most of the rough stone walls were crumbled into heaps; only the doorway and a lone window remained blindly staring onto the wild moor.

There is nothing so evocative of the mortality of man as his derelict habitations. The moment a building is redundant in the south, we have it down and build others in its place, probably high-rise flats or offices. There are so many of us and so little space. But less than six million people inhabit Scotland and the majority of these reside in the Glasgow and Edinburgh areas. Scotland has space and in the main there are plenty of rock and stones for the gathering. There is no point in carting them away to build elsewhere, so many of these epitaphs lie strewn on moor and glen. From the sixty or so small steadings once recorded in this area alone, less than thirty remain occupied now.

Cuckoos were far more common here and Galloway has one of the best barn owl populations in the British Isles. On the way to do our shopping in the nearest town, we saw greenfinches and swallows; a buzzard was being mobbed by crows. A weasel crossed the tarmac in front of us carrying a vole in its mouth. It followed the line of the road until it came to a trail through the grassy verge and bounded along it with the prey held by the back of its neck. She probably had hungry kits waiting. That long, lithe body is adapted to searching through the runways and tunnels of voles and mice that are too small to admit the larger stoat; mole runs are also frequented. The victim is always killed by a well-aimed bite to the back of the neck. Their bounding energy belies the fact that they must eat frequently, consuming a third of their body weight a day. They cannot survive without eating for much more than twenty-four hours and cache uneaten prey. The weasel we watched that day was not unduly nervous of us. If it had not been so preoccupied with carrying its prey, it would have probably returned like most of its kind, curious to see if we were still there. Experienced larger carnivores generally leave stoats and weasels well alone for they will fight back fearlessly if attacked, can produce an unpleasant smell from the gland beneath their tails and moreover, have little flesh on their thin, muscular bodies. I have watched weasels run (rather than climb) up trees to raid nests for eggs or young birds unbothered by the frantic calls of the parents. Unlike squirrels they can descend with equal grace and speed almost defying the human eye to follow.

I went out one night to watch the owls; there seemed to be some competition between the two species. I am used to tawnies, but the barn owls particularly enthralled me especially as they seemed so unconcerned at my standing there. They liked the damp places (they had that in common with the herons) and I tried to establish the extent of their territory. I felt that these species may be in competition with one another; certainly the tawnies that night seemed the aggressors. In England the white owl has decreased greatly due to road deaths and loss of habitat and the tawny has appeared to increase. Has the one filled a vacuum left by the other? It is usual when breeding barn owls to release them in areas unfrequented by others of their kind; not where there are no tawnies however. Released owls are on strange ground; they have to mark out an area and hold it against rivals, so released owls are stressed owls too. Such freed white owls have been found dead through starvation in areas where there is plenty of apparent prey.* I had a feeling the tawnies here would soon attack their neighbours or was I reading more into their aggressive cries?

Deep in my thoughts of owls I was returning at 5.20 a.m. when, turning a corner, I saw a badger grooming itself in the silent lane. Such an unexpected sight in the first touch of sunlight – foxgloves and wild roses trailing over the drystane dykes and the lone badger so busy there. It took its time, stretching backwards to reach a particularly awkward place and combing through its fur with those long-clawed paws. A sad sight too for so few badgers remained. What would be its future? There were old drainage pipes below in the field with holes in their sides and I wondered if this badger had made its home in these. This is not unknown in some areas of England.

That evening I showed Melanie where I had seen the badger grooming and walking home at 9 p.m. We spied the barn owl hunting across the back field and disappearing behind a clump of trees. We stood on the verge, I with the binoculars and waited till it rose up from the grass with a vole in its mouth. As it passed over my head, I turned following its flight; lovely heart-shaped face and gold-edged wings. It seemed unbothered by our presence. Later at the cottage, we saw the pipistrelles coming out from under the raised tile of the skylight roof – one after another – catch an insect and return. They would land below the tile and crawl up and under. Weaning their young we thought.

---

* In November 1992 it became illegal to release or allow the escape of barn owls into the wild in Britain except under licence. For more information or advice The Barn Owl Trust can be contacted, though an s.a.e. is appreciated. Their address is: Waterleat, Ashburton, Devon TQ13 7HU.

The badger's home was not in the old drainage pipes, but in the glen high up above the rushing burn. There were only two open holes; others had been infilled like those on the moor. Trails led down to the water, to the field above and along to the pipes themselves which were dry and empty. There were snuffle holes in the pasture and a play area in the long, flattened grass. The smell of badger musk was everywhere; it must come from more than one animal. They were nicely tucked away here, but from the old stopped-up entrances the sett would seem to have been interfered with before. Melanie had heard there was a vermin controller employed by the farmers but he wasn't from this neighbourhood. Did he come every two or three months and how had these badgers escaped his attentions? Provided the brocks were not seen on the tarmac by local people, they should go unnoticed for now. They had time to disappear as a vehicle climbed the hill; to descend, it must turn a corner and would be heard before the driver could see the animal ahead. Only a walker was likely to come upon one there and few were likely to be out walking that early in the morning. Even the shepherd came from the farm to the fields and moor in his van. We both felt however, that the badgers had found some safe hideaway and merely returned as the glen was their true home. Surely there were others, but where? A Bill to protect badger setts was currently going through Parliament. That brought by Tony Banks MP had failed last year, but another by Roy Hughes MP was making its way through the House of Lords. Even if it became law, it would be difficult to enforce in such isolated areas as this.

The hot sunny weather continued. One day I walked the moor as far as the OS bench marker; the views in all directions were superb. The track with its steadings lay on one side and the blue winding loch on the other. I went to sleep in the sunshine and woke to find an adder sunbathing a few centimetres from my face. I had never seen one so close; how wonderfully patterned was the zigzag back and the V behind its head. I waited for it to go to sleep before I moved, then remembered they have no eyelids! So instead I moved gently and watched as lethargically it slipped away. Repassing the marker I found another adder sun worshipping; this made three seen in one week.

That day too, we explored Dirl Wood. This was a lovely place and one that anybody might be proud to own. There were graceful, old lichen-covered trees above a disused slate quarry as well as some sitka and spruce. Its small clearings contained ferns and bracken, ideal habitat for the deer. It was possible the main badger clan was housed in the quarry, but summer's luxuriant growth and the huge piles of loose slates, made searching for it dangerous. It would be best left to the winter when the undergrowth died down. The owner was favourably inclined towards wild animals, so the brocks would be unmolested here. I had to return home the next day to finish typing the manuscript and Melanie had her own work to continue. We would keep in touch.

I returned to my village on 5 July and the realization of how much I had missed Dydor; seeing his dark shape from my window was like greeting a lost friend. That evening the solicitor who had drafted Roy Hughes's Bill to Protect Badger Setts rang to say it had passed its third reading in the House of Lords and returned to the Commons that day for approval by them of the Lords' amendments. It would receive the Royal Assent some time the following week, when it would be titled the Badgers Act 1991.* It would come into force after three months, longer than normal, to give MAFF time to work out the licensing provisions. It was these licensing provisions that might emasculate much of the effort put into protecting badger setts so there was still cause for concern.

That night I watched Spike and his clan eating bilberries further down the burnside. The black, ripe ones were carefully picked off in the same way as they eat blackberries, although such a small shrub like this without prickles, is far easier to pick from than high bramble bushes. These pea-sized blaeberries reminded me rather of sloes with that blue-black sheen, but were very sweet; they are also nutritious and filling. The dominant sow (I had nicknamed Millie) gorged herself on these before curling round amongst the shiny-leaved bushes and going to sleep. This was my first experience of the bil or blae berry for it is a lover of acid soils and occurs on moorland although as here, it also grows in open woodland. It was still light at 11 p.m., something else I wasn't used to. Other fruits beloved of bird and badger were ripe now – the ground was littered with the geans' wild cherries and the wild strawberries and raspberries made the waysides bright with their delicious food. All along the Cley the nettle-leaved bellflowers nodded their stately heads and meadowsweet dwelt in the damp places. Great clumps of perforate St John's wort shone like gold and the deep blue meadow cranesbill with its fruits like long, straight, pointed beaks flourished.

Two events occurred that July which gave me great pleasure. Mike Harris from northeast Grampian contacted me through the National Federation of Badger Groups (NFBG). Mike was involved with the Forestry Commission for North Scotland and the Nature Conservancy Council in compiling management guidelines for forestry operations near badger setts. I had written a much simplified one for NFBG, but Mike's was superb and far more comprehensive. As he worked closely with two such eminent organizations, these guidelines would not only be enforced by them, but hopefully would encourage the numerous private operators to adopt them too. We both knew from personal experience that at worst, badgers are killed and their setts destroyed by felling over them and at the very best, badgers become so stressed that they will desert their setts. Stress also inhibits breeding success. It was grand to find someone else in Scotland involved in badger welfare. Mike too was a white settler, but had lived in Scotland for fourteen years and made a lifetime study of the animal.

Then BBC *Wildlife Magazine* published an article I had written and

---

* Later it became amalgamated into the *Protection of Badgers Act 1992*, so consolidating the Badgers Act 1973, Badgers Act 1991 and Badgers (Further Protection) Act 1991.

mentioned I was now living in the Lothians. From this came several enquiries from young people in different Scottish regions (only one a native-born Scot), anxious to help badgers in their area. There was one badger group in Fife, but not the enthusiasm for badgers one sees in England and Wales which by then had seventy groups with the number still increasing. (It was significant that during the Badger Sett Protection Bill's journey through the House of Lords, Lord Burton had requested that it would not apply to Scotland; fortunately, this was overruled.) With the new Bill soon to become law, these enquirers began to record any setts they could find in their areas. It was a start.

Melanie wrote telling me she had been back to the glen and made a very careful examination over a period of some weeks, but found the same old story. There must have been quite a lot of badgers there at various times she felt, judging by the evidence of rocks, large and small stones, plus turf blocking sett entrances; many looked old stoppings as mosses had formed on some of the rocks. Often the entrances were under tree roots on the steep slope and one bore signs of being dug into at the side of the stone as if the badgers had tried that way to remove it. She did a badger watch one evening, but didn't see any emerge. However, there were fresh signs of activity during the following weeks with old bedding consisting of beech leaves and grass being pulled down the bank some way from the entrance. It should be borne in mind that setts in rocky places have no earth to be dug out and therefore no spoil heaps. The badgers' trails were by now clearly defined which worried Melanie lest the farmer or vermin controller should take an interest.

If my friend didn't see the badgers, the same couldn't be said for her colony of pipistrelle bats. One evening she watched a total of sixty-three individuals emerge from the tiles. Near the end of this time, two bats returned, flew round and round the entrances, sometimes gently touching the tiles and then crawled in. As some of the last bats to leave seemed small, she wondered if they were young ones enticed out by their mothers. There was however, a sequel to this. At 3.45 a.m. one morning she was woken by a loud whirling, flapping noise in the bedroom and found that an adult had entered by the open window. Throwing all the windows wide and leaving the bat alone, didn't encourage it to leave, so finally she gave up and spent the rest of the night in the spare room. However, it appeared to be the bats' tap-dancing class and in the roof space above her bed, a good time was had by all. For a brief while the colony seemed intent on taking over the wee cottage, even to one crawling out of the kitchen sink waste pipe and nearly drowing in the process. As Melanie remarked, 'I couldn't believe my eyes when his foxy face emerged!' It did however, survive the ordeal as did Melanie, who although interested in bats, found the sheer numbers rather daunting. She wrote:

> 'And last night I heard one in the wall behind the sink and sure enough when I opened the door to put some rubbish in the bin, there was a baby one this time, sitting on the lid. They get between the cladding and the walls, under

and all over the roof, flapping and banging, fluttering and chittering – yes, I'm now tuned in very well to their lively conversations! Even as I write, ominous flapping sounds at the head of the stairs tell me that another one is getting up to mischief where it ought not to be. Incidentally, I now know what bat droppings look like – the windows are covered in them!'

Eventually the bats vacated their nursery roost and Melanie had the cottage to herself once more.

CHAPTER THREE

The Otters

The otters came as a great surprise. I had gone to watch at the sett along the Wild Way one beautifully starry night. The midsummer hours of darkness are so short in Scotland, that it was a joy to be out in the brief night to see a velvety sky. Light nights are an asset of course, although you cannot disappear quite so well from human eyes. This area of Scotland wasn't like my part of Kent however, with all sorts of human night-life, sometimes for dubious reasons. Even camping tourists seemed in short supply.

I sat on an old, twisted rhododendron trunk and watched three well grown badgers bathing in the Cley. The river was shallow and slow-flowing here, winding to and fro along the valley. They splashed about with great enjoyment, sometimes sitting on the bottom to scratch with only their heads above water. Other badgers came and went not merely to drink, but to submerge and swim; seen like this they resembled black and white dogs. Back on the bank or on an exposed rock, they would shake themselves vigorously, the wet fur clinging unflatteringly to their chunky bodies and pot bellies.

Now they were gone. Quietness settled about the vacant sett as starlight filtered gently through the long, evergreen leaves to shine on their wide, smooth surfaces. It was a warm, close night with the thick leaves pleasantly cool to the touch. Only the river still murmured on its way with slight eddies and an occasional plop as something rose and dropped again. Several times a whistle sounded, once close to, when it seemed more of a high-pitched squeak. Now all was still. In the distance an owl hooted far over the fields and I settled more comfortably on the crooked trunk, my feet resting on a lower branch. It was well past 4 a.m. and the light was good when I was first aware of an animal turning over a large stone at the water's edge. It caught something in its mouth and then held it in its front paws whilst it ate – an otter, the first I had ever seen in the wild. It searched about for some minutes, then came my way in bounds not unlike a large stoat. It stopped and stoat – or weasel-like, stood upright on hind legs to reconnoitre and gave the same piercing whistle. I sat delighted as it whistled again. It seemed to be a contact call, 'I am here, where are you?' and I heard a chirruping. Sadly it disappeared into the dense foliage below me, but I was certain that the chirruping was another otter answering. However, on that early morning, I only saw the one.

Walking back through the shelter belt to the Wild Way in a daze of joy, I nearly bumped into two young badgers searching amongst the roots of an old beech! I stood holding my breath as their inspection turned into a game and a chase of tag began round the tree. One actually brushed my leg, but so excited and noisy were they (and by now my jeans were smelly and wet from walking through the dew-laden grass), that neither noticed at all. Just as suddenly, their game took them chasing off through the trees to the sett and then I did wander home along the road. No traffic, only hares eating the vergeside herbage till they saw me approach, then standing tall briefly before long-leggedly walking away. There were roe families browsing in the gentle light and blackbirds turning over last year's dead leaves for an early meal to a background of avian song. Surely the best part of the new day.

Another morning I searched for a sett recorded by the Mammal Society in a copse by a quarry. Sure enough it was there, but long abandoned. One part had been extensively dug but with spades that had destroyed the underground tunnelling, the other more recent holes had been gassed and stopped. There was a Cymag cyanide canister still lying in an entrance. This gassing was the first I had encountered in the Lothians and prompted me to contact the Scottish Society for the Prevention of Cruelty to Animals (SSPCA) in the city. We met and discussed the gassed sett I had recently discovered and found the land to be owned by a laird known to the SSPCA Superintendent. Badger digging was touched upon. Although not common in the Lothians now, it is by no means unknown. I told him of the setts that Melanie and I had found and the need to withold her name from any investigation. My friend was a white settler in a small isolated community where even the local policeman was a relative. Like myself she was happily established with new friends; it would be sad to spoil that and in the long term, not beneficial to the badgers. As it happened the SSPCA had recently wound up a long-running case of dog fighting involving the use of badgers in the Borders. The Superintendent pointed out that if they had indulged in name dropping, they would never have infiltrated the gang involved. They, like our RSPCA, had undercover men in plain clothes and unmarked vehicles and were well aware of the blanket gassing and stopping of setts in many areas. Now the Badgers Act was soon to become law it would be up to them to investigate, warn landowners of the new Act and its penalties and take action if the law wasn't upheld. He took details of the setts concerned and we shook hands on it. This was an enormous relief to Melanie and me – the SSPCA appreciated the need for anonymity and we could continue to monitor the situation. It was also good that the SSPCA were already involved in practical application of the new Act.

Now came a period of steady rain which the badgers enjoyed in their quest for worms. One night I mooched contentedly along the burnside before wandering upstream to the sett under the sitkas. I made myself comfortable on a flat rock very near a large entrance above the bole of a wych-elm pollard. It was almost dry under the close-growing spruce;

not until 6 p.m. did the early morning sunlight begin to shaft through the denseness of the trees. The burn dashing loudly over its stony bed far below and a breeze moving the tree tops were the only sounds until a sheep baaed in the fields beyond. A glimpse of a black and white head and a badger approached the holes nearest me. It had scrambled up the steep rocky burnside and puffed as it came by. A stop to listen, head raised and it seemed to stare straight at me. There was a movement behind me and two more badgers appeared and then the half-grown cubs. Only one to my knowledge was missing; the one with the split ear I called Spike. The goldcrest called his monotonous cry and crows began to caw over the sunlit pasture. It was still gloomy under the sitkas, but from the opening made by the burn the sun stole further in. All the badgers disappeared underground as quietly as they had come and there was Spike grubbing about in the bole of a long dead tree, snuffling and grumbling. 'Zi-zi-ziiit' went the tiny bird above our heads as he sneezed loudly and went below too.

Leaving the shelter belt the sudden brightness made me blink. I thought of Galloway's many miles of spruce and fir, glad that my part of Scotland was less afforested. I have heard a coniferous forest described as a biological desert compared with a deciduous one of like size. An obvious example is the insect species that trees support, for example: oak–284, willow–266, birch–299, hawthorn–149, compared with larch–17, fir–16 and holly–7. Conifer canopy like that of beech, shades out most of the ground flora so their woodland edges and clearings are often very important habitat especially for small mammals. Moreover, conifer forests have a beauty of their own. It is the size of afforestation in parts of Scotland that is worrying.

I followed the burn until it met the Cley to look at the many white nettle-leaved bellflowers growing amongst the more normal blue ones. Two foxes came down to the water's edge to drink; both were moulting and one was a very dark, dusky colour. This seemed not uncommon in the locality. A heron that had been fishing in midstream flew up with a fish in its long beak. As it flapped over my head and across the field, the catch appeared to be a roach. Time I went home for *my* breakfast!

I had to return to the Wild Way sett, not only to watch its badgers. I would leave home at midnight and several times saw members of the clan eating wild raspberries at the roadside a mile from their home. The otter was a bitch and one night I discovered she had two cubs; the holt was also beneath the rhododendrons. It was a wonderful area for roe, rabbits, foxes, badgers and otters with planted beech, ash and sycamore further up the slope. An area of bracken lay between the rhododendrons and the higher trees. The lower boggy areas were carpeted with the marsh violets' dainty lilac flowers. Beech, ash, sycamore, elm and lime have for centuries been planted as fodder for livestock and horses. Holly too, for only the lower leaves have sharp points along their edges. The wayfaring trees came as a surprise though, until I found they were introductions to the Lothians. Now they were bright with berries, some already taken by the birds.

Discovering the otter cubs had been a unique experience and a moral dilemma for theirs is a fragile existence even in Scotland. I decided not to watch again for fear of alarming their mother. They were safe here, but if she moved because of me, it might bring disaster to the family. Badgers were one thing, but otters with cubs were too precious to chance. Stealing back through the bracken that early morning with determination and a selfish regret, I chanced upon a roe buck, dainty hooves tucked beneath him, sitting at his ease as he chewed the cud. In spite of his deep russet fur and neat, pointed antlers I would have gone by unheeding deep in my thoughts had it not been for the glisten of his moist, dark nose. The bracken partly hid him and a low bough did the rest. I avoided eye contact and continued on, grateful for the close encounter.

The book was finished so I had more time now to explore. It seemed commonsense to name the Burn Badgers if I wished to keep a record of their individual habits and status within the clan. Spike's name led naturally to The Goons. Spike and Millie then were the dominant pair. Neddy was a yearling subordinate male and exuberant C. Goon was another. The cubs' names defeated me but their escapades found them natural ones. Grace was small and neat with a narrow head, whilst Disgrace her brother was a burly young fellow with well-pronounced cheek tufts and a penchant for mischief.

Gradually the Burn Badgers came to accept I was there. Sitting, my shape wasn't what they would expect of a human and I posed no threat. I made no noise and rarely moved, leaving them to go before I left myself. There would be considerable activity at the sett when they first emerged. One animal would back onto and mark another with musk from the scent gland beneath its raised tail and this would be repeated by a third. The mixture of individual musking gave each the clan scent and is a ritual with most badger families on emergence unless they live under stressed conditions when they may go off immediately to forage. The Burn Badgers had no such fears however and spent long periods musking, grooming scratching and playing in the vicinity of their sett before disappearing separately for the serious business of finding food. Only the cubs who were now independent of Millie, kept together. Over a period of several weeks, I took to following different clan members, always at a discreet distance.

Neddy in particular, proved interesting when I trailed him to the old disused moss-covered curling pond outside the village. Once every village in Scotland had its own curling pond. This one had been a large oblong area cemented across and about 12 cm deep and would have been filled with water. Frozen, this would take a long time to melt as the surrounding trees protected it from the winter sun. The game was played with heavy round flat stones often of local marble with a handle attached; the stone would be slid towards a target across the ice, rather like bowls on a green. Recent nights had been damp and misty and Neddy slowly worked his way across the area turning over the moss as he did so. Water collected here naturally so that all sorts of badger delicacies could be found beneath; beetles, slugs, centipedes, worms, all were eagerly taken.

C. Goon was a great wanderer and the only member of the clan that regularly musked my boots. I could go with him rather than follow; his favoured foraging area was around the old shieling, the far loch side and the lower slopes of the hills. Fishermen had permits to use these waters so at night there was a need for discretion. I often spoke to them as I returned in good light if I no longer was in C.Goon's company. Only once did I err. Fortunately, the badger was mistaken for a dog amongst the reeds as I talked to the man. I will be honest and say that from previous experience of discarded tackle, litter and hooked fish thrown back, I was prejudiced against fishing, but these men sometimes accompanied by their sons gave me a more balanced view. To their knowledge there were no eels in the loch; apart from the indigenous fish it was stocked with brown and rainbow trout. Angling was most successful at night or early morning when having caught one, two or three trout they returned to their cars and went home, often before their wives and the rest of the family were up. Certainly those early mornings as the slight mist lifted to panoramic views of the hills were an enjoyment in itself and a trout rising to insect swarms over the surface and a baited hook an added bonus. There weren't many night anglers, perhaps four round the entire loch, but two I came to know very well and they taught me a great deal. And like me they had encountered the otter! He was a large male – his size caught me unawares; part of his territory overlapped with the Burn Badgers and because they accepted me, in time he came to do so. I did occasionally return to watch the Clackmon clan, but now most of my nocturnal excursions were spent here in the shadow of Dydor the Dark Hill.

Much of Millie's time was taken up with digging out the old nursery part of the sett including her own tunnels and chambers. Perhaps inspired by her example, Grace did hers too. Soon bird and rabbit skulls appeared on Millie's spoil heaps which was rather strange; to my knowledge, brock tends to crunch up such small, fragile bones. Very old pieces of broken pottery and glass suggested an ancient midden; fortunately the glass was so thick and worn that it posed no danger to unwary paws. Heads of wheat and sheep wool were next amongst her bracken and dry grass bedding, but no sheep bones. The presence of wool reminded me of my first visit to the Clackmon sett in the shelter belt when the farmer had left a young lamb's body not far from the entrance holes. I thought either fox or badger would have scavanged from it, but that and another left similarly were untouched (except for the pecked-out eyes) and slowly rotted away. I spoke to Mr Robertson about the sheep wool and he suggested the sow might take it down for bedding in the same way as bracken. 'There's plenty aboot especially afore shearing. Ye can see yourself hoo it sheds; badgers an noo stupid beests.' That gave me food for thought, but it has never been recorded by others so I cannot say. Years ago in Kent however, a young sow well-known to me, stole my brand new lambswool jersey which later appeared on her spoil heap, so perhaps sheep wool for bedding is the real McCoy! Even had a fox denned in that part of the sett, the badgers would have cleared out all evidence of its stay before reclaiming it for themselves. The clearing out continued revealing on Grace's spoil heap a badger skull and pelvis with part of the spine still attached; judging by the teeth it had been a young adult. Sick and injured badgers will try to go underground to die and that part of the sett may be abandoned for a time or walled up, so there was nothing unusual about this. I collected all the bones and skulls out of interest and photographed them at the bole of a sitka spruce together with the heads of wheat. These last had been neatly bitten off where the stalk met the head and the ripe grains had either dropped or been picked out. I have seen Kentish badger cubs playing with such heads. Had Grace and Disgrace taken them back for a game?

The well-grown cubs stuffed themselves with wild raspberries and I couldn't really blame them. These sweet, luscious fruits grew everywhere at the shelter belt edges and along lanesides, tempting the hungry including myself with their fragrance. Bilberries too were still there for the taking and the blackberries were ripening. I'm not surprised that in other countries, bears fatten themselves on berries ready for a winter hibernation. Though these little Scottish 'bears' would not be hibernating, they grew plumper and plumper as the weeks passed. The hanging clusters of rowan berries would soon be ripe and dropping and when the harvest was over, they would glean the spilt grain. Like the birds, this was the badgers' season of abundance. Their dung changed from the soft, often shapeless mass denoting earthworms to solid droppings studded with berry seeds and grain husks that had passed through the gut undigested. There was plenty of time for play for adults and cubs on the burnside or in the clear water itself. Grace and Disgrace tried their paws at fishing, but only succeeded in falling in themselves rather than making the fish fall out.

The otter completely disregarded all these activities and the badgers were only mildly interested in his. I cannot recall that he was ever fearful of me though he kept his distance. Perhaps because the brocks took me for granted, curiosity on his part finally got the upper hand. He was wet from the burn and a vigorous shake gave his smooth, sleek pelage a spiky look. Next he rubbed his head, shoulders and flanks along the wiry grass squeezing the surplus water out of the guard hairs. He seemed to take little notice of me sitting there until suddenly, he was at my side. My immediate impression was of size. Here was a creature as long as a boar badger though the thick, flattened tapering tail added another 45–48 cm in length. His body was slender with a distinctive hump to the lower back. He turned his head to face me and I was aware of a veritable sprouting of stiff whiskers, a short stumpy muzzle with a dog-like nose, small, neatly rounded ears and a pair of sharp eyes. I averted my startled gaze to the flared nostrils whereupon the otter moved off a short distance and with tail raised and waving, sprainted several times. The odour wasn't fishy or oily as I have since read, or even spicy and 'sweet'. Like the badgers' musked droppings, otters' have a smell all their own. Attempting to translate the action into otter language, I would say he was informing me this was his territory, though with no hint of aggression. Having asserted his rights, he took himself off through the sitkas and that was the last I saw of the otter that night.

Spike sometimes padded down to the edge of the village where he might clean out some of the leaf-filled entrances to the Mound, finding and eating rabbit nestlings that an inexperienced mother had been foolish enough to house there, as well as pignuts growing in the horses' field nearby. I recalled an incident I had been told by the man who had shooting rights on the estate here; he lived in a cottage not far from a piggery housed in an old steading. One winter a few years ago it appeared, he was called out by Phil the man that owned the pig farm. Phil thought that a fox had been digging under the outer wall and up through the floor taking piglets of a few days old. As fast as he filled one hole, another was dug. Eventually a snare was set over the latest hole which caught, not a fox as he thought, but a badger. Knowing his neighbour was interested and used to wild animals, Phil asked the other for his help in releasing the badger, which he gave. The neighbour also pointed out that the badger was a protected species and what about avoiding future problems by making the old building more secure? This was done and Phil lost no more piglets. The badger had part of its ear missing so I suspect it was Spike when he was living at the Mound.

If the otter was midstream when the clan came down the burnside, he might climb onto a boulder to watch their progress. Then off he would go bounding along the bank to where the waters were dammed to form the pool. Here he slipped into the water to fish. His movements were smooth and fluid, only his head above surface left a large 'V' in its wake. Now he would vanish, but a line of bubbles traced the hunter below. He caught many very small fish which were eaten on the surface, but larger ones especially trout, he brought to the margins, usually chewing them from the head; in that way, the prey soon ceased thrashing. This pool was his favourite place; its depth and lack of obstacles gave the otter great scope and its damming ensured that the fish dropping in from the waterfall had then to get out over the rocks. The badgers rarely entered the pool deliberately, preferring the burn with its many boulders from which the more expert amongst them, might stand and flip fish.

It is believed that otters are nocturnal for two reasons. They are less likely to be disturbed by man and the water is much colder at night which makes fish torpid and easier to catch. In isolated places, otters may be abroad in daylight, whilst on seashores, their fishing coincides with high tides. I went to the sett during the day because it had once been the target of badger diggers and deep down I feared it might be again. Once there I would sit and write up my notes of the previous night under the sitkas, an occupation often interrupted by roe, pheasants, the resident vixen and her four well-grown cubs and the sheep from the field. These last would duck under the wire fencing to browse on the grass beyond. This gap under the wire was also a badger, otter and fox trail to and from the fields. On the far side of the burn was a footpath where villagers sometimes walked their dogs to the loch above. They couldn't be seen, but were occasionally heard at a distance. However, they meant no more to the creatures here than the sheepdogs and men's voices from the farmyard. Only twice did I see the otter like this, but it was enough to establish his lying-up place during the day; the entrance was a narrow crevice between rocks under the roots of a tree.

He deposited his dark, muscus-covered spraints in conspicuous places; on top of rocks and boulders, midstream or on the bank were the most popular. He left smaller spraints along his trails. These suggested scent warnings to other otters although I never saw any. I regularly took some home to dissect and found they not only contained undigested fish bones and scales as expected, but occasionally feathers, small mammal and frog remains too. His paw prints, or seals, were abundant in the damp places, but very hard to find elsewhere. They were five-toed and long-clawed like the badgers' but the toes were farther away from the main pad and in a sharper crescent. As I crossed the burn one sunny afternoon, something sinuous moved on a rock farther upstream. Nothing could be heard above the thundering water, but I'm certain he saw my movement and slipped behind the boulder into the burn. Sure enough when I reached the spot, his beautifully clear spatulate prints were beginning to dry in the sun. The centre of the rock was wet too where he had lain to rest or sun worship. I felt guilty at disturbing him, but an hour later sitting writing above the burn, I again spied a movement. He had returned to his rock.

Watching that otter especially at night in proximity to the badgers, I was reminded that both are members of the weasel family, the Mustelidae. Both have short legs, long bodies, small eyes and ears and possess musk glands beneath their tails which scent their droppings. The musk of neither is offensive, rather the reverse. I thought of the two young otters I had seen near the Wild Way. Unlike badger cubs they can be born at any time of year with no delayed implantation. Those cubs had been fluffy-coated and only just beginning to swim which suggested they were about three months old. Their mother was catching food for them and barring accidents, they would stay with her for another nine months or more. However, as with badger cubs, young otter mortality is high.

The area under the sitkas aroused my curiosity, for it seemed that once the ground had been disturbed by man long before these trees were planted. Judging by the fragments dug out by the badgers the immediate locality of the sett must have been a midden, but what of the rest? An old map gave me my first clue and early documents including the *1st Statistical Account* of the locality written in 1791–92 furnished me with more. If it was the pain of a bad back preventing me sleeping at night that started me on the wildlife trail years ago in a Kentish woodland, it was an earlier love of local history that answered my questions about that wood. The past tells us why the present was fashioned, just as the present determines the future.

The geology of the area from valley to hills was unusual. In the northeast portion of the range, the principal rocks were of volcanic origin, whilst the centre and southwest portions were mostly sedimentary. Two of the hills were sandstone beds, but the rest were made up of conglomerates, grits, vertical thicknesses of thin- and thick-bedded shales and occasional veins of limestone. Volcanic upheavals in earliest times had caused these layers to tip and what must have once been a great platform of nearly horizontal beds had now got valleys scooped out of it in every direction, some of them more than 300 metres deep. The harder portions of rock were left standing to form the hills. Large boulders, some of them ten and twelve tonnes in weight from far-off sites, now strewn over the hillsides were evidence of glacial action during the Ice Age.

When I first looked at the sett I noticed the slate lying about, some dug up by the badgers, some scattered further afield. At a distance I found a large piece of limestone partly fashioned and then abandoned by a stonemason. The slates I discovered were incidental to the quarry which had been started here, it was freestone that was wanted. Freestone was any fine-grained stone especially sandstone or limestone, that could be cut and worked in any direction without breaking. This limestone proved to be of inferior quality however so the enterprise ceased. The huge piece of stone fascinated me partly covered as it was with years of old pine needles. It was in the shape of a coffin; carving had been started on the head end but the foot had snapped off. It seemed a strange object half submerged now in detritus and needles and I told the kirk caretaker of my find. This prompted me to ask him the reason for the curious metal coffin-like structures I had seen outside churches in the city and I was told these were mort-safes, relics of the resurrectionists or body snatchers of the eighteenth and nineteenth centuries. The faculty of medicine at the university became famous and the number of students practising anatomy under such renowned doctors and lecturers as John Barclay and Robert Knox increased, greatly far outstripping the bodies of felons and criminals used in dissection. Grave-robbing by students or professionals was rife though, interestingly, not a crime in the eyes of the law. (Taking a shroud was however, so the body would be stripped before it was placed in a sack and carted off.) Religious feeling against despoiling the dead was far stronger north of the border. Here watchtowers were built in graveyards and traps such as spring-guns set up. A mort-safe would be placed over a fresh grave to stop the sack-'em-up men from stealing the corpse. Later it would be removed for the next burial. Only the wealthy or more well-to-do could afford this. At its height, corpses could command ten guineas and more and were even shipped secretly from Dublin to the Ayrshire coast where they were loaded and sent across Scotland in crates labelled 'pianos' or 'books.' A new verb and noun crept into the language – to burke or a burke, although Burke and Hare were never resurrectionists but murderers who smothered their victims for the trade.

The wheat was being harvested and some of the barley. The former has taken over from oats which were once grown extensively. There was a heap of last year's discarded wheat dumped in a patch of nettles at the field edge and for several nights the Burn Badgers fed mainly on that. Their dung was studded with husks, some in pits round the side of the shelter belt and some deposited on top of the pine needles close to the sett entrances. Then came two nights of gentle rain and the clan moved out onto the pasture to forage for earthworms.

One morning I walked down to the farmyard and spoke to Mr Robertson. He hadn't been aware of the otter and was very pleased saying he had never seen one. I pointed out that although I came from a part of Kent where once they had been so common as to have otter in one of the place names, I had never seen one in the wild either, until I came here! It was pleasant to have the farmer's goodwill. I had become attached to the village where the people were friendly to an incomer. It struck me for the first time how I had left my own country without a backward glance and settled with great happiness near the foot of the hills. I might be a white settler, but I was an accepted one and felt at home.

Sometimes looking at Dydor I had the curious feeling it was about to rise, stretch and amble off. I had only to scramble up its heather-clad sides to go to. It was never an inanimate object; it lived, loved and brooded over this part of Scotland and at some inner signal would rise up and walk. My love for it was a passion that surprised me, but I didn't fear for it as I once had for that far-off English wood. If I climbed to the summit, the view stretched from the hills to the lower slopes and the Cley. In the distance gasworks and towers stood on the skyline, those reminders of my own species spewing out in a sprawl on the landscape that ill fitted this perfect place. So mostly I preferred to sit in the heather halfway down from the summit with the 'go-baks' for company and a vista before me of hills and folds where the sheep safely grazed. The hills had not changed in a millennium and the only mark left by man was that of 300 years ago, the old run-rigs still clearly seen on their lower slopes. I came this way almost daily, yet never tired of looking across the loch at the curving lines imprinted on the pasture.

A week earlier on the Glorious Twelfth the grouse season had started. There were butts on the moor but so far there had been no organized drives, merely a few individuals out shooting. Muirburn, the patch burning of old heather, was practised here for the benefit of the grouse. Mature ling heather gives them cover, the young shoots are eaten and the clearings used by the chicks in which to sun themselves. Red grouse are a native bird and have to be tough to survive. Even when the sun shines the wind is often bitter. In winter they keep treading with their feathered feet to prevent being buried under drifting snow.

Slowly walking down Dydor's flank, I found myself amongst the swallows. They were all around me turning, wheeling, diving for insects – one brushed my face. The grouse still called 'go-bak, go-bak' as if I would! I sat in the heather to write with the green, green hillsides before me. I couldn't sit writing for long however, without slipping downwards from the steepness of the hill; perhaps the grouse had been right! Nearing the burn, I saw where the badgers had been turning over the nearly dried out cowpats to feed on the tiny white earthworms in and beneath them. Although an unusually hot August, the heavy night dews were encouraging *Lumbricus terrestris* onto the surface in some parts of their territory, but dew can be notoriously patchy. There were still many wet places however, even away from the burn and at night it was common to see great grey slugs, all of 20 cm long and beautifully marked, out in search of a meal. There were large patches of a vivid yellow flower clinging to rocks at the Cley's edge and I found it to be another introduction – the monkey flower (*Mimulus guttatus*) from North America. My landlady was away again and walking the dogs I met another dog-walker who told me his whippet had met a badger one morning 'bigger than him' going into the Mound. Fortunately the dog had put its tail between its legs and returned to its master, unlike the retriever I walked who some years earlier had accosted a badger at this same sett and received a bite that left her mouth permanently twisted into a grimace.

The heather bloomed on Dydor, changing its darkness to purple. That part of the lochan fed by the spring was awash with pink-flowering amphibious bistort. Further over were small white flowers that looked like frog-bit and water forget-me-not had turned its margins to blue. By mid-August there was a period of heavy rain and violent thunderstorms that gradually passed. In their wake came skeins of geese briefly glimpsed amongst flying clouds. The rain replenished the burns that thundered once more on their way to the valley. It gave new vigour to the flora. The bog below the sitkas was bright again with the pretty pink purslane (*Montia sibirica*) with its shiny, dark green leaves. Out on the moors the sphagnum moss turned a vivid red with many sundews stretching their tempting 'dew'-baited traps to lure unsuspecting insects. Now many of these were in flower, the tiny white blooms on their slender stalks rising high above the hairy leaves.

I spent much of my time day and night at the sett of the Burn Badgers. When Spike wasn't wandering off to the Mound, his part of the sett was the huge entrance above the wych-elm. Once the elm had been pollarded though the limbs on it were now well grown, but its roots held the earth and rocks on the slope. Each time I collected up broken glass and rubbish to leave in the village litter-bin on my way home; the place was beginning to look really good. One day I found more wheat heads lying by the sett and fresh, bitten-off blades of grass dropped inside two entrances from bundles of bedding that had been taken down. I made a rough sketch of the wych-elm; it was a fabulous tree clinging onto the steep slope. Spike's hole faced it so that his dug-out spoil had piled up high all around and even across the short trunk. The boar often stood on hind legs to run his front claws down one limb effectively tearing off the bark which hung in long strips. This is commonly done by dominant boars to elder trees in my part of Kent, but no elders grew by this sett. Both tree species however showed a surprising whiteness of wood beneath the torn bark. Though he may have been cleaning his claws, he had also left this visual marker proclaiming his right to the place. A yellow loosestrife grew by the drystane dyke, very beautiful amongst the long, green grass. A badger trail led past this to the wild raspberries which were still plentiful.

The fox cubs had lost their woolly coats and resembled young adults now, although their rich brown fur looked in far better condition than the vixen's moulting coat. One youngster had disappeared but the remaining three usually came together at the natal den amongst the rocks after a night spent searching for food. Berries and insects were easily found and their mother still left some food, for example, part of a rabbit, a mole or the occasional woodpigeon to supplement their diet. A few more weeks and their hunting skill would be sufficiently improved to catch such prey for themselves. They still played together, but the friendly games of puppyhood were degenerating into squabbles and they pushed one another as they stood on hind legs with tails raised, ears laid back and open-mouthed aggression. I never mentioned their presence to Mr Robertson although he probably knew they were there. One morning the trio found part of a fish the otter had discarded. While the two young dog foxes fought over it their sister stole off with the booty under cover of the noise.

The night of the full moon in August was the 25th and I still have the record I kept of it!

> A cloudy sky, though with the moon behind the clouds visibility is excellent. Honeysuckle in the hedgerows is perfuming the night with many moths and flying insects. At 5 a.m. it is first light and I've just been greeted by the jet black cat who sits by the entrance to the farm. He has the fiercest, glittering, yellow eyes I have ever seen in a feline, but these belie his nature for he is very friendly. He isn't waiting for me, but for the badgers who will cross the road here. This is another badger-friendly cat, although he doesn't go looking for them like my cat Flo did [see *Green-eyed Flo*], nor does he enter their sett. I can't cross the burn as it is still in full flood, so walk up to the loch and so into the top of the sitka belt. Since the rain there are many fine specimens of the stinkhorn (*Phallas impudicus*) pushing up and fruiting under the spruce. There was no breeze this night, although now a light one has sprung up. I stand leaning against a trunk by the sett and savour the gloom of the trees and the green light appearing beyond them through the bracken – a magic moment. The tawny pair that roost in the old dead oak call and answer from beyond the wood. Now greylags cry as they pass above the trees to their feeding grounds. A woodpigeon begins a cooing lament just above me. The mournful chant persists into my subconscious as the dark lessens. 'Hard times coming, hard times coming, hard times coming, hard,' it seems to say. Even after I return home, at the back of my mind, the refrain will repetitiously persist.

Ah, the cubs are here playing tag amongst the trunks. They race over the bare, hummocky ground sending up showers of dead brown pine needles over the gaping sett entrances and are gone just as abruptly. A small shape darts silently over the same ground, pauses, and slips to an entrance, only to pause again – a weasel! From beyond the sombre sitka shade where the green light filters, the fronds move and it is this movement that the weasel watches. There are rabbits feeding in the grassy space. Then a movement to my left. A roe buck jumps oh so lightly, into the bracken that earlier I passed through to reach this spot. He seems not to have noticed my scent which must surely have lingered there. Another jumps, followed by her two kids. Now the whole family feed on the soft rush in the gully. A shrill scream – I had quite forgotten the weasel – and a movement almost at my feet. Millie and Spike stare, heads raised in the direction of the cry. Unnoticed, the roe have vanished, though I suspect they slipped away along the gully.

The tawny gives a long, last, lingering curtain-call and a different cry comes of geese flying southwards but not I think, greylags this time. A woodpecker makes me jump with his first tattoo of the day and hardly daring to breath, I slowly look upwards. The great spotted tries again and this time skilfully extracts a long, centipede-like creature. C. Goon is flirting with Millie and gets a cuff from her unfriendly paw, whereupon the twins hurl themselves upon him with glee and another game is in full swing – the noise! Round and round the tree against which I lean, they are a blur of grey badger bodies. It is well light now. A pause in the hurly-burly as that gruesome twosome, sorry threesome, C. Goon, Grace and Disgrace stop for breath. The only sounds are those of Spike noisily grooming a safe distance away from their game. His claws raking through his fur as he sits back in one of the hollows and the clapping of wings as the woodpigeon goes in search of breakfast amongst the wheat stubble sound loud in the sudden quietness. Much later as I walk back out of the wood, there is a movement. The roe family lie up on the field edge chewing the cud. I feel much too excited to tamely return home, so walk the length of the burn and down to the kirk yard to decipher some of the names on the oldest tombstones. The rowan berries are ripely beautiful; a tranquil end to a wonderful night.

Sometimes I had the burnside to myself after the badgers had gone their separate ways to forage and the otter would be fishing in the pool. Insects were everywhere on the surface of the water and the otter was submerged. There would be a sudden flurry and turmoil of water and there he would be on the surface again with a fish in his jaws. Occasionally he brought fish ashore and eating them as he normally did from the head, the sound of his crunching came clearly to me. One really large fish however, he cleaned from the shoulder down and left just the head, spine and tail; a very neat job. The anglers on the loch said he sometimes left fish partly eaten, though I rarely found this; perhaps they had disturbed him at his meal? Usually it was the badgers returning to their sett much later in the early morning who smelled where the otter had eaten his fill. Then they would snuffle round and if the foxes were near, one or other of the clan would chase them off. Badgers do not appear to join forces to rid themselves of an unwanted visitor or intruder such as a strange badger or an aggressive dog. They never attempted to bother the otter however, apart from Grace and Disgrace who twice to my knowledge, tried to solicit him in their games with total lack of success. I suspect he regarded the clan as a necessary evil and since his territory was far greater than theirs, he need not have stayed unless he chose to do so. I enjoyed seeing him eat, holding his prey in those long-clawed, webbed forefeet, the small bright eyes always alert and with frequent stops to listen.

Otters communicate with various sounds but the only one I could even poorly imitate was the high-pitched piping known as the otter's whistle that I had heard the Wild Way bitch make to her cubs. I tried to copy it, though I doubted whether it was very much like hers. He stood up on hind legs to look over at me very carefully, then came closer. Their faces are indeed very dog-like, no wonder they are called dogs and bitches. The long stiff whiskers are an aid to finding their prey in murky or dark water. Like badgers they are reputed to be very shy, but clearly they can get used to human presence especially if they have no cause to fear it. This same otter I discovered early one morning well into the hills which gave me some idea of the extent of his territory. A dog's range will encompass that of two or sometimes three bitches though apart from a week or so when mating, all are said to lead solitary existences.

By the end of August the pink-footed geese were returning early from their summer feeding grounds in Greenland and Iceland. One night a great flock descended onto the wheat stubble where Millie, C. Goon and Spike were foraging for the dropped grain. I counted 128 geese and then gave up; there must have been hundreds on that field. People who say badgers are not fast movers should have seen those three run for it – and they didn't return that night!

By the loch one morning I stopped to watch two border collies rounding up the sheep to the shepherd's whistles. Slowly they were herded up and moved off to fresh pasture on the far hillside. Another man stood watching by the van and trailer that had brought them up to the foot of the hills, but engrossed in the dogs' work, I didn't heed that it was Mr Robertson until he came over and spoke. He asked after the badgers and otter and we discussed the harvest, the silage he was at present cutting and the barley straw soon to be roll-baled, wrapped and stacked in the barn for winter feed. I hadn't realized either that his brother was the shepherd; it was difficult to imagine two more physically dissimilar men. Sandy Robertson laughed, remarking that Will and he were never taken for brothers. The sheep were Will's responsibility, the cows his and the arable side was shared between them. It seemed to work well.

I continued my walk and in an area of grass moor with heather and sedges came across a great, green caterpillar with pink spots along its sides. It was crossing the track and I stood for some moments watching its progress before recognizing that it was a well-grown emperor moth caterpillar. Their vivid coloration gives them excellent camouflage on heather their food plant, but not so on a dusty path! There were not the numerous species of butterflies and moths in this part of Scotland as there are in Kent. Here I found the butterflies of the cabbage white, plenty of red admirals and peacocks (Tabby the cat ate a red admiral one morning!) orange tips, small and pearl-bordered fritillaries and meadow browns, but that was all. I came to where planks were laid over the bog to facilitate walking. Happening to glance to my right, I looked harder. There beautifully disguised on a patch of brown, dried-out moss and decaying wood was a grey partridge hen with four chicks. She stared at me a long moment and I wished myself far away. Then up she flew without any great haste and the young ones followed. I was amazed the chicks were such good fliers for they were still small until I discovered they can fly at sixteen days old. It was their mother's eyes that had caught my attention; if it were not for them, they would have gone unnoticed so well were they blended into their surroundings.

Returning I stood for awhile to watch the herons each standing on a stilt-like leg with its mirror image in the margins. They stayed so still one could be forgiven for thinking them to be asleep, but I knew from other occasions that the slightest movement below water would produce a stabbing dagger-like thrust on the fisherman's part and most likely, a successful catch. The herons nested at the top of a Scots pine, the spreading canopy ideally suited to the large, untidy structure. The loch was so plentifully stocked that it is surprising there was not more than one pair. The nest had most unusual bedding material hanging down over the untidy platform edge that blew back and forth in the slightest wind. Workmen had been laying pipes on the road to the village and one of their bright orange plastic strips of fencing had been requisitioned by the heron. I continued on to the sitka belt and looked at the sett; the sound of the tractor cutting the grass for silage receded and returned. I could see the glint of rushing waters far below me and above came the sound of magpies and crows quarrelling; who was robbing whose nest? Even as I sat watching Spike's entrance, the leaves were slowly drifting earthwards from his coppiced elm. At the field edge the birches too were shedding their foliage, each small pointed leaf a gentle spatter of gold that twisted as it fell. Not yet the end of August but already the autumn was come.

CHAPTER FOUR

Wildlife Records

I decided to walk the main peaks in the area for the heather was now fully out. It would be good to see what a difference a few weeks had made. Walking up from the village the path through the shelter belt was dark and cool and the vista of sunny stubble and hills beyond, the light at the end of a tunnel. The roll-baled straw was scattered about the top field. In the middle distance the tractor driver was manoeuvring a bale into position. Now it was grasped by the pick-up to be transported to the pole-barn where it would keep dry and well ventilated until needed. Beyond was a dark line of drystane dyke leading over the boggy pasture with a background entirely dominated by the purple heather-clad Dydor. The deep blue sky with its sparse fluffs of white cloud, purple hill and the golden stubble were a wonderful start to my day. But for the lone tractor and I, nothing moved in the landscape, even the birds seemed resting and silent. Already it was hot, though when I crossed the moor there was almost bound to be a breeze and through the pass in the hills too. Pack on back and all the day ahead of me with the sun shining above, what more could one want? There was a busyness of bees on the flowering ling, the marsh cinquefoil's star-shaped flowers were still in bloom together with the tiny white petals of marsh bedstraw and the milkworts' vivid blue flecks.

The terrain was becoming more rugged and the sheep sparser. The pass was a narrow defile through steep rock faces and the way scattered with boulders. A crow flew lazily from an overhead lintel like a discarded rag in the warm air. Now the ground was dropping. As from nowhere a tiny burn bubbled and gained momentum in its descent to the reservoir below. A glimpse of blue showed its presence, still no larger than my thumbnail from this distance with the purple hills rearing starkly upright from its edges.

It was tempting to linger by the water margins, but I was anxious to be on the peaks by midday. Now the path led upwards, twisting and turning upon itself and a wind blew sharply though the sun still shone. It was good to look back every so often to see the view of reservoir and hillside I had left. Once at the summit there was a sadder view looking down the far side to the site of the Covenanters' battlefield. The battle had been fought like so many, in the name of religion and the freedom to practise it. The Covenanters were Scottish Presbyterians who objected to English Episcopalian interference in their worship. They supported the National Covenant of 1638, hence their name, which pledged opposition to the English bishops. There were other bloody battles throughout the 1600s, but not until William and Mary came to the throne were the laws relaxed in an attempt to unite the country and bring about peace.

Galloway saw the start of this particular uprising that lasted only fifteen days, when Covenanters there fought with soldiers sent to arrest them. The Covenanters took the leader prisoner and marching nearly to the capital rallied many to their support until they were 1000 strong. Soon large numbers deserted, however, and the Covenanters turned back only to find the 3000-strong royalist force under General Dalzell in hot pursuit. They were followed through these hills and made their last stand below me on a bleak November day in 1666. Some Covenanters were killed and more captured; some were tortured then executed, but many fled to die in these hills. For most of them the area would have been strange country. It is one thing to walk with a map and rucksack in good weather, quite another when exhausted and wounded in bad. There are many memorials of the Killing Times in Scotland to those who died for their faith. There are a few in these hills. But for each monument here, hundreds died unmarked and unsung and the hills still guard their secrets.

I sat eating my sandwiches; no sheep or birds, only the sighing wind for company. Each point of the compass revealed a different vista. It might have been that high mountain from which 'all the kingdoms of the world were shown in a moment of time.' How insignificant and expendable is man.

The land with all its living creatures can well do without us, but we cannot do without them. Perhaps we should all go up into high places sometimes to discover ourselves. Now bees were entering a hole in a grassy tussock, their bodies dusted with gold and their pollen sacks full. There was movement everywhere on the heather; sitting amongst that company I had no more importance than one of those outcrops of rock. They had their place in the scheme of things; without them most flowers would never be pollinated and many species of flora would cease to exist.

The sun was well past its zenith when I moved on. Now came a series of steep gradients as peak followed peak, most clothed in purple so that the few bracken-clad hills came as a verdant surprise. Law is an alternative word for hill in the Lothians as in Lytlaw, Wooly Law and Hunt Law. Small areas of afforestation had been planted on some slopes. Unlike Dumfries and Galloway however, these were few and didn't destroy the contours of the hills. Looking across from summit to the lower slopes of another law I again saw lines of the ancient run-rigs, a series of ridges and furrows still imprinted on the rough pasture. Alone on the peaks, I had a strange sense of history, almost eternity; the past, present and future seemed merged into one. But for the seasons, little changed on these hills.

With several more miles to go, I spied my home loch and the village spread out below for a brief time, until a fresh hill looming before me, hid it once more from my view. Now I was on Lytlaw, more familiar ground that I walked regularly and so to the lower slopes of my friend Dydor and its Dark Spring forever feeding the clear waters, lifeblood of all living things.

I found many old otter spraints on a boulder in the margins of the loch; they become dry and crumbly as they age until only the fish bones remain. On top of all the old spraints, two fresh ones had been deposited about 5 cm long. I enjoyed watching the otter grooming in the pool. First he would rear up out of the water to check it was only me sitting there. Then he floated on his back slowly scratching his chest, the picture of contentment. All four paws were held well out of the water. He rolled over and over, then lay floating on his back again, bobbing up and down on the disturbed surface rather like a rocking cradle. One of his hind legs sticking up in front of him caught his attention. He drew it up and with his forepaws holding it steady, licked first at the fur of the lower leg, then the webbing between each toe and lastly, nibbled at the fifth digit set well back on the foot and then at the others. His teeth clicked on the long claws. The toes and claws of the forepaws were longer than those of the hind. Righting himself, the otter dog paddled slowly round the pool till something below caught his attention and with forepaws at his sides, dived into the depths.

I never volunteered information about the otter or badgers, but the loch fishermen often spoke of the former. One man went on angling holidays in the far north of Scotland and recounted how otters sometimes lie up in sheds and outhouses and are not particularly nervous of man. I said nothing about 'my' otter but it confirmed what I already believed namely, that the shyness of otters, like badgers, is greatly exaggerated. Yes, they are wary at first – that is natural, but provided one acts with discretion and poses no threat, they will come to accept you in time. I often lingered at the field edge near the sett before returning home, for a pair of greenfinches had made their nest in a small hawthorn there. It was a bulky cup of moss and grasses placed against the trunk. The parents fed their offspring by regurgitation and already had produced one brood. This second one was less than a fortnight old. One morning the flutterings and calls of the adults caught my attention. There on a branch near the nest was a grey squirrel holding one of the nestlings in his paws as if it was a nut and eating it. Having finished, he leapt easily to the nest again, but at that point I intervened, clicking and hissing at the marauder as squirrels do one to another. Confused though not intimidated, he followed me from the hawthorn along the tree edge and this way we kept parallel; at least he had forgotten his meal. Finally on a small bough he sat and washed, cleaning the chick down off his white chest and chin. Then he faced me sitting back on his haunches, right paw resting at his side. Walking home I hoped the remaining brood would survive his predations; I liked those greenfinches.

By now with Melanie's help, I had amassed a considerable amount of information on the history of mammals in Scotland. Some of the earliest records were by John Leslie (Scottish bishop and historian 1527–96) which translated into modern English said: 'The greater part of the nobility have their main recreation in hunting with the sleuth-hounds, for that, this recreation has our countrymen either in the fields to hunt the hare and the fox, or in the sands and hills the badgers, or in the mountains the wolf or the wildcat.' (The last wolf was killed in Scotland in 1740.)

This of course was for sport, but other animals such as rabbits were hunted as a livelihood for their skins and as meat. A picture of rabbits round their warren in East Lothian in the 1690s, indicates a regular source of extra meat (though not for the poor). Since early times, Scotland held a European reputation for its skins. In *The Influence of Man on Animal Life in Scotland* by James Ritchie published 1920, he says:

> Among the taxed items at the Port of Leith (Edinburgh) in 1482 are mentioned skins of calf, goat, kid, rabbit, polecat, otter and badger. Apart from this considerable export of Scottish skins, many changed hands within the country at local fairs of which the annual Fur Market of Dumfries was typical. Here there were on sale every February, the year's produce of Dumfriesshire, of the shire of Stewarty of Galloway, of the counties of Ayr, Lanark, Peebles, Selkirk, Roxburgh, and even of Cumberland and Northumberland:- hare skins, sometimes to the number of 70,000; rabbit skins, in one year as many as 200,000; fitches or foumarts (polecats) on one occasion 600 and skins of otters, badgers, foxes and wildcats as the supply offered.

Hecter Boece (1465?–1536) talking of exported skins says: 'among thame ar mony martrikis [martens] bevers, quhitvedis [stoats or ermines] and toddis [foxes]; the furrs and skinnis of thaim are coft [bought] with gret price amang uncouth [foreign] merchandis . . .' The Ayr manuscript written in the days of King Robert Bruce (1274–1329) lists among the commoner skins of fox, stoat, weasel, pine marten and wildcat, those of beaver and sable, as well as hides and deer skins. It was once suggested that beaver and sable were foreign skins re-exported. However, historical records now suggest beavers survived in Scotland into the thirteenth century. Sable could be a mistranslation of pine marten; in modern terminology the sable is a marten (*Martes zibellina*) of north Asian forests. Ritchie tell us:

> The customs duties levied upon exports of Scottish skins are interesting. In the fourteenth century an export duty of fourpence was levied on each timmer of skins and this was raised in 1424, to sixpence on every ten fox skins exported. [A timmer or timber was a merchant's term used to denote according to kind, a number of skins. For instance, a timmer of martens, polecats or ermines contained 30 skins.] The fox has from earliest times been regarded as vermin to be killed whenever possible, but it is well to remember that the value of its pelt acted like a price upon its head. By the beginning of the seventeenth century the skins exported and valued at 40s, a piece, numbered 1,012 a year

– no inconsiderable slaughter when there was added to it the number traded within the country.

There was no such creature then as the urban fox.
James Ritchie continues:

> In Scotland the decadence of the Badger is to be accounted for by a multitude of influences which told severally and directly against it. It was hunted for sport, it was caught for baiting, it was destroyed for its destructiveness, it was killed for food and its skins were a marketable commodity. Of all these direct influences the value of its skin was probably that which least influenced its welfare, for in Scotland the skins never created any great demand, and I mention the Badger here simply because the skins which sold at some 5s. or 6s. each, made an occasional appearance at the Dumfries Fur Fair up to about the middle of the nineteenth century.

I don't know when badger hair first became popular for use in artists' brushes or shaving brushes, or the pelts for the making of sporrans to hang over a kilt, but certainly both had been in vogue for some considerable time which seems to have escaped Ritchie's notice. In the *Zoologist* for January 1882 comes the comment: '1842 was a sad year for the poor Badgers, owing to the revival of the Highland dress after the Queen's [Victoria] visit to Scotland.' These sporrans began as modest purses, but for regimental dress became very elaborate affairs. An officer's sporran dated about 1832 of the 93rd Highland Regiment of Foot at the Edinburgh Castle Museum shows virtually the whole badger except for the legs used as a sporran with the head as the flap to close it and six ermines hanging as decoration. This practice would still appear to be flourishing as the National Federation of Badger Groups (NFBG) had a request from a gentleman in Scotland in 1991 for members to send him badgers killed in traffic accidents to be made into sporrans; this request was rejected. A year later at a farmers association ball in Aberdeenshire, one of the organizing committee sported a badger's head sporran on his kilt.

Dr Campbell wrote in 1774 that: 'the Badger is hunted and destroyed, whenever found and being by nature an inactive and indolent Creature, is commonly fat, and therefore they make his hind Quarters into Hames in North Britain and Wales.' (This was common throughout England.) In the *Spectator* of 29 September 1917, a correspondent gives many recipes for cooking the badger, which he said were familiar to his mother and practised in the Outer Hebrides. While the recipes may well be correct, the locality seems at fault, for at least in recorded times, badgers were unknown there.

Badger products were also in demand. *Baily's Magazine* 1880 gives:

> A cure for ailments of the bladder was said to be provided by pills made from the gall of a living adult badger mixed with hare's blood, flour, dill seeds and

wormwood. And a Clever Nanny made a salve from badger's fat which at one time was in great request over the counties of Stirling and Perth as it was felt to be useful for treating burns, scalds, and indeed for all sorts of hurts and wounds.

But the best-known of all the sovereign remedies obtained from badgers was published in 1800 in *The Sporting Magazine*: 'The flesh, blood and grease of the badger are very useful for oils, ointments, salves and powders. These were said to cure shortness of breath, the cough of the lungs, for the stone, sprained sinews, aches etc. In addition a well-dressed badger skin was said to be very warm and comfortable for ancient people who are troubled with paralytic disorders.' It it interesting that recent studies have identified corticosteroids in badger fat, so the folklore cure for rheumatism and sprains using badger grease could have some scientific basis.

James Ritchie discusses the effects of the destruction of the forest by early man upon animal life. By the same token of course, one can see that recent afforestation has increased cover for it too. I found many references to flooding and in particular, 'the more sudden and serious flooding of the rivers after heavy rain has had accountable effect upon their inhabitants and those of the low lying valleys, drowning such creatures as Badgers often in great number – the two great floods of the Findhorn in 1829, say the brothers Stuart, drowned in their holes most of the badgers in the lower banks, washing them into the stream . . .'

Otter pelts were used for making gloves, vests etc. as they were not only very durable, but retained their softness and pliancy after being repeatedly wetted. Of all pelts, those of the otter had the best fur or underwool; the top hair was pulled out before the skins were manufactured. It was also in demand for linings, collars and cuffs of men's coats. 'Yet,' says Ritchie:

> the demand for the skins of Scottish Otters, has been long on the downgrade. The Otter skins which were exported in the early seventeenth century – the annual export averaged only some 44 skins – fetched 40s. each but thereafter the price seems gradually to have fallen. About 1800, according to the *Dumfries Courier* of February 21st 1829, a Dumfries dealer who purchased 60 otter skins from a single individual, paid close on 30s. each for them; but the statistics of the Dumfries Fur Market show that from 1829 to 1869, when otter skins ceased to be forthcoming, the price averaged rather under 10s. a skin and although it rose in 1840 to 13s., it frequently fell so low as 5s. and 6s., and touched its lowest ebb of 3s. to 6s. in 1866.

One might be forgiven for thinking that the declining fashion for wearing otter skins might now give the creature an opportunity to gradually increase its numbers. However, the tale of a single 'vermin' list will indicate the penalty paid by the otter for its depredations real or imaginary in fishing streams. On the Duchess of Sutherland's estates during the three years from

March 1831 to March 1834, a reward of 5s. offered for each head was paid on 263 otters.

Ritchie finishes by remarking:

> The case of the Badger and the Otter, however, is typical of most of the fur-bearing natives of Scotland, and in concluding an account of the influence of the trade in skins upon the Scottish fauna, I would emphasize again that skins alone seldom formed the whole subject of the persecution to which their possessors were subjected, but that other and varied objects and especially the protection of game and minor domestic stock, combined to intensify the pursuit of most of the fur-bearers. The destruction of Otters for their fur, because of their raids on Salmon and Trout, and for sport, has made inroads on their numbers, occasionally attributed to other causes.

Coming closer to the present and the Lothian area of Scotland where I now lived, I made some sobering discoveries. *The Mammalian Fauna of the Edinburgh District* by William Evans FCSE published 1892 states:

> That the Badger, or Brock, as it was called, was a common animal throughout the district in olden times goes without saying. At the time the *Old Statistical Account* was drawn up – the closing years of last century – it was still well known as an inhabitant of many localities, though even then its numbers were greatly reduced; and the adverse conditions continuing to grow, its extermination in most of its former haunts was apparently accomplished by about the middle of the present century. Here and there a miserable remnant lingered a few years longer, but it is very doubtful if more than eight or nine pairs of the original stock now exist anywhere in the valley of the Forth, and these mainly in its remotest parts among the Perthshire hills. In the valley of the Tweed it maintained its footing better, and a few favourite habitats are known to be still occupied.
>
> In the *Old Statistical Account of Duddingstone* (vol.xviii, p. 374) we read that a solitary badger at times may provoke a stubborn chase and contest, and it is interesting to know that at the present moment a few are to be found within a very short distance of that locality, though I fear we cannot claim them as the descendants of the sturdy beasts just mentioned. I refer to the policies at Edmonstone House, where Badgers have taken up their abode for some years past, and are known to have bred on several occasions. Unfortunately, the gamekeeper seems to think they are already too numerous, and has taken to killing them. In May of this year (1891) I saw two of them in the taxidermist's hands. It is supposed that this colony originated with a female which escaped from the stables at The Ince, where Mr T. Speedy has kept several in confinement. The Badger seen in a field near Greenend in June 1883, and mentioned in the *Scotsman* at the time, was doubtless the same animal.

The name of Mr Tom Speedy was to occur again and again.

The list of badgers found (and inevitably killed) makes depressing reading, but there were also some surprises. A paper submitted by Charles

Campbell entitled 'A Badger Colony in Dalmeny Park' and published in the *Transactions of the Edinburgh Naturalists Field Club* 1897 records:

> For some time the papers bear reports relating to the capture of a badger at some part of the Lothians or neighbouring counties. It was only at the beginning of this month that a letter appeared in the *Scotsman* giving an account of the capture of a badger near Roxburgh. Some of the nearer of these records I am inclined to believe may be set down to animals which have migrated from the colony which I will now speak of, for although it still seems to hold its own, it has not increased of late, and the question of food supply alone would cause some of the younger generations to seek a new home.
>
> In a secluded corner of Dalmeny Park there has existed for some years now a colony of badgers. Their history, briefly related, is as follows. In 1881 the Earl of Rosebery brought a pair of badgers from the south of England, and had them liberated in Dalmeny Woods. Nothing more was seen of them inside the policies, but a badger killed at Hopetoun shortly afterwards was supposed to be one of the pair. In 1889 three others, one male and two females, were brought to Dalmeny. Profiting by experience, these, instead of being liberated in the open, were let into an old fox earth. Here they at once took up their abode, and seemed to adapt themselves to their new surroundings.

These badgers thrived and have populated, amongst other places, an area now well within the boundary of the city of Edinburgh. Lord Rosebery was Master of Foxhounds and believed that the reintroduction of badgers to the area would improve living conditions for foxes suffering from mange. The badger is built for digging; his claws are continually growing. Occasionally one sees a 'lazy' brock whose front claws have grown completely under so that it hobbles, though fortunately this is rare. Foxes will dig their own dens, but will take over a disused sett readily. A fox suffering from sarcoptic mange deposits pieces of its crusty skin containing the mites that cause it on anything it squeezes through or under including the earth of its underground home. Mange is unusual in badgers, but not unknown. Dr Ernest Neal in *The Natural History of Badgers* (1986) cites a head keeper in the north of Scotland who found a badger lying in a fox's den that had no hair except for a small tuft on its tail. Three years earlier a fox using this den had also had mange. It is doubtful whether introducing badgers to an area would decrease instances of mange in foxes, but it was certainly a widely-held belief and led to many reintroductions of badgers to areas where formerly they had been wiped out for their so-called destructiveness. Ritchie remarks that: 'In several districts of South Britain, foxes and badgers also are actually imported from the continent and from Scotland, and are set free to establish themselves in the hope that the hunt may benefit thereby.' The fox population of an entire district may be exterminated by mange within a few months and can take considerable time to build up again. Obviously this is a loss to the area's fox-hunting community.

The naturalist's transactions or published records, covering many areas of Great Britain, usually began in Queen Victoria's reign which heralded a great upsurge of genuine interest in the natural world. Values are sometimes very different to today's however for this interest brought with it the vogue of collecting and rivalry amongst collectors and not only for birds' eggs, butterflies and rare plants. Tom Speedy was an interesting example of this. He spent a few days with an old friend who had seen otter prints in the snow. Speedy says:

> I was anxious to make a collection of the rarer of the fauna of our country and having already procured specimens of the badger, the wildcat, the fox and the small quadrupeds, I was exceedingly anxious to acquire a couple of otters. This was no easy matter, as I preserve those only killed by my own gun or rifle. The badgers I procured in one of the Border counties by climbing a tree above their 'earth' and shooting them at the mouth as they came out in the moonlight. The wildcats I shot as they were 'bolted' from a cairn of stones by fox-terriers, while assisting a keeper in Ross-shire. It was with a feeling of reluctance that I destroyed two of these, the rarest of our wild animals, but the enraged keeper, whose game had suffered the previous season from a couple of broods of wildcats, declared in emphatic terms that their presence could not and would not be tolerated.

He successfully hunts and shoots his otters – a male at one location and a female at another and concludes: 'I returned southwards, highly gratified with my winter's ramble and proud of the splendid specimens which I was fortunate enough to obtain.'

A paper read and published in the same transactions in 1892 by J.T. Mack entitled *A Day with The Dumfriesshire Otter-Hounds With A Few Remarks On The Otter* is equally revealing. Mack believed otters killed off sickly and diseased fish and enjoying eels as they do, otters must help the fisherman for eels devour large quantities of salmon and trout ova and fry. He complained that the otter was a much maligned animal, but still enjoyed accompanying the above hunt and finishes: 'As a health-giving pursuit during the summer months, nothing can equal otter-hunting.'

Victorian naturalists were very observant and Tom Speedy was no exception. 'Badgers,' he wrote 'are becoming scarce, the traps of the rabbit catcher being instrumental in reducing their number. It is gratifying to learn that some proprietors are now reintroducing them on their estates and giving orders that they are to be protected.' Judging by present-day reports I receive from contacts in many areas of Scotland, it would appear that snares intended for rabbit and fox, frequently kill badgers. I suspect this may be the answer to the continuing low badger densities in parts of the country that could easily sustain many more.

Speedy gives a detailed account of the baiting of his day:

> Drawing the badger never failed to gather a crowd, a badger frequently being kept for the purposes of low public-houses. This cruel sport however, was

prohibited by Act of Parliament in 1850. Yet long after the passing of the Act it was now and then indulged in by the lower stratum of society in rural areas. (As a boy) I have an indistinct recollection of a band of travelling gipsies camping on a disused road, and having with them a badger in a box for carrying on this illegal sport. My remembrance of the box is that it was six or seven feet long and about eighteen inches in width and depth. A number of people brought their dogs to 'draw the badger.' Not one of them could accomplish it, and those game enough to try generally came out with ugly cuts about the head. Some of the terriers got hold of the badger, and for a time it looked as if they would fetch him out; but in every case they failed, and the reason was obvious. Being largely endowed with curiosity, I got down on my knees and looked into the box. I saw the white stripes of the badger's face and his small eyes like fiery orbs, no doubt expecting an encounter from another adversary. For half the length of the box next the badger spars were nailed across the bottom, so that he could get a hold for his feet, and consequently it required considerable strength to dislodge him. On the other hand, it was alleged that the bottom near the entrance had been rubbed over with a soft soap, so that once past the spars, the slippery floor rendered 'drawing the badger' impossible. I was not old enough to take notice of the stakes, but I remember money changed hands and the language used, as is generally the case in such low species of gambling, was more expulsive than refined.

I wonder if the language of the Scots regiments was much different? From *Baily's Magazine* published 1880:

This use of badgers as a spectacle was not only a rural pastime for they were also taken to towns to provide sport as at Colinton in 1880 when badger-baiting was arranged to entertain the officers based in Edinburgh Castle. [The 1850 Act of Parliament to which Tom Speedy alluded, seems to have been disregarded by all classes!] Apparently a disagreeable impression was created for brock had to be smoked before he would leave his earth. He was then seized by a dog at the entrance and a terrific and bloody struggle ensued.

Dog succeeded dog until eventually the badger was overcome.

Baiting seems to have been common in the Edinburgh area. There are records from the estate of a Mr Inglis on the banks of the Leith and of baiting organized by a farmer to entertain his visiting Stirlingshire tenants. In this instance the badger killed three dogs before it was 'bottled up for another day'. A report by J.A. Harvie Brown in 1882 contains the comment under Fifeshire: 'The sea-cliffs east of St Andrew's were their breeding haunts fifty years ago, and it used to be the practice to 'draw the Badger' in a hole on St Andrew's Links.' J.A. Harvie Brown FRSE, FZS attempted a regional assessment of the badger's status in Scotland in the *Zoologist*, Third Series published January 1882, but like so many recorders of Scotland's fauna only succeeds in giving the numbers of animals taken into captivity or killed, rather than those observed. Again there are accounts of introductions in parts of the country where they were fast becoming extinct and a few (though a pitifully few) records of enlightened landowners anxious to preserve their wildlife.

Perhaps the last word should go to William Evans:

> From the earliest times man has ever exercised a modifying influence on mammalian-faunas, adversely affecting some species either by direct persecution or by rendering the country unsuitable to their habits, and directly or indirectly fostering the increase of others. He has, moreover, long been in the habit of importing certain species from one country or district to another, so that it is not always easy to separate the indigenous from the introduced. The more populous a district becomes, and the more its agricultural industries are developed, the greater will be the changes on its fauna. Add to these factors the existence for many centuries of a large and influential class of landowners holding strong views regarding the preservation of game, and it will readily be understood that the district around Edinburgh was probably the first in Scotland to witness a radical change in the character of its mammalian-life within historic times. The larger predaceous animals, such as the Wolf and the Bear, which carried destruction among the flocks, and even threatened the life of the herdsman himself, would be among the first to succumb. Many species would be hunted for their skins or their flesh; others mainly for sport. The smaller Carnivora would receive further attention on account of their visits to the poultry-yard and Hares and Rabbits because of injury to the crops. Then came the game laws – another interference with the balance of nature – accelerating the destruction of the predatory animals, and facilitating the increase of the rodents. The inordinate increase of the Rabbit led in its turn to a universal system of trapping to keep it in check, and from that day the fate of most of the remaining terrestrial Carnivora was sealed.

A comment to this is interesting: 'Evidence of the former existence of the Bear, the Wolf and the Wild Boar, even within historic times, is not wanting; and remains of the Wolf and the Reindeer have been found on the hills above Dreghorn.' But perhaps the last record should go to someone we have already met when William Evans tells us: 'Mr T. Speedy, obtained from this and other parts of Scotland several hundred Weasels and Stoats for transportation alive to New Zealand in the hope that they may provide a natural remedy for the Rabbit plague in that country.'

By late August nearly all the silage grass was cut in the field next to the Burn Sett. Not only did this leave numerous short, fallen blades that were ideal for bedding, but the remaining grass was close-cropped; excellent for badgers worming. I often went before dawn to sit by the sett under the sitkas. With the glint of water rushing below me, it was a lovely way to end the night. I chose a different rock one morning that gave me a closer view of the steep incline down to the burn. Spike padded silently up the slope, came to inspect my boots, then had a brief search around his home and went below; it was 5.30 a.m. The tawny couple began to call somewhere above and a little to my right; she doing her husky invitation and he answering his clear, tremulous hoot. A roe barked, paused and barked again.

C. Goon also came the same way and like Spike, began searching the ground. Suddenly he looked up, caught sight of me and dashed into the nearest entrance – which as it happened, wasn't his. I was taken aback until I guessed that sitting in a different spot and with the badger's poor sight, he had taken me for something else. C. Goon well named; after all, he had been foraging close to me earlier that night! I was determined not to speak however, or in any other way reveal it was in fact me. A striped head appeared after a pause; he came out, looked and ran back! Again his head appeared, then more of him until standing tall he looked directly at me. He looked truly regal and splendid like that, not a C. Goon at all. I knew the very moment he realized it was me – he looked, yes, he looked so sheepish. I spoke softly and he trundled over, backed onto and musked my boots carefully, first one, then the other. Then off he went to his own entrance, glancing back every so often in my direction as he crossed the needle-strewn ground.

Outside the trees I could hear geese overhead, their wild calls a thrilling, most musical sound. It had to be a flock of pink-footed. Going home later by the loch, another flock (or perhaps the same) were circling above the water, a wonderful sight. Pink-footed were the commonest geese here with the greylags a close second. Each night now they fed over the stubble finding grain, sprouting grasses and roots. The badgers spent much of their time on the boggy area where the burn disappeared underground after leaving the loch. The moss was alive with slugs, snails, spiders and insects.

This was an idyllic period with so much to watch under a waning moon in a soft, silky sky. The otter seemed as content in his solitary condition as I was in mine. Sometimes as I sat quietly observing some small creature, be it hedgehog or vole, he would appear watching me, often coming so close that I could see the water droplets on his whiskers. It amused me to think that each of us was as curious as the other. The climax occurred one early morning when his whiskers came in contact with my jeans and he noticed a long thread hanging from the knee I had earlier caught on barbed wire. For some moments he chose to worry at it, pulling until it broke. It was only on my journey home to the village, that I saw my knee showing through the hole he had made!

Some mornings I might come up from the shelter belt to look out over the dimpled, misty water of the loch. There would be geese on the far side, preening after a busy night's feeding and fish jumping for insects on the surface. A trout caught by an angler leapt, twisted and turned on the line until it was finally netted. Another catch lay nearby on the grass. The slow, dark hump of Dydor was a slumbering leviathan crouched at the water's edge. Whether seen from my window as I wrote, viewed from the village or the loch, it had a friendly, warm aspect; it was always *my* Dark Hill.

Sometimes I would leave my work and walk up and onwards, scrambling through bracken and heather-clad flanks till I reached its sloping shoulders. There would I stay in Dydor's company, watching over the world below. How is it that high places call us? Yet this was one of a range of hills, not mountains. I had never seen the Highlands, nor the Cairngorms. I remember walking the loch shore when the pink-footed geese could be heard, though not seen, somewhere on its waters. The sun's rays tried to pierce the gloom and I willed that my small 'mountain' might be revealed to me. A grey, diaphanous scarf moved to show a purple curve and was gone. The calling geese sounded more stridently and now I could pick out their murky shapes floating near to me in the margins. Suddenly the sun was all about and the Dark Hill revealed itself. How beautiful it was; the Great Beaste was awaking. Grey water, sky and air were transformed to blue skyscape and bluer water, green grass and purple moor. The geese preened, turned and bickered as a fisherman called from the distant shore. A gentle breeze touched the birch leaves that drifted away in golden showers. The curtain continued to lift from the farthest peaks; they too were revealed. Now the panorama in all its glory was complete.

I took the terrier out one afternoon and walked her in the late sunshine along the track to the kirk. It was 5.30 p.m. and long tree shadows crept over stubble and green grass. A few people were tending their ponies and an occasional shot rang out from further away. I looked to my right as we walked alongside the old tower ruin. There were three deeply red shapes at the far tree edge near the Cley. The tallest turned, showing a light patch of rump. A family of roe were quietly browsing at the field edge. I bent and put the dog on the lead for my rapt interest had communicated itself to her, but for that, she would never have noticed. Sometimes they shook their heads; there were many flies about. We stood for long moments watching the three taking the herbage till distant voices caused them to disappear into the cover of the trees.

As the shadows deepened we walked round the ruined tower which was once a fortification of great strength. The Second Statistical Account for the parish prepared in the 1830s and 40s by the minister, the Revd Thomas Barclay says:

> It was an occasional residence of the lovely but unfortunate Mary, and also a favourite hunting place of her son and successor, James VI. In consequence of his pecuniary embarrassments on one occasion, it is said to have fallen into the hands of the celebrated George Heriot, and by him bequeathed to a daughter, from whom, along with the adjoining land, it was purchased by the ancestor of the present proprietor. Tradition reports it to have had a subterranean communication (with another tower) and, about the beginning of the last century, a piper attempted to explore it. The sound of his pipes was heard as far as the bridge, where he is supposed to have perished. It certainly had a communication with the Cley and with another building on the opposite bank of the river. Persons living a few years since have descended a considerable

way down the hidden passage. It is supposed that the garrison secured by this means a clandestine supply of water, and that, during a siege, when they were hard pressed for provisions, and the enemy in confident expectation of starving them, one of the soldiers in the act of drawing water, accidentally caught some fish in his bucket, which the governor boastingly hung out in sight of the besiegers. On seeing this unexpected store the assailants hastily raised the siege, deeming it a hopeless attempt to starve a garrison that were so mysteriously supplied. The town appears to have been surrounded by a moat, and there are still traces of a deep ditch.'

I tried to imagine the piper and how he would have lit his way. Both hands are needed to play the bagpipes, so a candle would have been fixed to him. From my own experiences of exploring a disused mine, I knew that small lights in enclosed passages cause flickering shadows. If the story is true, it is likely the piper fell down a shaft without seeing, until too late, what was at his feet.

Flocks of swallows and house martins were gathering to feed over the marshes, sure sign they would soon be gone for another year. I saw one of the sparrowhawks drop onto a flock of meadow pipits as they fed upon insects in the heather. It glided in circular flight above the pipits, to plunge with folded wings upon its victim. Earlier that year, I had watched both parents hunting such small passerines for their growing chicks. The world seemed full of small, active birds. Linnets and redpolls searched for seeds in the little birch and alder wood by the marsh and even in the garden, blue and great tits as well as greenfinches, feasted on the berries below my window.

A dog fox frequented the gardens, coming in from the shelter belt via the road. He made a regular tour of inspection in the early morning and we met if I returned home before dawn; not that he was particularly concerned at my appearance, far from it. The resident cats however, were something different. As well as the two dogs, a cat called Tabitha belonged to our household, but unlike a cat I had once owned, this one disliked foxes as much as she detested her own kind. Tabitha or Tabby was an old cat, made older by a bad bout of cat flu years ago which left her health impaired. Other cats might threaten and claw her, from which behaviour she had no redress, but she certainly made up for her lowly position in the local feline hierarchy by her persecution of the fox. He would come slinking round the corner, ears forward, eyes alert for the slightest sound or movement. The other cats took little notice of their tawny visitor so he merely avoided direct physical contact or eye contact with them. It was only Tabitha that he feared. If more than one feline was on the premises he knew she would be indoors – usually sleeping on my bed – but if the garden appeared empty, then he would hesitate for long moments testing the air with his nose. Once I returned nearly to be bowled over by a fleeing fox hotly pursued by the furious old cat; his nose bore the scars for some weeks. Why did he like our garden in preference to the others? I suspect because it was much larger, longer and more overgrown than those of our neighbours with their trim lawns and neat flowerbeds. Our garden had plenty of tree and shrub cover, tall plants and shady places where an exploring fox, like the hedgehogs, could find a tasty morsel unobserved by human eyes. Having seen the fox off that morning, Tabby followed me up to my room purring. A welcome mug of tea for me and milk for her; she enjoyed buttered toast as much as I. One couldn't really blame Tabby for the fox feud; it probably gave her back her self-respect to see him run.

The first of September was my last night in the Lothians for a few weeks. Melanie and I were going to a conference in England together, then I would be leaving her to continue on to friends in my home county of Kent. It was a night of deep, deep mist and very cold. Millie had been digging out; her paw-prints showed clear in the fresh, sandy earth. There was no sound but for the tumbling burn; no geese and even well after dawn, no cooing of stock doves or wood pigeons. (The doves had nested in a rabbit burrow in the field bank earlier in the year.) I left at 6 a.m. and walked home in the freezing greyness. The past few nights were turning the beech leaves and bracken to bronze. How would they look when I returned in October?

By noon however, it was so hot and sunny that I was tempted back. I sat on the boulder near Spike's entrance under the cool sitkas, though the sunshine slanted in to touch some of the further holes. I thought I could hear sounds of a badger 'aaaaring' above the rushing waters, but told myself I must have badgers on the brain! Still it continued until I was convinced that I hadn't mistaken the sound. Silently on the dead pine needles, I edged over to the far part of the sett nearest the field. There was Spike grooming himself in a hollow amongst the bracken where the sun lay warm. I stared and stared – partly in surprise, but partly because I had never seen him (or any others of the clan come to that), in such excellent light. He grunted and 'aaaared' and wriggled his shoulders against the cool bracken. Then lifted his chin, eyes closed to the golden sun that had lost its way into the wood. Slowly I edged back under the sitkas and their gloomy depths, smiling to myself. Several times in Kent I had found day nests; once still warm from its occupant, but never till I came to Scotland did I find one badger-occupied! I stood awhile gazing around me. Here and there sunbeams lit the darkness, a patch here, a shaft there. One hit an entrance so that I could see far down its tunnelling, until it turned a sharp corner. I locked the memory in my heart and walked back to the village to pack my case.

Chapter Five

Badgers in Four Regions

It was good to see Melanie again and bring our news and wildlife experiences up to date. The weather continued sunny with Galloway at its best. On the way to the moor we stopped to speak to a farmer's wife and coincidentally found she had been born and brought up in that area of the Lothian hills I had walked the previous week. Sheep farming was going through a bad phase; the black-faced breed was out of fashion and their lambs were selling for less than £12. Her husband had gone to market to buy some of the continental breeds. Dairy farming in the valleys was unaffected and was subsidized too which helped. Not so the sheep however. We asked how long she and her husband had farmed here; he was an Ayrshire man. When they first came they had used horses to plough like their neighbours, not knowing these would succumb to horse-sickness, believed to be caused through micro-bacteria in the soil on their land. Thus they were the first farm locally to own a tractor; that was about thirty-two years ago. The lady laughed as she recalled how 'newfangled' they were considered with a few less conservative amongst their neighbours daring to do the same. It was from her I learnt that 'mains' in many Scottish place names originally meant 'home farm' even though many mains farms have disappeared now from the landscape.

A young buzzard was flying and calling as we continued on to the moor and the ruined steading with its nearby trees and distant glimpse of blue from the loch. Deserted dwellings may have a sad air about them, but it was a beautiful place. Walking here we were very unlikely even in midsummer to meet anyone else unless like earlier, we stopped at a farmhouse, and these were few and far between. The moor swept on rising and falling with distant vistas of hills. Returning much later, we collected the dead adder I had found earlier that morning; a small, immature specimen I wished to dry out and keep. My friend who had never shared my love of snakes, generously allowed me to lay it outside on the sitting-room windowsill to dehydrate in the sun, merely remarking that she hoped the postman did not mistake it for a slumbering adder and make a quick getaway without delivering her mail!

We did a badger watch that evening above the high bank of the burn. Someone was shooting further up the valley and young roe looking like small adults, barked and chased amongst the trees. Greylag geese landed on the field behind us feeding on the blades of grass. Three badgers emerged on the lower path and went down to the water to drink and splash about. The tawnies were vocal and their fledglings well-grown, though still being fed by one of the parents. This feeding is usual, for these owls need to fly well and learn the limits of the adults' territory before hunting themselves. No sign of the barn owls though. A neighbour of Melanie's had reported them still to be seen further down the glen. Was the movement of territory seasonal on the barn owls' part, or something to do with the tawnies?

The day before we journeyed to Shropshire and the conference, I followed the burn out of the valley to the edge of the moor. The Galloway climate of warmth and wet encourages luxuriant ferns to hang from the rocky ledges the waters have carved out through millennia of rushing from their source. Small, wind-tortured trees gripped the upper reaches, their roots deeply probing the fissured rocks in search of life-giving earth. The loveliest of these were the rowans, their ripe, hanging clusters of berries making splashes of vivid colour above the clamouring burn. Hidden amongst this overgrown lushness I found a bridge, deftly made of small trunks lashed together and sat on it awhile watching an adder swimming below my dangling legs. There was no discernible path to or from it so it wasn't recently used. Someone had taken a great deal of trouble to build this tiny bridge that appeared to lead from nowhere to nowhere – how strange. There was a flycatcher bird-box nailed to a tree, another small sett further upstream with a well-marked trail above the burn, a free-running wire snare fixed on this trail and kept in position by a partly-broken branch and much evidence of the roe on the trail too, from their slots or hoof prints. (It is an offence to set snares intended for deer or badgers and this was in fact two snares joined together to form a much larger, stronger one; certainly not intended for rabbit or fox.) Something beautifully patterned beneath a tree caught my eye – bars of buff, beige and rufus, wings and tail stretched out in death by the mossy bole; the missing adult tawny owl. I knelt with bitter regret and touched the softly-rounded flight feathers. The shot had pierced the back of the skull. Surely the marksman had known he was shooting a tawny? What else could you possibly mistake for an owl?

Walking home I ran my hand under the roughness of the metal gate that led into the field of the Highland cattle. It came away with several wiry bicoloured hairs clinging to it; so the badgers went under here once they crossed the lane. That evening I showed Melanie the snare and some of the flight feathers I had brought home with me as we discussed the owl and then the badgers. To have survived the continual persecution of snaring, gassing and sett-stopping, the clan must have found a safe refuge on private property; somewhere tucked away where they could breed in safety, only moving out when their numbers slowly increased. As we had agreed on my last visit, that only left Dirk Wood and the disused quarry in its midst. Come the winter, we would search for it together. That weekend was the conference after which we parted; Melanie to return to her cottage, I to continue on to Kent via Somerset.

How fortunate we are in these islands to have such a varied landscape within a few miles. Just as the Lothians and Galloway are complete contrasts each beautiful in its different way, so are Somerset and Kent. Somerset is well populated badger-wise, but many of the towns such as Yeovil have experienced rapid housing development in the last forty years which has swallowed up these animals' feeding grounds, leaving their setts in gardens or isolated amongst building complexes. This causes many problems for the human population some of which are tolerant, but many are not, and the county's badger groups work hard to resolve these conflicts to the benefit of both sides. Road casualty animals are high and may occur in the centre of towns. It was in Somerset that I saw my first road sign warning of badgers crossing – an exclamation within a red triangle and the word 'badgers' beneath. This was erected long before the badger groups existed and no one seems to know who suggested it be placed there, but certainly this speaks volumnes for an enlightened council. Whilst many counties might be unhappy at advertising the presence of their badgers in this way to those who would wish them harm, in Somerset the feeling prevails that since these animals are numerous anyway, badger diggers and lampers don't need such signs to find animals to bait. Clearly the clan of this area were living there long before that stretch of road was built and in the badger manner, still travel on their ancient trails irrespective of passing traffic. Road casualty badgers I was told, rarely occur there now, but whether that indicates more careful driving thanks to the notice or fewer badgers from this clan because of past mortalities, I have no way of knowing.

At the time of writing, conservation bodies are calling on MAFF to agree to a moratorium on badger culling in the name of bovine TB. For twenty years the Ministry has been killing badgers in cattle-infected areas, believing them to be responsible for spreading the disease to bovines, although this still remains unproven. It was interesting therefore, that in this county of very high cattle and badger densities, the incidence of TB was extremely low.

Somerset's deeply sunken lanes intrigued me with their sandy slopes and exposed tree roots. Its follies did too, those poetic reminders of the eighteenth and nineteenth centuries' great estates and love of landscape gardening. The ones I looked at were true follies, either deliberately sham ruins, Gothic-arched or broken pedimented, or best of all, the towers often hollow inside with no means of ascending and built purely for decoration or self-expression. Somehow these towers suited the landscape as they rose gracefully above the tree line or stood sentinel over the parkland, no two ever the same. The fascination of follies! One tower had a small rounded opening at its base and bending down, I stepped inside. Tawny owl pellets lay at my feet and looking above, the rough stonework funnelled upwards to a small patch of sky overhead. Somewhere the owl would be roosting, but impossible to see from the ground. This old parkland was now fenced off into fields dotted about with stately trees, living remnants of a bygone dream.

In Kent and my old area, there was a different story. Two months earlier I had been told of a farm in process of being made into a golf course. The work had continued well until the manager, when checking the grounds at first light as he did each morning found a dead, mutilated fox and then a badger cub lying on the fairways. Within a week he picked up two more badgers, adults this time, and the district's RSPCA inspector confirmed amongst other injuries, those of dog bites; they had been baited. It was known that the land was lamped; indeed, during the farmer's time he had given permission for lampers to hunt the area, also shooters by day and one of his woodlands had been hired out to motorbike scramblers. This farmer had told Paul Hoskins, the new owner, that the 500 acres contained badgers and expressed a strong dislike for the animals. Although he would not actually encourage terrier-men to dig them out, if they happened to, he merely looked the other way. This conversation had so interested Paul that he employed a firm of consultants who specialized in leisure facilities to find the setts on his new property and design the course in such a way as to leave those areas in the rough. The land had been pasture and some areas were now planted with trees and wild flowers. It covered two deep valleys and took in part of three woods on its borders. There were public footpaths across it.

I stayed for a while with Dave and his wife. Dave was a member of the local badger group and since I had left Kent, he tried to look after my old area as well as his own. He regularly cleaned the badger reflectors spaced out along the lane outside my village as I had done and kept an eye, where possible, on the setts. He and other members of the group had made several all-night vigils on the golf course, taking it in turns with the manager and Paul the owner as well as the RSPCA inspector. However like all offences, the criminal has the upper hand and can strike whenever he chooses. There were many fruitless nights when nothing happened and periods when all seemed quiet. Then the baiters would strike again leaving one or two freshly baited badgers on the fairways.

There were several theories as to who might be doing the baiting. The owner had ordered hunt terrier-men off his land a few weeks before the start of these incidents, when he caught them fox 'cubbing' without permission. Needless to say, the farmer had always welcomed the hunt. Could this be the terrier-men's way of getting back? However, anybody could have borne Paul a grudge – the lampers, shooters or come to that the motorbike riders; all had lost out to the golf course.

Only once had lampers come near to being caught. Two beams had been seen approaching from different directions and the badger group had contacted the local police who unfortunately were inexperienced in such matters, coming in to the area with headlights blazing and blue light flashing. The lampers merely turned off their lights and disappeared into the nearest woods. Since then it seemed to have become a 'catch-as-catch-can' game with the baiters versus the group. Privately I wondered if all the ten badgers found to date really came from that area? The incident with the patrol car upset the RSPCA inspector who complained to the police station and as a result the group were given police cover for a couple of nights without success.

Dave took me to meet Pat the manager who showed us round the course indicating where the bulk of the animals had been found. It was a beautiful area and an isolated one bordered by two small winding lanes. Much further over into the next valley (and out of this police area) was a caravan site and a small hamlet with a public house. Even if people *were* discovered at night crossing the golf course, with the footpaths, they could easily say they had been drinking at the pub and taken the dogs for a late walk (I have known this with lampers before), and unless caught well away from the paths, they would not even be trespassing. A van could be parked almost anywhere off the lanes; tucked behind a hedge, in amongst residents' cars, in any of the three woods, or even alongside farm vehicles by outhouses or barns. The possibilities were endless.

Pat was very upset about the baiting. When first given the golf course work he had taken books on badgers out of his local library, looking forward to seeing them as part of his job. Paul had even agreed to make a permanent hide overlooking the main sett; now it had all turned sour. He felt helpless and more bitter at each fresh body and showed me three, two sows and a boar, the latest victims. I asked to have a proper look at them so we laid them side by side. Yes, there were many dog bites, but something else rather strange. Each had a deep, neat, round hole roughly in the region of the throat and a corresponding one in the chest. What could have caused these wounds – something like a two-pronged pitchfork? The dogs would have been set upon each badger until it tired. Then it had been pinned down with the two-pronged object and what then? One sow's chest seemed particularly red and placing my hand over it, I pressed gently with the palm. Immediately I felt broken bones; the whole chest was soft and mushy. I did the same to the others and a splintered rib broke through the skin. My guess was that one baiter pinned the badger down whilst another jumped up and down on its chest.

That morning I was very angry – angry at the pathetic bodies, angry at the futility of the nightly vigils, but most of all at the big man's distress. Why should Pat stay up all night, or his boss come to that, to protect badgers? Most golf course owners aren't too keen on brock who in dry weather will often make snuffle holes and worse in turf to find the fat white cockchafer grubs living beneath. But here were people who had made their greens in consideration of the badger population, planting trees as cover round the more exposed setts and modifying the amenities to suit the badger as well as the human clans. And they were not to be left in peace. I spoke to Dave suggesting we take these latest victims to the police station and put them on the counter under the duty sergeant's nose. It is one thing to talk about badger-baiting, quite another to look at the end results. This we did and although at that stage the police couldn't give us any more manpower, the sergeant did get their Scene of Crimes officer to take photographs and also measure the distance between the holes on the bodies. Even if lampers were accosted by the police at their vehicle and later a baited badger was found on the golf course, in court it could not be proved that these men had actually done the baiting. However, if they had in their possession an instrument capable of inflicting the pitchfork injuries, it would certainly help a prosecution.

I did my first night watch with the group on 23 September. Dave drove us slowly up the rutted tarmac. It curved as it rose higher and looking back, the lights of the village receded. A badger appeared from our right and grunting, ambled off in front of us. Slowly we followed at a discreet distance, its big, whitish tail and shaggy rump swaying as it went. It was a steep incline and brock was becoming puffed. After several backward, disgruntled glances our way, he took the easy option – up the left-hand bank and into the field. Laughing, Dave said, 'Well, at least there's one still alive.' The journey continued upwards past a sign denoting the golf course ahead; neat lettering on a green board and still the car climbed. In spite of myself the long journey made me yawn. Another neat notice to our left and a beautiful model of a tawny owl carved above it. 'What a good idea on Peter's part,' I was thinking as the car crept past and the owl turned its head at a 90° angle to watch us go! At last we reached the first cottage. No lights showed as we came to the next. We parked at Pat's office and waited for the two members of the group we were to relieve at midnight. Moments later they came down the hillside and through the yard; no problems, all had been quiet. Dave and I in warm gear with rucksacks containing biscuits, flask, binoculars and radios, walked quietly up the hill and positioned ourselves looking out over the valleys.

I didn't know the area as well as my companion, so after an hour I left him keeping look-out with his two-way radio, and with mine in my hand walked into the 'killing fields' as Pat called the fairways in the valley bottom. There were sudden showers, but clouds were blown too fast over the sky for them to last long. At 3.30 a.m. there was a full moon with a strong, warm wind. I saw two figures walking a wood edge but they disappeared into a fold of land. By the time I came up from the valley there was no one to be seen, but I walked into the edge of the woods and looked out onto the golf course and up the valley as I followed the path. I sat for a while writing and watching. Dark trails of cloud moved smokily across the face of the moon as the wind tried to tear the sheets of my pad as I wrote. Later I returned noting that the nearby sheep were huddled together in the lea of the trees. Dave had seen nothing; all was quiet. We waited until daybreak and slowly walked back down to Pat's office. I was staying with other friends by now, so Dave dropped me outside their cottage.

It was still too early to disturb them by going in so I decided to walk round to a nearby sett in a sand-pit and see what the badgers had been doing there that night. Birds were just beginning to sing at 6.20 a.m. as I reached the top of the quarry. I walked in having ducked under the leafage where it was still fairly dark. Too late I found I had barged into a hive of activity. One badger was scratching himself hard to my left and another viewed further down the steep slope was slowly coming my way with head down searching the ground as it approached. I took a deep breath and did the next stupid thing – crept round to my right – and directly into the path of a badger backing upwards carrying bedding! I stood frozen to the spot hoping frantically it would go into an entrance lower down. Instead, it continued up – right up to my boots. Here by necessity, it had to stop. It grunted and pushed hard. I stared down at the rough, hairy back not quite believing what was happening. Again it humped its hindquarters and pressed against my legs – my, it was strong. It grunted and grumbled trying to rearrange the bundle clasped between front claws and against its chest. Already pieces of grass were slipping out. What was halting its progress? Suddenly it looked round as best it could, caught the briefest glimpse of booted legs and froze. Slowly the hairs on its shoulders and back stood on end. By now it had dropped the bedding which did a graceful slide back the way it had come till it rested against a beech's bole. The badger took another furtive look round, then slowly up at the owner of the legs. Next moment amid a haze of musk, it vanished back down and round a corner. I could actually hear its progress into the fastness – and safety – of the sett.

Carefully now, I edged backwards to find the first badgers had gone home to bed. I stayed with most of me hidden behind a tree with just a bit of my head out to see what might be the next move. Moments passed but I was in no hurry and leaning comfortably against the trunk I almost began to doze. Then I heard a faint noise and opening my eyes, saw a striped face looking my way. It smelt the air, but couldn't get my scent, then hesitated before gathering up the nearest pieces of grass it had earlier abandoned. As it disappeared downwards and backwards into the entrance I had unwittingly been 'guarding' on its first return, I could almost hear it sigh. Poor old badger! I did go indoors to my friends then and over breakfast we discussed what their badgers had been doing that morning. The incident at the sand-pit was a tonic to me, presenting as it did, the other side of the coin, although the memory of those three baited bodies will always remain.

I was resolved to walk all round the woods and farms off the golf course, so Dave drove me over one early morning before he went to work. Peter Hoskins had warned other landowners of what was happening on his land, suggesting they all keep a lookout for dumped carcases and suspicious vehicles parked in isolated places by day or night. Peter felt it wasn't merely happening on his golf course and he was right. A farmer backing onto Peter's land picked up three dead badgers, one well decomposed that were dumped underneath a hedge near a gate leading from one of the lanes. The word spread and other farmers further into the county were reporting the same. This left me wondering how many are never detected, either buried in shallow graves or more likely, placed in black bin liners and dumped on municipal tips. The Mammal Society's records of badger setts in the area showed these were plentiful, but the records were nearly twenty years old.

That morning I spoke to a farmer's wife I had known from several years earlier when still living in Kent. I felt that prospective lampers watching the area could see car headlights going up to the golf course. Apart from the two cottages and Pat's office, the long track didn't go anywhere. Yes, the farmer would be perfectly happy for any of us to park a vehicle behind his house, provided we telephoned beforehand to let him know. Although this meant a walk through an unknown wood, it was quite easy from there to come onto the golf course. Now I began to check the area's setts; this was quite as depressing as the lamping. Each one I came to was now disused with many old crowning-down holes and other human interference. In two of the woods there were dug-out trenches, the type made by army cadets, with sandbag barriers and the charred remnants of old camp fires. It wasn't merely Peter's farmer who had allowed his woods to be used for multifarious activities. That day I checked twelve setts and at only two were there any signs of badger occupation.

I walked on and so to the far end of the golf course, where I met a very disheartened Pat who had made another grisly discovery. I had previously asked him to leave any more bodies where he found them so this one was *in situ*. Again the bites, the pitchfork marks and the reddened chest and belly. I lifted it up and found no blood on the grass nor anywhere around. So it had been brought here and dumped, but baited elsewhere. Had any of the others shown no signs of blood in the immediate location in spite of massive injuries – yes, several. This prompted Pat to tell me something he hadn't cared to mention the other day. One or two bodies had been slit, the entrails pulled out and partly eaten. The RSPCA inspector told him that this was sometimes done whilst the guts were still warm to encourage the dogs to attack more ferociously the next time they met a badger. The Inspector was right; I had met this before.

Two evenings later Dave and I did another night vigil. He had made enquiries at local pubs including the one by the hamlet and had picked up one or two scraps of information that would need checking. It was a beautiful night as we walked uphill and by 3.30 a.m. there was a heavy dew. I sat down and sketched the scene whilst Dave went walkabout, then left him to rest as I took his place. We both had radios so could keep in contact at all times. There had been an incident at the weekend when the sheep that grazed parts of the old pasture, had been found loose in the wood and the tup caught in a thicket at the far side. Someone had opened the gate and left it open, but the shepherd was convinced the flock had been chased and harried from the state they were in and the distance they had travelled. Pat said we would know of approaching trouble by the actions of the sheep, but that night was quiet human-wise. I saw a badger and later, a fox and heard a tawny owl and a little owl. The fox disturbed the sheep as it passed between them and the tup stood on a hillock acting as lookout. Sheep like horses and cows, like to graze at night. All was quiet, all was still. Now the moon was fitfully shining as a wind far above sent the clouds trailing over, but no wind touched the trees or myself down below. I walked to the big main sett and looked at the place where Pat had so wanted the hide. It wouldn't interfere with the badgers' lives as it would be well above them on the hill, but by the time the golf course was finished would there be any badgers to watch? As I stood deep in thought, a badger (probably the one I had seen earlier) came snuffling along and I wondered not for the first time, whether many of the dead badgers had really come from this clan? I looked for other setts and found one at the edge of the lower wood and another amongst nettles above the fairway in the valley of the killing fields. They were one or two-entrance outliners, but were well occupied. My feet were leaving a bruise-trail through the dew-sodden grass. By now it was cold, but so beautiful. I walked the lampers' route, that is, where Pat believed them to come in, back along the wood edge and found myself in the lane above the farm where we were allowed to park. It was all so simple for the lampers for they choose the time. Never mind. Although we felt helpless and frustrated, 'They also serve who only stand and wait.' Give the baiters time and they would slip up; they were too clever for their own good. The wood was wonderful to walk in at night with its wide grassy rides and views over the golf course. A public footpath led through here out to the lane beyond and the pub. It was easy to see how lampers could go drinking there and leave perhaps at closing time to come into the area unnoticed.

Dave arranged a meeting with the group's chairman, myself, the RSPCA inspector and Peter at the local police station to discuss the situation with the head of the Force Support Unit one evening. Unfortunately everything was happening with several emergencies running together when we arrived, so although we did talk briefly to the police inspector and gave him some facts and figures already prepared, that was the sum total of the discussion. However sympathetic the police were to the problem, it was obvious to all of us that at present they were too overstretched in their everyday duties to actively help.

Before I left Kent I spent several nights in my old study area not more than five miles away from the golf course. Last April I had left for Scotland leaving nine adult badgers with five young cubs. These badgers treated me as one of themselves, musking and grooming me and although five months had elapsed, I felt sure the adults would not have forgotten. Those left certainly hadn't, but now they numbered only four. The dominant and sub-dominant boars were amongst those missing and the dominant sow I called Crisp had most of her right hind leg torn away although the wound had healed. Three-legged badgers are greatly handicapped in the wild and stroking Crisp I wondered how long she would survive. Returning from my last night's watch I met an elderly couple from one of the villages out walking their dog; I had known them for many years. It appeared there had been an upsurge of lamping on this farmland too. Badger cubs often die of natural causes, so counting the cubs merely as two, that still left only four out of eleven and seven probably lamped.

En route for Scotland I stayed with Karen, my daughter, in her South Yorkshire village and caught up on her news. She had a five-month-old Rhodesian ridgeback puppy called Harriet to keep her company which I walked each day. It was an excellent method of getting to know the countryside and I found several small woods and copses in the vicinity. Many woods in the county had been owned by the Forestry Commission (these were deciduous trees), and were now considered uneconomical so were being sold. I was told that they tended to be reasonably priced and the Yorkshire Trust took an interest, but there were so many that undoubtedly some would be bought privately and felled.

I met Gary Baker of the local badger group and together we did a tour of setts in the Doncaster Metropolitan Borough Council area. This is the largest council area in the country amounting to 264 square miles. Gary and his group had made eighteen artificial setts of which twelve were now badger-occupied. These were necessary as past diggers had destroyed so many setts in their trenching efforts to take their victims. Few natural setts now had many entrances; two or three here is usual although Gary's father could remember when setts were much larger and covered wider areas. He recalls that the 1960s saw an upsurge in badger-digging and then the late 1970s. It seemed Gary said, to go in cycles of every eight or ten years. Baiting too has changed in Yorkshire. Up to modern times it consisted of tying a badger in a barrel and testing a dog's gameness to 'have a go'. Now it has more sadistic refinements with several dogs simultaneously, so that no one wins and pieces of dog and badger are left at the scene. Gary found a terrier's ear, also lower jaw amongst many badger pieces at the scene of such a baiting which took place at a sett in a remote area between Doncaster and Sheffield. Sadly, there are many such places, with 80 per cent of all known setts here now deserted or destroyed.

It was because the group discovered badgers living in land drains, that they conceived the idea of creating artificial ones with clay pipes. The drains were made in Victorian times to clear waterlogged farmland and store it for irrigation. Most of these have become broken and disused. Sometimes the old drains are dry all year round and badgers can live in them freely. Often however, they are wet in winter and the badgers have to find other accommodation. A drain only gives you two entrances, that is, the ends of a pipe. There have been criticisms by the public of artificial setts, but I feel South Yorkshire have proved they can be and are suitable habitat for badgers.

The area is quarried for limestone and sand, as well as coal; there are clay deposits too. As in Cumbria, badgers have taken over disused mines. Gary took me to 60 hectares of private grounds where the landowner had allowed him and two other members of the group to build a small two-entrance sett in a release pen in his woods. A sow and boar (orphaned cubs of that year) had been placed here in August and were settling down well. Gary and Co. had made a 2-metre high wire fence round the compound with plenty of room for the inmates on the wooded slope. The fence went into the ground and turned inwards at a 45 degree angle to prevent the animals digging themselves out. In a few weeks, two badger gates would be erected at points where their trails led to the fence. The occupying badgers had already sited dung pits near the fence instinctively marking the limits of their present territory. There was oak, elder, ash and bramble inside the compound and felled timber that the young badgers were digging under to make their own sett. This too was a good sign. They were wild and acting naturally with a desire to dig and extend. Soon they would make use of the gates to come and go as they pleased. There were no other badgers for many miles.

Walking by day with Harriet in a wood close to Karen's house, we watched grey squirrels running in the oaks. The dog's large ears pricked and she bounded the length of her extending flexi-lead with excitement. Suddenly, amongst the foliage of one tree I seemed to see a striped bewhiskered face watching us intently. Could it be? I wasn't sure, but it seemed to be a tabby cat.

Karen and I had moved from Kent together the previous April. She had kept Flo my tabby cat as the household I was living with in Scotland already had Tabitha and the two dogs. Flo's hatred of her own kind was only exceeded by her feelings for dogs. Flo had been abandoned as a youngster at a stable and taken me over when I came to live in the caravan nearby. She was by nature a feral creature, liking the company of the resident badgers and foxes and only condescending to visit me when she chose. I didn't feel I could leave her for several times she had nearly come to grief with four Dobermans that were allowed to roam as a pack, but neither would she settle easily into a suburban life. For some time she had stayed with Karen (who didn't have Harriet then), but was absent for increasing periods until she finally disappeared. I had always said to my daughter that Flo would find a fox to befriend and be off and we hoped this was what happened rather than some ill fate.

That night I walked the area, but although I saw three foxes, I found no trace of the cat. Nonetheless, I had the most peculiar feeling that she was there. The following night it was raining slightly as I entered the wood. Water drops pattered on the leaves overhead masking my footsteps. A fox glided across the winding path and coming to an opening under beeches I spied a small, striped feline as if waiting. Squatting down I called 'Flo, Flo' and indeed, it was she. Casually she wound herself round me and accepted a stroke before she moved off to rub her chin against the nearest trunk. I walked on filled with a great elation in spite of her offhand welcome. Something shot past my side, ran up the bark of an ash and hung there calling piteously. 'Oh Flo, what an old trick,' and I laughed as I continued on my way. Deep down I longed to stop and fondle her but that was not the way to deal with independent Flo!

We approached the single-gauge railway line with its depots and industrial estate on the far side. A man was calling and in the ring of light by a building I made out a fox and then another, heads bent as if eating. Flo slipped stealthily over the unelectrified line. These rails were only occasionally used now, but had once taken coal regularly from the local colliery to power stations some miles away. I waited some time as the rain became heavier, then sought shelter beneath a warehouse overhang. Foxes and cat were gone and only the empty bowls remained. I walked into the depot as a dog growled, then barked. Two men sat there, one calling the Alsatian to him. They listened cautiously to my story of Flo and how she came to be living in the woods. I described her carefully – neat striped coat and vividly green eyes, sensing they were afraid I was intending to reclaim her. Karen now had her dog for company and protection. The cat had found her own level and chosen her favoured environment, the woods. I was relieved that someone was prepared to feed her if necessary for come the winter months, she would find mice and voles scarce. She feared dogs, I continued, but enjoyed the company of foxes. Could I leave my phone number with them? If a problem should arise or anything befall her, I would rather know and perhaps help. They were welcome to reverse the charges as Scotland was a long-distance call. Both men unbent. The one holding the Alsatian saying, 'Aye, she does like foxes and no mistake.' The dog was merely walked round with him for security. With public footpaths through the complex there was no way of closing the place at night. The other asked how old I thought Flo was. I replied five/six years and described how she had been left at the stable. That morning I recounted the night's events to Karen who was very happy to know that Flo had found a friendly wood and night watchmen, rather than a fatal car.

Later that day I took Harriet in the woods and met a middle-aged man walking a young Patterdale bitch. The owner was short with a big, bulbous grey nose with large pores and wearing a cloth cap. I admired his dog and he admired Harriet. Did he put his terrier to rabbit yet? Aye, she went down a hole only yesterday and he had gone to a friend at the gypsy encampment nearby for a shovel to dig her out. 'Gosh,' says I 'she will be good at the black and whites when she's older.' Oh, his other Patterdales were great at the brockies. One was badly scarred from its encounters, but all were game little dogs – I should see them! 'With luck,' thought I, 'and a few more chats, I might even do that.' Gary Baker had told me that men around Doncaster were proud of their dogs' prowess when put to badger and not at all reticent on badger-digging topics and apparently he was right!

Yorkshire has the worst record for long-standing badger abuse in the country. It also has a reputation for coal mining; mining and the breeding of small terriers seems to go hand in hand. This is true also of the Midlands, Wales and the Lake District. *One Man and His dog* is a romanticized portrait and not all working dogs are kept to herd sheep and cattle. There is a great deal of unemployment in these areas, so some men are left with plenty of time on their hands and the need for money in their pockets. The fighting/baiting dog provides a macho image for its owner who, interestingly, is often a little, weedy type. The owner of such a dog gets his kicks from the prowess and aggression of his canine for he is often a physical coward himself. A badly scarred dog is living proof that *his* tyke is game for anything and such dogs sell for high prices. An unemployed man has time to breed terriers and to work them; they are money in his pocket and prestige in the eyes of his friends. Badger-baiting and dog fighting go hand in hand. A badger has been brought in to ring the changes at many a dog-fight. They are used to train dogs to fight, just as badger cubs are useful to train young dogs. A puppy may be put off fighting for life if he gets the worst of his first few encounters.

Owners bet on their dog's gameness and big money changes hands. Many women know their menfolk are involved, but either see little wrong in it (after all, grandad did it and dad, so why should silly laws change what generations have practised?), or enjoy watching fights themselves. Women so involved are sometimes more bloodthirsty than their men. Only time will alter the situation – time and education. This is why I feel that the talks most badger groups give to primary school children, is time well spent. Many children brought up in these areas have only seen one side of the badger – when the boar is fighting for its life or the sow, fighting for her cubs. To bring a stuffed road casualty badger into the classroom, to talk about its normal way of life, its cleanliness, playfulness; to let children touch the long front digging claws or stroke the rough fur, shows them the true creature. A shy, normally timid badger leading its nocturnal life out of sight of man and his dogs, its only enemies. Whilst I can sympathize with those that do not like to see stuffed badgers, Micky, the road casualty I had, did more good for his kind (and still does – Dave has him!) in death than he ever could in life.

The day before I left Yorkshire three men in the north appeared at Harrogate magistrates' court charged with offences relating to dog fighting. Two injured Pit Bulls were found on an RSPCA raid in the cellar of a cottage at Nesbrough. Nothing unusual in that; the only surprise was that they had been caught. On talking to Karen I found people had been taking an interest in Harriet. She was thinking of having the dog tattooed inside one of her ears in case she should be stolen for fighting. Harry hadn't an aggressive streak in her, but others seeing her size and breed would not know that and in any case, dogs were often stolen for others to practise on. It would be best to have the tattooing done on the inside of her thigh however, for the RSPCA had found that such stolen dogs may have their ears removed to prevent identification.

It was time to say goodbye. The train beyond Newcastle was restricted to 80 mph because of the gale-force gusts, but that gave me more time to enjoy the changing landscape. The sea was so close now below the windows. Bamburgh Castle stands stoically on its site of a sixth-century fortress, then the Holy Island of Lindisfarne comes into view. We pass over the curving viaduct to Berwick-upon-Tweed and the end of the train is visible to those in its front compartments. It is 5.52 p.m. and the train still lopes by the sea as the hills roll, turn and delve. We are approaching Scotland and my heart throbs in my throat. I like its people but it is the land with which I feel so akin – a sense of belonging. Oh deserter, to neglect the country of your birth and love another so readily! The day is dying. Deep swirling clouds hide the last glow of the sun. The train quickens as if hearing my unspoken wish. I am going home.

We are in Scotland now passing the Bass rock. Jagged formations rear and disappear and the sullen sea vanishes, a hard grey swell. The land is ploughed here, furrows running to the headland to disappear still flowing, over the cliffs. Forty miles from the city, huge straw bales covered in plastic, lie dimly on the stubble; helpless giants waiting for the tractor to take them away. The gloom deepens, but I note that the trees are only thinly covered in leaves. There is a clear half moon some nights away from the full and I wonder how *my* badgers have fared, under the Dark Hill.

CHAPTER SIX

Back to the Dark Hill

My first task now I was home was to check the area's badger setts. Those of Clackmon Farm and the Wild Way were fine and I even discovered a large sprainting site under the rhododendrons at the latter, proof that at least one otter was present, if not all three. I left the home of the Burn Badgers until last. They had cleared and dug out at seven entrances and the earth of four had old bedding amongst it. There had been much rooting for grubs and beetles under the sitkas. The roaring burn was full, sending plumes of spray high into the air. A fox lay curled up asleep in the long grass at the side of the sheeps' field, his thick brush covering his face. The thundering water far below made too much noise for him to hear any footfalls I might make and the wind was blowing in from the pasture, bringing his scent to me. I walked silently over the needle-strewn ground picking up pieces of glass recently turned up by the badgers. There had been a great deal of rain; everywhere was waterlogged. Like the Borders I had passed through in the train, roll bales still lay on the shaven fields by the loch.

I watched my first goldeneye and widgeon bobbing up and down on the choppy surface together with a huge flock of pink-footed and greylag geese. It was good to be home and in a country where there was little animal persecution. Reflecting by the lochside however, perhaps I should have said little *obvious* persecution. Gassing and sett-stopping can account for more badgers in one fell swoop than any amount of digging and lamping. It can and has wiped out entire clans, but there is no obvious cruelty to show for it; the evidence lies underground. Out of sight and out of mind to those who illegally practise gassing with most of the human population blissfully unaware. Up to 1982 MAFF had killed badgers with cyanide gas pumped into setts, in their campaign to eradicate badgers from bovine TB-infected areas. Experiments at the Chemical Defence Establishment at Porton Down however, found gassing to be inadequate to kill quickly and humanely. Only rats and rabbits can legally be gassed today. Setts may consist of many metres of underground tunnelling and chambers and badgers are large animals. Almost certainly many thousands of badgers had died slow, agonizing deaths before this simple fact was established. Now MAFF cage-traps and shoots as the main means of badger control. I fervently hoped the SSPCA *would* check the farms Melanie and I had found, but of course, this was but a tiny fragment of the entire region. What of the north of Scotland and districts we knew nothing about?

The flowering heather was over, its dead blooms a dull brown. Fieldfares and redwings were arriving to feed in noisy flocks on the hips and haws. Most of the leaves were gone from the birches whose branches were so covered in lichens as to resemble grey frost. Springing up from the grass beneath, the fly agarics' brilliant caps with their white spots were splashes of scarlet amongst the green. There were linnets, greenfinches and redpolls feeding in the birch wood and a tree creeper amongst a roving party of tits along the wooded shore. Unlike the great, blue, coal and long-tailed company however, this mouse-like creeper was moving upwards in jerky spirals, stopping every so often to probe with its long, slender beak into the fissured bark of an oak for small insects, spiders and woodlice concealed there. Those jewel-eyed, long-tailed tits particularly attracted me as they noisily investigated a hawthorn. Their combination of pink and white feathers, white crown bordered with black stripes, diminutive size and exaggerated length of tail as they balanced, pecked for insects and called to each other, was a pleasing sight.

Now it was 4.30 p.m. with the late autumn sun low in the sky, its beams filtering their way to me sitting near the sett under the sitkas. A tractor crossed the pasture at a distance, but could not compete with the surging shout of the burn. I caught tantalizing glimpses of its white torrent below me through the trees. A last wych-elm leaf dangled from a sun-touched thread; it reminded me of the limes in the village streets that were showers of falling gold. There were so many snuffle holes, the needle-strewn ground was covered in their neat conical shapes. I thought it was beetles these badgers had been seeking, for this earth was too acid for worms. I dug down with my fingers and turned up chrysalis cases and yes, three small beetles, one black and two brown. The needles were wet under the dry top ones. There was a hollow between tree roots that had been used as a dung pit. Some dung was old and crumbly and other quite fresh; all studded with wheat husks. One must have been a grain rather than a husk for it had sprouted two long green shoots! The sun was gone with the last twitterings of birds soon to roost as a chiller air beckoned the night. Geese called overhead though I could not hear their wing beats above the urgent burn.

There was a glint of light on water as something humped into view and was gone. I smiled knowing the otter had betrayed his coming and was content to bide his time. The moon was rising. I could not see its face – only the beams amongst the far birch softly touched, flickered and touched again. My life's happiest moments have been alone in a wood at night. There is comfort and pleasure in the knowledge that the constellations are eternal and do not share our own mortality. Day follows night, rain follows sun in endless progressions. A movement interrupted my reverie. Whitely under the sitkas, a badger peered out and scented the air; Spike of the damaged ear and massive shoulders, deciding it was time to come above. He settled back onto a fallen branch and began to scratch. His hind leg was so vigorously employed as to blur before my eyes. He snorted with the sustained effort and in the sudden silence, bent to investigate his leg. The nearest conifer had exposed roots writhing up in tortured coils around the bole like snakes in a pit and I thought of the adders on the Galloway hills.

It was still only 6.10 p.m. although well dark under the trees. There was a whirr of feathers as a pheasant flew up above me to roost. It startled Millie who was using the tree-root dung pit; she froze a moment, then relaxed and lounging backwards began grooming her belly fur. I didn't recognize Grace and Disgrace at first – they seemed to have grown so much in my absence. It was they, however, who came up to inspect me, first backing onto each other with tails raised, then musking my boots. I might never have been away. Through the straight, bare tree trunks I saw other members of the clan coming together briefly to scent-mark each other and mutually groom before going their separate ways. Sharp sounds further down the slope suggested that someone's long claws were tearing away rotting bark to reveal the badger delicacies hidden beneath. Just as suddenly all was quiet; the badgers had gone.

Outside on the open fields, frost was settling. I went down to the burn delighting in the flash and glitter of tumbling waters; how I had missed this place. Something long and lithe rose out of the water and tail raised and waving, sprainted on a flat-topped rock. I dared a whistle half afraid I might frighten him, but I need not have done so for he well knew I was there. Again there came the curious feeling that I hadn't been away; the seven week's absence with all its sadness of baited bodies melted and dissolved. Light from the sickle moon came filtering into the rocky chasm bouncing off the water drops as the otter shook himself, his smooth fur altering to spiky tufts. Now he was next to me, standing upright the better to look at the whistler, small eyes above his bewhiskered muzzle bright with interest. Next he was down amongst the sedges and lesser spearwort, its buttercup flowers bobbing as he passed through. My boots were inspected. What did he make of the badgers' musking I wondered? Was I classed as part badger and part creature of alien smell? His whiskers touching my bare hand tickled. Then a skein of geese flew across the moon as the otter bounded downstream to fish in the pool.

A mist was settling over the landscape as I stood by the margins of the loch, gazing over to where I knew Dydor to be. I couldn't see his curve through the shrouding grey any more than I could see the calling geese, but I knew the hills were there. No wonder so many others before me had fallen under their spell. I felt a great surge of joy whenever I looked upon their humped backs. They have the patience of eternity; they will endure beyond the span of man. Standing quietly I was aware of short, squat bodies moving on the turf, one at my feet; Grace, Neddy and Millie were worming snout to ground at some distance from each other. This rabbit-grazed grass was ideal and they often fed here. However, that early morning their stay was short-lived as one by one the pink-footed geese came out of the water to feed too, though in their case it was the blades of grass they were taking. The badgers soon moved away, not from fear I am sure, but the worms were very conscious of the big birds vibrating movements and ceased to come above ground to feed. Badgers are such skilful creepers, stealing along with silent tread.

At dawn I returned to the sett to find a bundle of clean, dry grass and elm leaves lying discarded by Millie's entrance. It would seem she had been taking in bedding, but left the last bundle outside. Badgers sometimes do this and may never take it down. In time the heap of bedding becomes covered in soil from fresh digging out or is blown away by the wind. Would she collect it later or leave it I wondered? There was more old glass dug out which I collected. It wasn't misty under the trees though the field was. I spoke to a ewe regarding me through the wire netting and noticed the tup was with them, promise of new lambs next year. Here was the gap under the wire through which the badgers passed and a wonderfully lichen-patterned boulder stood close by.

The morning sun had banished the mist as I left the shelter belt. Walking home to the village many small insects flew about my head and I thought of the swallows, alas long gone. The night's frost had lifted the last leaves from the trees. An elderly man walking his dog pointed at the glass I was carrying and called out 'Good for you.' in a strong Scottish accent as he passed. I must be getting the oddest reputation – a small, scruffy, middle-aged woman always walking villagewards clutching rubbish!

Friday, 25 October 1991 was the long-awaited day when the Badgers Act came into force. Now setts were legally protected as well as the animals themselves. Section 9, however, dealt with exceptions within the Act and provisions for the issue of licences for legally interfering with setts. These exceptions covered damage caused by badgers, including the undermining of railway banks and buildings etc, all of which was acceptable to most conservationists. However, licences would also be granted 'for the purpose of controlling foxes in order to protect livestock, game or wildlife, to inter-fere with a badger sett within an area specified in the licence by any means so specified.' This clause could be open to abuse from all sorts of people claiming to exercise fox control – the genuine and the dubious – farmers, fox hunts and others practising 'vermin' extermination. It has long been known that terrier-men working for fox hunts may be badger-diggers too and a recent case highlighting this sobering fact was very worrying. The Isle of Wight prosecution had convicted two men of badger-digging that May. Steve Clifton, a professional huntsman for the Isle of Wight Fox Hounds, and James Butcher, paid terrier-man for the Essex and Suffolk Fox Hounds, were each fined £500 with £500 costs. Unless MAFF were extremely careful as to whom they issued licences, the Act to protect badger setts would be in name only. Licences apart however, the biggest battle was going to be to prove that the farmer, developer or whoever destroys a sett knew it was there, for just as some would be destroyed deliberately, others might well be demolished in ignorance. Rightly, the Act decreed that there had to be a degree of intent or recklessness in the action.

Having fed and watered the ponies and walked the dogs, I had the rest of the day to myself. It was a cold, wild morning as I left the village, the fierce westerlies bowing the leaning trees until they twisted and moaned. I checked the Burn sett *en route* for the hills and found Millie's bundle still lying where she had left it some nights earlier, with pieces gradually dispersing in the wind blowing through from the open fields. Squirrels were quarrelling above me in the gusty trees and a host of fungus had appeared after the night's rain – saffron milk caps (*Lactarius deliciosus*) growing out along the sitkas' roots from the sandy soil and dozens of slimy, olive brown caps of *Hygrophorus hypothejus* pushing out of the needles. Under the pines at the loch edge were more toadstools including the violet-coloured caps of *Gomphidius glutinosus* with their thick, colourless, veils which in some young specimens still stretched from the cap border to the stems. Fluffy aspen seeds and larch needles showered the boletus pushing through the mossy grass as sullen waves slapped and foamed on the stony shore. Dydor humped darkly in a slate-grey sky seemed to beckon, an invitation difficult to resist. I passed the steadings lying open and forlorn and walked on across the waterlogged ground. But for the sphagnum all was grey with the cry of a lone crow sounding through a torrent of wind.

The sheep had been brought down to lower ground for the winter and suddenly they ran downfield as one, causing the pink-footed geese feeding amongst them to rise in a great flock and fly calling to the loch. Were they chasing the geese or did something startle the sheep? I walked over to the fence of their field, but found nothing untoward. It was strewn with fodder beet that Will had brought up on the trailer from the farm. There was sleet in the wind; it seared my face and I opened my mouth to taste it. Now I was on Dydor's flanks as following the sloping path through the dead bracken, I picked my way over the treacherous mud. In all their moods these hills had a beauty. It was good to be without human company alone on their peaks. The pass briefly sheltered me from the gale, but on the next narrow summit, its violence made walking impossible; the only answer was to crawl across. White flakes spun in twisting columns as the wind, crying with many voices, pried into rocky crevices and deep defiles with pitiless fingers. I was warm, protected from the worst in my waxed jacket and knew the route well enough, but I thought of the Covenanters in the Killing Times on another bleak November day in these hills.

It was in the comparative shelter of the leeward side of the next law that I came upon the black grouse. Although I had never seen one before there was no mistaking that lyre-shaped tail nor the red head wattles and black plumage of this handsome cock bird. The red grouse were common enough, but I thought its black cousin was absent from these hills – obviously I was wrong. It stretched its wings on seeing me, so I diverted my path and it remained in its refuge. Out of the wind, the silence was pleasant and the clouds occasionally parted to allow a weak sun to wash briefly over the landscape. Flakes still moved in the chill air, but lay for barely a moment before fading into the wiry grass. I took the winding track to the reservoir and stood a long while watching the scree slopes reflected in its depths. Fieldfares squabbled in the ragged hawthorns and a collie barked from the nearby farm.

Walking homewards towards the village there came a sudden trumpeting 'ahng-ha' and a whistling of wings as five beautiful white whooper swans flew overhead. Near the steadings, the fields of autumn-sown wheat were well up and already being sprayed, the tractor leaving neat 'tramlines' marking its progress. I walked indoors to my telephone ringing and found a friend from Essex speaking to me. Two members of his badger group had missed cubs they regularly watched and suspected lampers as bright lights had been reported in the vicinity. A search was instigated and both cubs found dead, a sow and a boar, lying in the grass at a considerable distance from their sett covered in bites consistent with attacking dogs. It was felt this must have occurred at night for the badgers would not have been at such a distance from home in the early evening. The sett showed no sign of interference. I told the caller of the badger lamping in Kent.

I had heard from my old group since I returned home to Scotland and more baited badger bodies had been discovered. An autopsy had been done on the most recent one. It had first been pierced and held down like the others by the two-pronged instrument and then either jumped upon or beaten; lungs were punctured, diaphragm ruptured, liver and kidneys grossly misplaced and both hind legs broken. As with the first twenty-five badgers, death had been slow and hard. A meeting took place with the local police inspector and head of their Support Unit; MAFF Special Investigations Branch expressed an interest. A similar branch of the RSPCA was heavily involved with investigating dog fighting and other cruelties, and the Gurkhas stationed in the county, who had already done night-time exercises protecting red kites in Wales, might be asked to help out. Like myself, those at the meeting had felt that the bodies had mainly been brought in from outside and dumped as an act of defiance because: a) the area could never support that number of badgers, and b) usually there was little or no blood on the ground in spite of gross injuries.

Although the lamping of badgers was now prevalent over many parts of England and Wales, it was the sheer number of baited bodies that was giving rise to concern. Kent might be the worst hit but the Richmond Park area of London also had a bad problem as did a golf course in Sussex. Although the suggestions of help were encouraging, nothing came of them for the remainder of 1991. However, things quietened on the Kentish golf course and at least the meeting had brought the concerned parties together. The badger group continued with their night vigils at weekends and at any time that they felt the area's wildlife threatened. Again I wondered how much badger-lamping was carried out in places where the perpetrators didn't leave the evidence to be found. Scotland seemed a far cry from England with its barbaric cruelties.

Walking towards the farm entrance one morning a car drew alongside and I found it was Sandy Robertson. He asked about the badgers and I said they were fine. I was going up to their sett now and often sat under the trees there writing, it was so peaceful. He asked about the otter and where it fished, so I told him it favoured the pool. Just then another car came up behind his so we said goodbye. Mention of the pool caused me to drop down off the footpath and linger by its side. Although a grey morning with rain in the air, it was mild and pleasant gazing at the rushing, foam-flecked cascade and the quieter water below. Farther up, I crossed the burn carefully to avoid the water coming over the tops of my wellingtons. I preferred the farm side to the banks I had left which were completely sitka-clad, but these had ferns and birches till higher up the slope near the badger sett.

Spike had dug out his entrance the previous night leaving deep paw-prints in the soft earth much of which now covered the great bole of the wych-elm close by. In the damp places there was a late flush of that pretty, five-petalled flower, pink purslane. I found some ripe and juicy blackberries at the side of the loch. By now there was a serenely blue sky with towering clouds and heavy grey waves lapped the shore where a solitary heron was standing on one leg. There were many more fungi – stinkhorns, fly agaric, boletus, honey fungus and the tiny stagshead. Amongst the dark foliage of the conifers, the larch needles were yellowing and falling underfoot, splashes of gold amongst the green. They reminded me that the holly berries in the shelter belts near the village were ripe and those of the yews were dropping. I walked on awhile to the Dark Spring and its great rush of water somewhere beneath my feet. Now sombre clouds were scurrying over a deepening sky and the red grouse chided 'go-bak, go-bak' from the depths of the moor. The heather-burning season had started in October and would continue now as the weather allowed until the following April. On Dydor patches had already been burnt under controlled conditions to encourage the old heather to regenerate and so provide new growth to feed the grouse. Not only did this benefit other wildlife by providing a mosaic of nesting and feeding habitats, but also ensured the survival of heather covering the hills.

Snow came again in early November but didn't settle; ice lay on the road above the village cladding the puddles that the rain had left. The badgers still foraged under the trees where it was sheltered from the bitter blast and collected grass bedding from the leeward side of the sheep field. I had missed the otter for a few nights but knew from his fresh spraints that all was well. The temperature steadily dropped. Though the village saw little of the snow, it covered the hill peaks and the long, smooth curve of Dydor. By day the sun reflected an azure sky in ruffled waters and the wind was a whetted knife. The loch was teeming with geese, the pink-footed greatly out numbering the greylag and occasional barnacle. To the golden-eye, widgeon and mallard were added teal, tufted duck, pochard and goosander, until now all strangers to me. My greatest delight was to stand under the tree cover by the lochside at dusk watching the geese and swans flying in for the night – such an incredible sight – the noise was deafening. If the birds descended onto the fields below the hills, the sheep would run for the safety of the drystane dykes. I wondered what the farmers thought of their aerial visitors, though on two such occasions the sheep retaliated by chasing the birds into the water. The badgers no longer feared the geese after their initial fright and on several milder nights I was to see sheep, geese and brocks all feeding in the same field. The clan had put on weight that autumn ready for the lean times ahead for although not a hibernating animal, a badger can stay below ground for many nights without food, living off the yellow fat stored beneath its skin.

For thirty-six hours strong gales swept Scotland. The trees outside my window heaved and turned as drapes of blackened cloud hid Dydor from me. By the afternoon it was raining too, the water rushing down the streets too fast for the drains to clear it. The burn frothed and roared, an awesome sight. Quite suddenly at dusk the battle of the elements ceased, the ensuing stillness a peaceful harmony. Now I found the burn too deep and powerful to cross and it was to remain so well into the following spring. Flowering red campion and herb robert still clung from its craggy walls, their petals made brighter by the constant spray. That night the badgers came above ground briefly. The bitter cold of the day had gone, but snow was in the air again. Soon they went to earth and I walked back to the village as fluffy flakes floated lazily around me. Large numbers of roe deer were gathered together in the lower shelter belts, more than I had ever seen in one place before. The next morning I awoke to several centimetres of snow, my first real snow in Scotland and as is often the way, it was no longer so cold, certainly not as bitter as the earlier gales.

How was the otter faring? There had been no apparent sign of him for some time. Unlike the badger clan that had no need to forage beneath the snow, he still must eat to survive. The badgers had the advantage too, of warmth. In winter their underground tunnelling is about 5°C higher than the outside temperature, whilst the sleeping chambers may be far warmer where several animals are curled up together. In spring where green bedding has been taken down, such as fresh grass or bluebell greenery, these chambers are said to be as warm as 18°C from the heat given off as it decomposes. I walked out that morning intent on finding otter spore in the unblemished snow. In the event, not only his prints were visible, but the otter himself. Why did he choose to hunt by day? Perhaps the fish he sought were torpid all the time in the very cold water and it was warmer for him to hunt diurnally. Fish dropping down to the pool tended to stay hidden at the bottom amongst the weeds, but the otter would soon disturb them into view and make his catch, trapped as they were in a relatively small space. Had the occasional dog-walker paused to look down through the trees to the distant pool, he would have been sharp-eyed indeed to spot the hump-backed dive, the line of bubbles tracing its underwater progress or that bobbing to the surface of the otter's head. I was careful to keep myself concealed, lest my watching drew unwelcome attention from my own kind.

By now I had learnt to smell the otter's presence close by even if I couldn't see him, in the same way as I could the badgers and foxes. This wasn't to be confused with urination, spraint or dung sites, but the personal scent of the creature itself. My sense of smell has always been good; I hope it never deteriorates. It is a sobering thought that animals such as these with this sense so highly developed, must find human scent overpowering. Our surface area is so much greater than theirs and unlike them, we sweat through our skin. One day I took the otter by surprise and he 'huffed' as he shot off to the relative safety of the pool, but there he stopped head clear of the water, recognized or smelled who it was and returned. He shook himself all over me, then rolled in the grass, pushing himself along on his belly, then on one side and the other, so squeezing the surplus water from his outer coat. It transpired he was in a playful mood. I thought of the Gaelic name for the otter, *Cudoun*, or burn dog, so Cudoun he became.

When he rolled amongst the grasses and spearwort I saw the uneven whitish throat patch under his chin. As yet I had no need to identify Cudoun but this was a good sign for me to know him by should other otters enter the neighbourhood. For the first time I saw him in good light when his coat was dry. He was a dusky brown with the chest and belly fur a lighter hue. Slipping from my rock seat I knelt by the lounging form and he paused there on his back, bright eyes ever watchful. Greatly daring I stretched out a hand touching the thick webbing of a forepaw and again his whiskers tickled as their owner sniffed my fingers. Now I straightened and began to slowly walk upstream along the bank – a chit, chitting and a lithe shape passed me, traversing the rocky margins with an agility far surpassing mine. I was to find that Cudoun had little vocalization; his contact whistle that we already exchanged, his huff of concern or anxiety and other soft sounds variable in quality, impossible to describe in words. These were intimate sounds made only when very close. Certainly these tones (that I will call whickerings) were signs of friendship and the ones that bonded us.

That was the day I found his holt, or rather he revealed it to me by going in and out its entrance several times. At a glance this was merely a hole between exposed tree roots, but closer examination found it dry, snug and well away from the surrounding dampness. I was curious about it however, for it looked remarkably like an old badger outliner – and so I believe it was. Later I was to find that this is not uncommon. I had read that otters do not dig their own holts but make suitable dens, natural or mammal-made, their own. Actually, this is not entirely true, though I suspect they prefer a ready-made vacant one. They will also take in bedding such as reeds or dry grass. That winter I discovered Cudoun using two other dens; one farther upstream, a hollow between rocks, and another far below the pool and very near human habitation, in the bole of an enormous sycamore tree. It seems to me that the importance of human disturbance in the otters' environment has been exaggerated as has their shyness. Walkers with unleashed dogs could pose a more serious threat to the burn dog however, especially where cubs or half-grown otters are in the vicinity.

Only the loch shallows were frozen, not the deeper water or the burn. Very soon the snow melted in a warmer air flow, but I wondered what would happen to Cudoun and his kind if all froze. He wouldn't become torpid like the badgers, nor had he their thick layer of fat on which to live. (Otters do have a layer of subcutaneous fat that together with their water-repellent coat, makes them resilient to near freezing temperatures, provided they are not forced to remain too long in the water as they once were when hunted.)

My last visit to Melanie and Galloway that year was a memorable one. On a moonlit night I wandered up the back lane towards the moor and watched a pair of barn owls hunting over the fields. There had been no snow in this southwestern region of Scotland and the weather was mild. I believed this pair not to be those we had watched from the cottage windows for there the white owls' territory had been around the hamlet and along the loch edge. I left them hunting and walked onto the hills above. The moor is a secret place at night, but not a silent one even when there is no wind. A plop-plopping sounded nearby and another too further over in the waterlogged areas where the sphagnum flourished. Most of the sheep slept in the shelter of rocky outcrops, their front hooves tucked beneath their recumbent forms. Occasionally a ewe would pass from one group to another to lie with them. At daybreak a dot appeared far above in the sky. It dropped lower wheeling and mewing, the wild mournful cry like a lost soul. The sheep took little notice of the buzzard; they were up and grazing as a curlew probed beneath a tussock and a distant cow lowed from the glen. Time to return. Where the burn flows near the lane I heard a commotion and recognized the sounds as those of badgers quarrelling. By the time I rounded the bend, the trio were nearing the burn and still arguing loud and clear. I watched until a rise in the lane hid them from my sight. How good to know that badgers were still here in spite of the persecution.

That afternoon Melanie and I went to explore Dirl Wood for the badger sett. Its disused quarry was a wonderland with trees, lichens, ferns and liverworts growing from its walls. Melanie told me that quarrying had ceased here when the slate was found to be too soft; cheaper and better could be brought from Lancashire. There were few trees then with dwelling places for the workers erected amongst them, now reduced to occasional heaps of lichen-covered stone and mostly concealed by ferns and bramble. I suppose some could claim this was an eerie place, but it was also wild and lovely. There were many rabbit holes and signs of roe deer and plenty of ideal places for badgers to den. Several deep crevices in the rocky walls had been worn smooth by the constant passing of bodies, although with no soil to dig out there were no spoil heaps to prove badgers denned there. We discovered two passages into the mine that led deeper underground. These were brick-lined, wet and overhung with ferns so we didn't venture down them. It was a tempting site to explore, but we soon found it could be dangerous. Under the wet, dead leaves of many autumns the loose slates readily slid downwards on the steep slopes. Above the quarry and throughout the wood, animal trails wound to and fro and at one point, the badgers appeared to go over the drystane dyke. A large stone had come down with moss torn off it and claw marks were visible on its surface where the animals had reached up and pulled themselves over. Down below and slightly to one side, another rock had been pushed away from its site on the ground; a badger had searched for some titbit beneath. Melanie checked where she might safely come and watch this little clan. A splendidly curved oak tree made a convenient seat overlooking the entrances in the quarry and a nearby trunk had the typical scratching marks on its mossy bark. Later we walked round the outside of the trees amongst the sheep. Dirl Wood was larger than appeared at first glance.

On the last night of my stay it was still very mild with the full moon seeking out the darkest crevices. There were five barn owls perched on the dyke and I suspected that three were youngsters that had not yet dispersed to find territories of their own. A short time elapsed and first one tawny and then another appeared. Almost immediately, the first brown owl attacked a white in mid-flight. None of the other owls interfered or seemed particularly interested. The two birds flew at each other screeching and hissing with talons outstretched. At one point they engaged and continued to quarrel in the grass. Finally the second tawny landed on the ground and the white owl flew off. The other barn owls seemed singularly unmoved by the whole performance. I slipped away and hurried down the lane and along the main road. As I hoped: a barn owl pair were hunting along the loch margins. So these white owls from the loch area were those we watched from the cottage and the family of five had their territory above in the glen.

The following morning I went to post a letter and continued up to the area where earlier I had watched the owls fighting. I met a taxi driver and we stood talking. He too had seen five barn owls the previous evening as he drove his fare up the lane. We agreed that the end of their territory seemed to be the junction of the lanes and he went on to say that more than anything, he would love to see a live badger. Once he had found a dead one on the road outside Dumfries in the Nithsdale area. Not that he thought he would ever watch one around this hamlet, the farmers saw to that. I said nothing but was very interested when he commented that badgers had been cleared out – mainly through gassing – for fear of bovine TB. He too came of farming stock and knew old habits die hard. All the old prejudices are difficult to erase, but perhaps one day he would see a live badger. We said goodbye, but not before I mentioned the new Badgers Act 1991 protecting their setts.

As he so rightly said, however, what chance had that of being enforced up here?*

I returned to the Lothians and my village to find high winds blowing over the hills though the air was warm and mild. There had been heavy rain. The burn was a rushing torrent and the deciduous trees quite bare. Grace and Disgrace found me as they returned home from worming on the pasture and in playful mood, head-butted my legs and ran circles round me as I sat. They also encountered Cudoun. Everywhere was very wet and he was searching the rushes and long grass between sett and field. The badgers came forward whickering, hopeful and hesitant, which considering his size was probably wise. Otter-boy stood up on hind legs and regarded them thoughtfully, then made to bound off with his distinctive humped gait. A few metres away however, he turned and looked again as Grace made a little run forward. This must have convinced Cudoun that badgers are best seen and kept at a distance for he changed his mind and disappeared at speed to the burn.

It was pleasant to stand in the gloaming of a November evening watching the perfect reflection of the peaks in quiet waters. Then came a distant throbbing of wings; geese were flying high over the loch. Another flock, now a skein, as more and more came into view, were all flying from a northerly point to circle in a great cloud. A multitude of voices, geese and swans, and a great swell of sound that grew and grew as the sky darkened further and more birds joined the throng. Used to the nightly invasion now, the sheep took scant notice. A whooper swan dropped, surf rising, onto the mirrored surface – another and another. Slowly the swirling sky cleared as birds descended some onto the pasture and the calling eased, so that I could hear individual voices.

I wandered back up to the path with birch and pine to my right and the flowing ditch and drystane dyke that borders the farm on my left. Something dropped from the low wall and disappeared into the ditch. Sounds of lapping came clear and up it came to my path, black stripes on white turned to regard me standing there. It was C. Goon and I cannot think who was the more surprised, badger or me! By now it was 4.45 p.m. I spoke softly and he made to pass, paused at my boots and tail raised, backed onto and musked them before vanishing through the scrub beneath the pines. It was so peaceful walking by myself in the dark that really wasn't although the night had already come. Inevitably my feet led me to the gap in the fence and the night *was* dark there in the sitkas' shade. At the sett someone was digging out; great bundles of old dried grass and bracken mixed with pieces of sheep wool. Mounds of it were appearing and three entrances were already cleared of wych-elm leaves and needles that seemed determined to creep back into the clean tunnels beyond. Far below the burn tumbled and twisted over

---

* Fourteen months later, an entire herd had to be slaughtered on a farm in the district after an outbreak of bovine TB. This outbreak was traced to imported animals with no badger connections – but the fear remains.

its rocky bed and still the badger worked on beneath my feet intent on cleaning its home once more before its winter rest. A pheasant called and shifted uneasily on a branch by the waters as a tawny figure stole to the bank to quench its thirst before setting out to hunt. It was so mild and still under the trees. No breath of wind touched their outspread arms and across the fields, stars sparkled in a soft sky.

It was the same story at the Clackmon sett when I went for a walk one afternoon that way. One entrance dug under a rock beneath a pine tree was particularly impressive. Fresh bracken had been collected here also for clean bedding and taken in together with long, dried grass stems and leaves. It is worth noting however, that from late autumn to early spring, holes may appear quite disused with dead leaves partly filling them. This can be very deceptive as badgers may well still be present. The trunks of the Swedish whitebeams at this sett showed clearly now they had shed their dark glossy leaves. The smooth grained bark with its horizontal bands of diamond-shaped lenticels, or corky warts, was an attractive sight. There was fresh dung in a pit by the burn itself, but also some lying on the top of the ground beneath the pines together with many snuffle holes. Beech mast lay at the shelter belt edge. Whilst I was there a V-formation of white-fronted geese, their flight punctuated with cries like hunting dogs, came overhead and shortly after the higher-pitched whistling wing beats of whooper swans flying towards the hills.

We were in early December when the temperature dropped giving way to nights of heavy frost. If my visits to the Burn Badgers didn't synchronize with their brief appearances above ground, I might miss seeing them for several nights. I often saw Cudoun however, catching a meal in the pool at first light. As the winter progressed I discovered him with an eel at the point of the burn where it joined the river. Having been told by the loch fishermen in the summer that its waters were empty of eels, I concluded that either they lived lower down in the burn or more likely, in the River Cley itself. That winter I found that eels did frequent the Cley though nowhere did they appear numerous, probably because these waters tended to be rather acidic. Watching Cudoun eat one reminded me that eels are said to be the otter's preferred fish – certainly, it was Cudoun's! He lay on the bank gripping the fish some way down its long body and chewing from the head. It made a large meal and he continued eating until the tail end was reached and nothing remained.

I decided to walk the hills by night and started out one early evening, the darkening sky a palette of violet, pink and apple-green. There were geese feeding amongst the sheep and I soon left the sparkling loch behind me as I climbed the lower slopes. Even as I walked the white rime thickened and a bold half moon swum above me in the freezing air. I was determined to see how far I could walk in the long December night and return the next day. For this warmly clad white settler with a chocolate bar, flask of hot tea and the inevitable notepad and pen, it was something of an adventure.

Soon all signs of life were left behind – no sheep, no bird; only the soft crunch of my shoes on frosted grass kept company with me and the whimpering wind. I turned aside from the way for I wanted to see from the top of Lytlaw at night. Dropping my pack on a boulder, I scrambled up to its peak and stood enjoying the distant glimmer of the loch I had left and far over on the horizon, the twinkling lights of the city. I could *smell* the night. On my way up I had briefly entered small pockets of warmth trapped from the day between rocky outcrops, but on the heights it was cold. The broken moon was a deep yellow hung in a starry vault. Looking carefully, the other half could be seen as a black twin, so close I might have reached up and plucked it from the sky.

There were no trees or bushes for the faint wind to stir, nor water falling. I took off my gloves and hands outstretched, let it whisper through the fingers and lift my hair. I might have been at the beginning of time – or its end, it made little difference for here was eternity. I suspect that centuries ago before the advent of artificial light, man had good night vision, far better than mine. True he dwelt in a world of superstition and omens, but he carried charms to ward off evil and worshipped the sun, moon and life-giving rain. Musing on Lytlaw's peak with the range of hills all around and Dydor's humped back crouching to my right, brought me close to my origins with a sense of belonging. Solitary and at peace I was fortunate indeed in our modern world, to be alone on these laws at night.

Returning, I retrieved my rucksack and continued on my way. The trail skirted a slope then rose up to ascend the next. It followed the edge of a sitka plantation and crossed a bubbling burn. Now I was walking that great expanse of moss and wiry grass known locally as Strathmuir, the flat moor. It was two hours past midnight and the temperature had dropped. My breath vaporized before my eyes though I was warm from walking. The route led to the foot of another range of hills unknown to me and the glitter of a small water ahead. I found a comfortable resting place at its margins and spread out the map. The lochan was called Blinkbonny, a popular name in the Lowlands often given to views; somehow it suited this spot. Steaming tea from the flask, some squares of chocolate and such a view! As if determined to live up to its reputation, Blinkbonny gave me something further that night – my first Scottish sighting of a long-eared owl. It probably roosted in the strip of coniferous woodland to my right. The notes of its call were regularly spaced and not loud, more a cooing moan than a hoot. Not far away the cry was answered, although I only saw one owl that night. For some time it hunted amongst the grass tussocks before veering away towards the trees, calling once more.

Ascending the slopes I passed the ruins of a shieling. It was very cold now on the heights with the grass crunching loudly at each step. The temperature usually drops to it lowest before dawn and I wanted to watch the sun rise from the hills. There came a distant burst of cackling as a skein of geese crossed the face of the fading moon. Now the steep, winding path flattened

A white head with its startling black stripes appeared disembodied above the spoil as if looking straight at me.

Badger at its sett on the edge of a wheatfield, Lothian Region.

Old, purblind boar badger.

Relaxed and grooming.

The tall, upright stance of a bark-scavenging badger who is quite capable of climbing that tree!

Nothing quite like a thorough scratch!

Except grooming in good company perhaps?

A steading nestling below the hills.

There is nothing so evocative of the mortality of man as his derelict habitations.

The downstream pool was a good place in which to hunt.

Bringing the catch to the bank.

Then he faced me, sitting back on his haunches, right paw resting at his side.

The swans on the lochan beneath Dydor.

Otter with remains of fish; the head is generally eaten first.

For the first time I saw him in good light when his coat was dry.

Typically, a circular area under and around the snared badger had been clawed into fresh earth in her long, protracted agony.

One more grossly baited badger was to appear on the golf course, bringing the total to 29.

Dirty from a good night's worming.

Badgers on the spoil heap of their sett.

Typical badger sett dug under sitkas in the Grampian Region.

A sett, also in the Grampian Region, dug into an open field.

Mike Harris looking at tree-felling over a badger sett where the Forestry Commission's guidelines had been carried out.

Many dead sheep are left to rot.

In the times of King Mainus huge stones were erected in a ring . . .

. . . . and the biggest of them was stretched out on the south side to serve as an altar.

Rabbit nestlings dug out by a badger. One left uneaten near the culprit's paw print!

Badgers frequently climb trees at night to take slugs, snails and insects hidden in the bark.

There was something about the tall, graceful stance; I had seen him before . . .

Enjoying a good scratch.

out and I found myself on a scree plateau high above the peaks of other braes. Light was spilling gently from the east as the sun climbed high enough to peer above the far range. Below, the panoramic landscape was scattered with rocks as though by a careless hand. Something moved between the nearest and I saw it was a fox hunting, probably for voles. It appeared to be listening, its large ears upright and well forward, then suddenly it rose on hind legs and pounced into the grass. A quick dig down and something small was picked up and chewed briefly before swallowing. A crow landed on a nearby boulder with a harsh croak and the fox glanced towards it before continuing its search. I looked back from whence I had come and saw hill upon hill disappearing into the far horizon, still dark from the night. Dropping down from the plateau the path forked here and I took the track that would lead me in a wide arc, back to the village I had left. By 10 a.m. the sunshine was bright though not warm enough to melt the frost. This had been the fifth deeply frosty night. Such a large build-up of hoar made the ground appear snow-covered as well as the trees I was approaching.

I passed a limekiln and quarry now disused and abandoned. Lime has an ancient history for building purposes, but was not appreciated as a fertilizer until the mid-1660s. Unfortunately, liming was often overdone and not accompanied by regular underground draining for another two centures resulting in unproductive land that in the Lothians and Borders particularly, often reverted to grazing. Once the need for good drainage was realized however, liming produced better crops of oats and bere – a type of barley used in the making of bread and bannocks and the brewing of ale.

There was another abandoned quarry further along my route and this time I left the track to sit in its shadow and finish the still warm tea in my flask. Vegetation hid the once raw scars of man's excavation and blasting. Heather and gorse clung to its sides and ferns traced a watercourse that dropped out of sight below me into an open shaft. Far overhead a valiant rowan tree struggled for survival, its roots searching for sustenance in a deep fissure between the rocky walls. I finished the tea and followed a faint trail that wound its way steadily upwards, the only sounds being those of sheep faintly bleating from a distant steading and the irregular drop, drop of water directly below within the shaft. I rounded a rocky outcrop, my feet tending to slip on the frosted grass and quite unexpectedly came upon a sett entrance! In my enthusiasm for this new countryside, I had given no thought to possible badgers existing here. The hole had been dug beneath a great boulder, but the small spoil heap had long ago been worn almost flat. I lay down and peered into a dry, sloping passage with rock on three sides. Higher still on the quarry face was another entrance, this time a mere squeeze between boulders worn shiny and smooth with use. The whole area smelled strongly of the animals' musk – someone had been out this cold night however briefly, and scent-marked their property. Unlike the territory of the animals I watched, there were no fields here and poor grazing rather than lush pasture. This clan would need to forage widely and I wondered how far they roamed in search of food.

Clouds hid the sun by mid-afternoon as I made slow headway against a strong, moist wind that quickly melted the frost. Shadows raced one another across the moor turning my familiar hills to shades of mauve and green. The bog near my feet was treacherously beautiful with an occasional sound of escaping gases from the wet, spongy ground. I walked through the pass to behold Dydor and stood by the loch as the evening light made corrugated foil of its surface – a silvery shimmering. The dying sun over his crouching form touched the birches with a rosy gold. Now great black clouds appeared behind the Dark Hill, spilling over and down towards me. The water's surface changed as the light altered and the shimmering, silvery quality was gone. For a few precious moments dark-sided Dydor remained etched black in the loch as a jackdaw's strident voice called a challenge from a lofty pine and a sheep bleated from the fold.

Chapter Seven

Hoolit

The New Year brought periods of snow alternating with a warmer airflow, wind and rain. It also brought a great surprise when I happened to visit the Wild Way and found Cudoun there. Perhaps I should not have been surprised. The loch and pool were frozen, so the less turbulent stretches of the more sheltered river itself were the only source of fish left open to him. Strange to think that the otter bitch and cubs that I had seen there last summer were Cudoun's offspring, but really, I should have guessed. I had read that a dog otter's territory may vary enormously and can take in that of more than one bitch, so it could well be that Cudoun had another family elsewhere.

At that time – January, the adult otters had no obvious interest in one another, each hunting for itself. True they registered each other's presence, but tended to avoid a head-on encounter if possible. If they did meet face to face, both would stop abruptly and cautiously sniff the other in the manner of dogs. They would then move aside and spraint several times in the time-honoured fashion of tails-up-and-waving and the bitch would continue on her way. Cudoun might spend some time sniffing her spraints, before urinating over them. I imagine they told him much about her sexual condition. Inland otters are reputed to breed at any time of year, but for most mammals, giving birth correlates either with a plentiful food supply for the mother or for the young at the start of weaning. Would this bitch breed again this year and would her youngsters stay in the area?

About this time I came across a query in a sporting magazine from a reader who tanned otter skins for the making of sporrans. He was a Ross-shire man and a member of a fox-control club sponsored by the Department of Agriculture and Fisheries for Scotland (DAFS). The otters drown in lobster and crab pots close to the shore and rather than let them rot, he was in the habit of sending a few to a taxidermist and tanned about four a year for his fishermen friends. He had, however, been warned that the possession of such a Schedule 5 protected animal might rightly land him in trouble, unless he could prove the otters had come by an accidental death.

I was amazed that these accidents still occurred. True, the old books and papers I perused on Scottish wildlife made frequent reference to such fatalities, some going back four centuries, but then of course, the otter had not been protected – rather the reverse. In my ignorance I had thought such drownings were part of the 'bad old days', but far from it. Nor did these drownings only apply to Scotland, but to Great Britain and the continent as well. Probably more British otters drown today in traps though their deaths are usually unrecorded because they are unintentional and the animal is protected from deliberate actions. They have a love of crustaceans such as lobsters and crabs and their special delicacy, the eel, has already been mentioned. Before the advent of synthetic fibres, otters often escaped before drowning by tearing through the basketwork of the lobster pot or creel and the cotton mesh of the eel fyke net. Since this is no longer possible, otters entering such traps now have no chance of escape before asphyxiation occurs.

One clear, breezy morning after a night of deep frost, I took the camera intending to photograph some of the deserted shielings in the lower hills. I would follow the path round Dydor through the pass to the old reservoir. There were three whooper swans mirrored in the lochan below the Dark Hill, two of them last year's cygnets judging by their dusky buff plumage. I found the path easy walking for the mud from early snow and rain was still frozen. It turned out a beautiful sunny day still well below freezing, but good walking weather. As I dropped down off the ridge I saw the reservoir was very full and had overflowed across the far side of the track partly submerging a line of hawthorns and was frozen into steep ridges by the wind. Most of the pink-feet were feeding on the grass of the lower slopes and showed no concern when my path took me through them. As I returned at 3 p.m. a half moon climbed the darkening sky and the air grew chill. Nearing my lodgings, the clamour of fieldfares and redwings settling for the night was as noisy as the rookery inhabitants over the way.

Soon after this I moved to Hoolit (owl) cottage on the Robertsons' land well beyond the village so was now much nearer to the animals I watched. That winter we had little snow, although the weather continued bitter. As dusk fell, a cold hand would settle more surely onto each grass blade and naked twig. The cottage had no garden, merely a wide area of rough-cut grass around it leading to a tumbledown steading belonging to the nearby farm. A fox might wander into view having come across the old wooden bridge from the pasture beyond the burn. It would look cautiously round and continue out of my sight. One evening I was suddenly made aware of an upright bird sitting on the drystane dyke by the gate. Even as I puzzled and lifted the binoculars, it darted away in low direct flight. The dying sun cast a blood red glow on its barred tail and I saw it was indeed a sparrowhawk hunting at dusk. A few evenings later there came a great cat-like noise of quarrelling; a dog fox was trying to mount a reluctant vixen beyond my kitchen window. The argument continued round the side of the steading and I slipped out hoping to watch the proceedings unobserved, only to find the vixen had crossed the burn with her suitor following at a discreet distance.

I was to regularly see both foxes and sparrowhawk. With the latter I noted it rarely hunted in the same place consecutively. Dusk, when small songsters

were intent on settling into their roosts amid scoldings and twitterings, was
an ideal time to swoop low, pluck up an unsuspecting victim and be well
away without pause. Too late, cries of alarm would punctuate the gloaming
to follow in the hunter's wake. That element of surprise meant a repeat
performance in the same place could only be successfully accomplished after
a ten- to twelve-day interval. The hawk dined well, following the outline of
dykes and steadings and best of all, the edges of the shelter belt round the
farm. It was a joy to dwell so near the burn's continual calling. I was to
pass many happy hours in its company by day and night and came to know
its many moods. In flood it was an awesome sight, spray rising high as it
thundered foam-flecked through its craggy walls. Surprising that the delicate
ferns growing in its shelter withstood such onslaught, so steadfast yet so frail
they appeared, but survive and flourish they did. In its gentler moods I didn't
need the bridge to cross, but could scramble over its water-smoothed rocks.
Buds on the primroses here appeared very early and their flowers in such a
sheltered place continued long after those in more open aspects had ceased
to bloom.

Sandy Robertson found me there one morning and we fell to talking of
the old days when the burn's power was harnessed to work the mills. Apart
from flour, there had once been paper, snuff, yarn and sailcloth industries
along the watercourses, from burn to river and leading to the city itself.
I told him of my findings in the archives of the *1st and 2nd Statistical
Accounts* of the area. These cover all of Scotland and are divided into
parishes, many written by local ministers. Although they contain general
sections, each Account is dependent on the interest of the writer and many
make absorbing reading. They are of course, a vital historical account of
local affairs written by educated men. The 1st Account written in 1771–2 by
a physician, Dr William Nisbet, records the first paper mill in the village.

> While the advantages of manufactures in Scotland cannot be too strongly
> inculcated, those in particular, that employ the very young and the aged ought
> to meet with every encouragement. The paper trade employs children from 10
> to 12 years of age, a period when they can do nothing very laborious, and
> when their morals from idleness and neglect, are very apt to be corrupted . . .
> Till within these few years, the people of this parish, were sober, industrious,
> and economical. The vices of the capital, however, are beginning to spread
> fast amongst them, and the introduction of those baneful articles to the poor,
> tea and whisky, will soon produce that corruption of morals and debility of
> constitution, which are already so sorely felt in many parishes, and which
> must soon materially injure the real strength and population of Scotland.

By the 2nd Statistical Account fifty years later, the Revd Barclay writes:
'The food of the peasantry consists of the various preparations of oatmeal,
potatoes, wheaten bread, tea and sugar,' so by now tea was presumably,
an accepted drink of the poor. In writing of the river he comments: 'In the
early part of its course it abounds with small (wild) trout; but the chloride

of lime and other chemical substances used by the papermakers have almost entirely destroyed them at the village and downwards.' With the mills long gone and a new generation conscious of pollution and its effects, the Cley and its attendant burns are probably cleaner and healthier than they have been for several centuries, bearing in mind that watercourses of bygone years were also general dumping grounds for domestic sewage. It is from the Revd Barclay too, that we hear that poaching was 'no uncommon crime' (meat was a luxury for the poor), and 'The establishment of the rural police has been of essential service to the tranquillity and order of the parish.'

I strolled out one evening about 11 p.m. as a dog barked and a man's voice called 'Good-nicht.' Sandy and Jacko, his little Jack Russell, were turning in for the night having done the rounds of the steadings together. Will's border collies were strictly working dogs not pets and slept in the barn near the house. It was mild now after the earlier rain with the moon not yet up and mist in the hollow places. The damp vegetation smelled fresh and alive; there seemed new scents everywhere as I passed by. Sitting on the big rock opposite Spike's entrance, I was reminded of another sett and another clan I had known (how long ago?), but this was a far cry from that Kentish woodland. Here was a wilder landscape with no human activity likely after dark. It is difficult to describe the joy of being out alone at night; such a peaceful, solitary existence. I feel so close to the earth and the meaning of life as the universe shines on far above me. I am infinitesimal, a mere link in a chain that joins me with my ancestors and with those yet to come. But each link is vital. The past forged it and that link will help forge the future. Every living thing be it plant or animal has this same potential, but the human species has something more – the power and the will to care and cherish this world of ours . . . or destroy it. We are the guardians of this earth for only we have the ability to reflect on past actions and plan for the future. And the future that may be distant to us is but a grain of sand in the hourglass of time.

A strong smell of fox disturbed my thoughts and I strained to hear any movement, but heard nothing. Then something stepped from the edge of the logs and looked carefully ahead, then left but not to the right where I sat. It was indeed a fox, the long fur damp from the wet grass outside. There was something about the tall, graceful stance; I had seen him before more than once from the cottage and yes, what was that he was so intently watching? Ah, the vixen! He bounded over the clear area in front of me making a high-pitched whine. She however, would have none of it and gave a series of sharp, rasping clicks to warn him off. This gekkering as it is called, sounds rather like a stick being run along a wooden paling fence and can reach explosive heights if two foxes fight. Submissively, Romeo lowered his head and trailed after her out of my sight.

It was too late to wait for the badgers this mild night; they had probably emerged long ago. Leaving the shelter belt and the burn's urgent flowing, the tawnies sounded clearer to me as they called one to another over the pasture. I followed the stone walling with the great mass of Dydor brooding ahead. It was pleasant to stand with the soft breeze whispering, the owls and an occasional bleat of a sheep for company. Probably the geese were feeding on the slopes by the loch for they were not here. Something shaggy searched along the farther wall, snuffling here and digging awhile there. He was finding beetles that he crunched gustily before swallowing. A big boar with heavy back and shoulders, the hair of his chest, long and luxuriant and a lively mask. I knelt, spoke softly and C. Goon came up to sniff at my hair with a grubby snout. True to form he next head-butted my legs, then ran round me inviting a game. He had grown into a handsome creature. A week later I watched the foxes in the shelter belt, who it would appear from their attitudes towards each other, had mated. They were busy digging a den under the heap of trunks and branches left when a path had been cleared through the trees.

An invitation came to stay a few days in Kent with Dave and his wife to be present at a meeting with my old badger group regarding the lamping problem there. Attending were the group's survey officer and chairman and seven police officers including the Inspector (as head of operations in his division), who had organized it. Apart from local beat officers and the Kent police force Wildlife Officer, the Inspector had invited the local RSPCA inspector (who had a last minute emergency call-out and could not attend) and two local officers from Essex police, who did.

The Inspector related the circumstances in which the group and police had become aware of the succession of badger deaths (now totalling 28), centred on the golf course from July onwards. Of all the incidents, only on one night were any suspects observed by the group who were carrying out surveillance. Police were called, but were seen approaching the scene by the suspects who made good their escape. The Inspector then gave an outline of crime in his area for the last six months of 1991. He pointed out that the level of crime was such that resources were not available to mount an operation, even in conjunction with the RSPCA, to combat the problem. Indeed, we all appreciated that Kent's rising crime rate had to take precedence over wildlife matters.

The Essex sergeant then described the local Watch Scheme he had initiated involving farmers, members of the public and gamekeepers, plus the use of information in local newspapers. From what had been described that evening, he agreed with the general opinion that the badgers had been taken and killed on the surface, not dug out of setts and that the most likely method was by lamping and the use of lurchers. He stressed the importance of building up intelligence and passing information between *all* interested parties. Also the lack of success when trying to catch poachers in open country. Far better to find their vehicle and wait for their return if possible, than following offenders back to it. He added for the police benefit that a thorough search was necessary for spades, blood, hair, trophies such as ears, tail, paws from a mutilated badger.

The group's chairman reported that it had been quiet for some time but he was expecting fresh activity. The RSPCA had an investigations team who were prepared to conduct an operation if offences were regularly committed, but not on the off chance. The Inspector asked that clear information be given beforehand showing map references etc. and a local Kent officer enquired if names and makes of vehicles together with their registration numbers belonging to patrolling group members could be passed on to the police to avoid confusion when investigating incidents.

Three very positive results from the police came out of this meeting, however, in spite of their pressure of work. The Inspector had sent a sample of blood from the most recent badger autopsy to the Central Forensic Laboratory at Aldermaston, Berkshire. This meant that any bloodstained article now seized by the police could be tested to see if it was indeed derived from a badger. This facility was available to all police and would be up to individual forces to apply through their local forensic department. The problem with lamping in lonely places at night has always been *proving* the dead badger or badger parts found the next morning were in any way connected with the suspects of the previous night. (When I telephoned a solicitor later, who was well versed in badger-related cases, it was good to hear him say that a successful conviction could probably be brought on this evidence alone.) The Inspector then explained that he would draw up a contingency plan for use by all stations in advising patrols on initial attendance at the scene, details of types of badger abuse, legislation, police powers and possible courses of action. Such plans were already available for unusual incidents not normally familiar to officers such as chemical spills, etc. Kent force's Wildlife Officer felt that the problem needed to be highlighted throughout the force and at headquarters level. He would liaise with the Training School for the Badger Act to be included in future update information. I was surprised at this, as a few years earlier, wildlife abuse lectures were part of force training. It appeared, however, that these had been axed with the first financial cutbacks. He also felt that a training video should be devoted to the subject, although he doubted that his superiors would show any enthusiasm. The excellent video produced in the 1980s by the Derbyshire force was now unobtainable and in any case, well out of date. All these promises were to come to fruition, although it was Cheshire police force who eventually initiated the video.

Strangely, it was the informal discussion after the meeting that contributed most to the cessation of the problem that had brought us all together. A name was mentioned; that of a local vermin controller who had offered to help one of the badger group catch the baiters. He wasn't known to this station's police, but his name certainly rang warning bells to a couple of officers present whose beats were further into Kent. True he had no police record, but they knew him as someone actively involved in animal abuse with other unpleasant characters who had past convictions. This highlighted what the Essex officer had said about passing information between all interested parties. The man had been very plausible. Not only had he given information, but on one occasion had phoned a group member telling him that lamping was actually taking place, then acting as a public-spirited citizen, had driven round the lanes searching for a parked vehicle! It is easy with hindsight to be critical of this trust, but very understandable when there are few of you trying to be everywhere at once with very little backup (for whatever reason), from the authorities. Over the next few weeks one more grossly baited badger was to appear on the golf course bringing the total to 29. The police searched his house without finding anything to relate him to the badgers, but they removed a shotgun for which he had no licence. The suspect's girlfriend informed on him and although her evidence was unreliable and not sufficient to bring a prosecution, the unsavoury episode ceased at least in this police area.

Before I left for Scotland, Dave drove me round my old haunts. I should have tried to locate Crisp again, but fearing the worst for my old favourite, lost courage and decided to do so on my next visit. Curiously, it wasn't the woods that had meant so much to me that I remembered on returning home, but the searing beauty of the golf course area and the flowing folds of Kentish downland like vivid green cloth dropped by a Titan's hand.

With February came snow on the hill tops and a time of deep frosts. One early morning I chose to follow the further burn that fed the loch away from Dydor and the Dark Spring. Hoar crackled underfoot and even the bog was deep frozen and safe to walk upon. The sheep had long ago been driven down to the home pastures, but eloquent evidence of them was everywhere. The first fleecy back sheltering behind a cluster of rocks, proved to be that of a long dead ewe, frost crystals glinting on a protruding rib. Some more recently dead were almost untouched by scavengers, except for the inevitable crow evidence of the pecked-out eyes. This reminded me strikingly of my 1981 stay in Cumbria and ewes on the fells that had died in the shelter of drystone walls. It would seem that hill sheep mortality is high and farmers accept this is so. As a native of Kent with its fertile land and healthy flocks with few obvious signs at least of disease, this mortality struck me forcibly as did the regular signs of foot rot amongst hill sheep. The cattle I saw grazing in Scotland looked healthy and well-cared for; the same could not be said of its sheep.

The shelter belts were soon left far behind as I gained the open moor. A wandering wind sighed and moaned, sending small flurries of ice against my face. Thick hoar hid the dark scars of an earlier muirburn, but where it lay on the untouched bushes of heather, glistening patinas touched each tiny leaf in a delicate tracery. A 'go-bak' called from its depths at my passing. I stood awhile inwardly smiling as tiny clouds of white rose in a wavering course betraying his route beneath the stubby ling. A ray of light crept through the grey sky, retreated, then triumphantly shone. Ten minutes later the frost was melting as a strengthening sun sped the last of the clouds away. Its warmth steamed, the bog myrtle perfuming the air with its fragrance and abruptly, a small flock of black birds rose from their feeding place in the bog and I saw they were carrion crows and rooks. It struck me forcibly that I had never seen hooded crows or ravens in village or farmland, moorland or hill and talking to Will that evening, I found these are indeed rare species here.

I followed the path rather than the burn for at times that seemed to meander through treacherous bog, reappearing later to murmur nearby, or sometimes tumbling between rocky, bracken-strewn defiles worn deep through the years. Occasionally the glitter of sun on water betrayed pools unrelated to the burn. I resolved to cross the heather expanse to explore one on my return. There were five springs feeding the burn. Discovering the last, I reflected on that word 'spring' with so many meanings; the first season of the year, a new awaking, the spring of one's life, to spring up – all definitions seemed to suit this apparition of clear, fresh water leaping from the earth.

The sun was on its downward journey as I returned. There came a movement of the wiry grass below me and another. Frogs wet from their hidden travels beneath the vegetation were strewn about my way, their gleaming skins a sharp contrast of browns and greens. I sat on a rocky outcrop and watched these gaudy travellers. Had they emerged to migrate to their breeding pools and if so, how far had they still to go? There was a frog nearby me on another rock, its forelegs clinging to the sharp-edged angle, the long hind legs relaxed and boldly marked. It was amusing to speculate why it was up so high, like a sentinel keeping watch or checking how far they had to go? Commonsense told me it had probably emerged from a dark crevice, stirred by the same biological urge as the others. So suddenly it startled me, the frog leapt in a long, smooth line and followed the company below.

It was idly sitting on that rock, watching the dying sun reflected in the pool some distance away over the moor, that I saw the otter. It took me awhile to recognize it as Cudoun partaking of an easy meal of frogs as they made their way under cover of the heather to their journey's end. Many successfully reached the water to spawn, but Cudoun had only to pounce as one emerged from the concealing heather, eat it and fall upon another. A ball of fire slid slowly behind the hills as a lone grouse called stridently in the quietness and the burn dog continued to feast. My whistle arrested him, a pause and he continued to chew carefully as I approached. I noted again how meticulously otters chew before swallowing unlike the Canidae family. He seemed to leave no pieces, but ate those frogs entire. Now he was sated and slipping soundlessly into the pool, lay on his back and began to groom. The highly sensitive whiskers of his eyebrows, throat and cheeks were thoroughly cleaned of any particles. His small ears set into the head which barely projected beyond the thick fur were thoughtfully rubbed. Now and then a frog would bump against the busy otter as his partly submerged body bobbed slightly with his exertions. The water was barely thirty metres across and as the migration into it continued, was becoming somewhat crowded. Cudoun floated, head and four paws clear of its surface, content and at ease. Something swam onto his submerged stomach, then jumped up with a plop onto a hind leg! The small eyes of the dozing 'island' opened bright and clear. A lightning forepaw came up and held its pop-eyed prisoner in a webbed embrace. Long green legs threshed in the air as the terrified frog had a close encounter with Cudoun's bewhiskered mouth and muzzle. But the otter was no longer hungry. Instead he toyed with the other, holding it in the water, lifting it out to watch the frantically flailing legs. Finally he raised his body slightly, released the frog, then grasped it. Suddenly tiring, he let it go and rolling slowly over, swam to the edge and shook himself over me before rubbing himself on the grass. Burn 'dog' indeed; that had been a favourite act of my bitch Wendy.

The short northern day was gone as I returned. I thought the otter still on the moor, but stopping at a carcase of that morning's sheep, he bounded forward to inspect it too. Why more of these sheep were not scavenged by foxes was a good question though undoubtedly, some were. Sandy and Will seemed impassive towards the foxes on their land. I wasn't so sure of their neighbours, however, for in many hill-sheep areas of Scotland, the fox as vermin is gassed, shot, poisoned and snared, but in spite of this I had been told that foxes have increased in recent years. This affects other animal populations too, as shooting apart, such methods of predator control cannot guarantee to kill the target species only. The widely held belief that foxes are automatically lamb-killers hardly holds water here. Why use up vital reserves of energy trying to take a new-born lamb from under the nose of its mother amongst a flock of ewes, when there are pickings aplenty with absolutely no effort from the dead?* I was to find several pregnant ewes dead later in the spring; pregnancy merely hastens death in ailing animals. It was the same on all these hills. Surely it made more sense to clear these carrion away for numbers of any wild species fluctuate according to food supply.

Later that year I corresponded with Don MacCaskill, a Scotsman living in Perthshire. He wrote:

> Badgers are indeed diminishing in numbers here, where 20 years ago or so they were very common. One area in particular on Loch Awe where I was stationed for many years had large numbers, introduced again from England by a local estate in the late 19th century. We went back there some time ago to check and every sett was empty and obviously had been so for some period of years. Exactly the same applies here where we now live – badgers have vanished . . .
>
> We are absolutely convinced that the main cause for the disappearance of the animals in the places I have mentioned is due to the use of fox snares, never checked as required, and set in holes in fences used by both foxes and

---

* Foxes actually seem to prefer well-decomposed carrion. George Pearce, a Shropshire farmer, told me that when he kept pigs, the new-born dead piglets were put in a shallow pit (no lime or chemicals applied). Foxes coming to scavenge from the pit, took bodies beneath the freshly dead, seeming to prefer decomposing, maggoty ones. This is logical enough when one considers that these latter are more easily torn apart and the maggots an added bonus.

badgers. We have been trying for years to get this barbaric instrument banned completely, but sheep farming interests have a very strong voice up here. Setts are also gassed just on the off chance that a fox might be using them.

The argument that foxes are predators of lambs is one that is held to strongly by some hill farmers and shepherds. They contend that even if predation is not the major source of lamb losses, this is only because foxes are rigorously controlled and if they were not, the numbers of dead lambs would rise considerably. Dr Ray Hewson, a scientist from Aberdeen University, has studied both foxes and shepherding for many years for the DAFS. The areas used for this research were Ardnish during 1975–77 and Drimmin from 1977–79. His studies revealed that as many as 24 per cent of lambs may be lost in the Highlands due to malnutrition, hypothermia, disease and stillbirths and only 1/2 per cent are taken by foxes.

Dr Hewson was invited to conduct a three-year study funded by the League Against Cruel Sports (LACS), the results of which were published by the League in their report *Victim of Myth*. During those three years from 1987 to 1990 no fox control was carried out in the study area, a 70 square kilometre estate at Eriboll in Sutherland. (Overall, Eriboll was surrounded by areas that maintained intensive control of foxes including the operations of the grant-aided Durness Fox Club.) Throughout that period, Dr Hewson monitored the effects of no control in his area on fox numbers, fox food habits and lamb predation. Interestingly, neither fox numbers or their breeding dens, nor lamb predation increased even when natural fox food supplies, i.e., voles, rabbits, hares, etc. were scarce. (Oddly enough, lamb losses were slighty lower than in the areas where foxes were rigorously controlled.)

It is worth quoting from Dr Hewson's conclusion:

> Some losses of lambs to foxes seem inevitable. They should be seen against the general pattern of losses of hill lambs. The average production of hill lambs surviving to June per 100 ewes in west Scotland over a five-year period varied between 66 and 71, but ranged from 45 on high exposed ground to 91 on sheltered holdings near the coast. Production varied greatly between adjacent holdings. It is against this background that predation by foxes of up to one to two per cent of the lambs, and often much less or none, must be considered. Lloyd (1980) estimates the figure for Wales at 0.5%. Many shepherds in west and north-west Scotland, including some of the most experienced, do not complain of losses. Killing of lambs by foxes appears to be a random and unpredictable process.
>
> There are no foxes on the island of Mull but production of lambs over a three-year period was no better than on similar ground on the mainland, in other words predation by foxes are part of, rather than in addition to, the normal scale of lamb losses . . .
>
> No one change in land use can explain the increase of foxes in Scotland over the last forty years. More afforestation provides in the early stages an abundance of field voles as food for foxes. Fox dens may be more secure when

the trees reach thicket stage but the field voles will largely have died out, and because of food shortages foxes may fail to breed. If the rate of new planting diminishes there will be less food for foxes.

Foreseeable developments in Scotland include increased game shooting, more people going to the hills, more tourism, a decline in sheep farming in favour of deer forests and changes in the rate of afforestation. Increased game shooting may lead to more rigorous control of foxes on low ground. Tourism and hill walking are unlikely to have any effect. Foxes are not inimical to the interests of deer stalkers. While the effects of a change in land management to deer forest are difficult to predict, they may well include less carrion and consequently fewer foxes with more voles and rabbits to feed them. So far as hill sheep areas are concerned, sheep carrion in winter is likely to determine the level of the fox population. Improvement in management leading to fewer dead sheep might reduce the fox population more than the current methods of control.

It is noteworthy that this report mentioned that sheep carrion is the principal factor that maintains eagles as well as foxes at higher densities in west Scotland than would be expected from the scarcity of live prey.

LACS questioned why DAFS should be grant-aiding twenty-nine 'fox destruction clubs' in Scotland since several studies have now proved that foxes are not a significant cause of lamb mortality. How could the Department justify such spending of public money? The Forestry Commission too killed 1682 adult foxes and 794 cubs on its property in 1988 to 89 as part of its 'good neighbour' policy towards surrounding sheep farmers. Since the staple diet of foxes is rabbits, hares and field voles which can all be serious pests to forestry, this was rather a curious practice.

Perhaps the final word should go to Don MacCaskill who deplored: 'It is quite unbelievable what some people will do to protect their so-called way of life and to hell with tomorrow — we have lost all faith that much wildlife will survive.'

The shelter belt around the farm and its steadings was of beech and sycamore as the foliage of both was widely used in bygone days as cattle fodder. These trees gave protection from the bitter winds not only to the buildings but to beast as well. At dawn and dusk I needed only to sit on the wide cottage windowsills (the stone walls were 60 cm thick) to see the roes' behaviour close to my home. Unlike other deer, the roe buck casts his antlers in November and December, so now their growing new ones were encased in dense velvet like short, furry stumps. The normally dainty bodies appeared chunkier now that their foxy red summer coats had given way to the thick, grey-flecked ones of winter. They have no external tail except for a tiny stump not visible within the rump hairs. I noticed when one of the dogs barked, however, that the does would erect their 'tush' or patch of anal hairs (which now were white, but are creamy in summer), like large powder puffs as they bounded off, warning the rest of the family that danger threatened. They liked to browse on the soft rush that grew everywhere round the cottage, bending down their graceful necks with front legs slightly splayed to reach it. Then up would rise the head, its large, liquid eyes ever watchful, pointed ears turning to catch the faintest of sounds. They only took grass when little else was available, especially the young grass in the early spring. They preferred leaves of trees and shrubs including bramble. Ferns, ivy, heather and blaeberry were eaten too. Later on in the year I saw them take flowers – wild roses and the diminutive harebell being most favoured. Like foxes, these roe had distinct facial markings. Black fur descended from nose to lower lip in striking contrast to their white 'moustaches' and chins. The skittish yearlings resembled small adults and the young males had well-formed pedicles, that short outgrowth of frontal bone on which their first antlers were developing. Several family groups of roe lived that winter amongst the trees and I had great joy in watching them.

I rarely saw the badgers now. Snug amongst dry bedding in their underground home, they were well adapted to living off their thick layers of fat built up in the autumn's season of plenty. It snowed halfway through the month, the howling wind making it feel far colder. A white carpet around the entrances remained untouched by badger paws, though fox spore, roe slots and the fine marks of birds' claws were everywhere. In the lull of the wind could be heard the constant twitterings of a myriad tiny birds. Siskin, goldfinch, linnet, brambling, greenfinch and many chaffinch with an occasional yellowhammer within their flocks. One afternoon there were four crossbills extracting seeds from the Scots pines that bordered the loch. The males' crimson plumage coupled with their mates' yellowy-green, small splashes of gaudy colour against a drab, grey sky. Best of all I saw my first snow buntings in some numbers on the heather moors, their flash of white wings as a hare startled them came as a surprise for, feeding, much of their white was not obvious and they appeared mostly brown.

One evening there was a small party of waxwings near the cottage feasting on the last of the rowan berries and less eagerly, the hips and haws. At dusk the long-eared owls sallied forth from the old ruined steading. Like the sparrowhawks, they would take any small birds disturbed from their roosts, though a commoner prey seemed to be mice, voles and the rats that frequented the farm. Their low, moaning hoots echoed through the shelter belt as they flew on wings longer and more pointed than the tawnies. Several of these birds roosted together communally and sometimes I might see one quartering the fields at dawn or dusk in search of prey in the manner of barn owls.

Gales swept the hills and with them came rain to melt the last of the snow. Even the sheep in the more sheltered valley looked wretched, huddled together in the lea of the drystane dykes. Their fleeces heavy and sodden, some brought forth the first of the season's lambs. I'm surprised that the stone walls or 'stells' built for sheltering sheep in the Borders aren't more common nationally on the mountains and hills. Like anything built of stone gathered *in situ*, they can give the appearance of great age, but were invented by a William Napier of Ettrick Park, Selkirk, who built his first stell in 1882. Some are variants on his design, but the circle has proved itself the most successful as not only is it wind proof, but unless there is no wind, snow is blown away from, not into it. These stone walls are about $1^1/2$ metres high, 10–12 metres in diameter and are open to the sky with a small entrance for the sheep to pass through. They are also useful to confine some of the flock to examine them. No stells here though so these sheep had to make do with walls and rocky outcrops.

Unexpectedly April was here. It seemed one moment gales were raging and the next, spring had crept in on gentle feet. Snowdrops gave way to the earlier snow and the opening primroses turned their pale faces to the sun. Along the tree-lined river banks, lesser celandine thrust up their shining yellow flowers and the warmer air encouraged midges that were attracted to the green tassels of dog's mercury by their fetid smell. Only the hill hares were still partly white (they didn't seem to go entirely white like those further north) as they browsed amongst the heather whilst snipe drummed overhead. These last, swooping in territorial display were a new experience for me, although the sound made by the rush of air vibrating through their stiff, outstretched tail feathers was perhaps more of a humming. (Will, with his usual aptness, described them as 'heather bleaters'.) Occasional snipe could be found throughout the year in damp spots along the Cley or in the boggy margins of the lochs, but several males displaying like this over the moor was an exhilarating sight.

Neither badgers nor otters in the area bred that year although the dominant sow of the further Wild Way clan produced a single cub. I had no sustained observations to know if this was the norm for otters, but lack of new badger cubs when food and places to den appeared sufficient for larger numbers was saddening. Both these members of the Mustelidae family become sexually mature in their second year. Although dominant badger sows infrequently miss breeding years in England, one cub only for the two clans here made a poor showing and boded ill for their future. The den under the wood pile on the Robertsons' land was soon home to the vixen's cubs that at five weeks old would play unsteadily at first and later with carefree abandon, around their earth. All young creatures have a certain attraction, but these four fox cubs in their woolly, chocolate-coloured coats were very appealing as each tried to usurp their leader's position as king-of-the-topmost-log-castle. I would watch the family well away from their home lest the vixen be unsettled and move them. Behind the glacial rock covered in lichens was an ideal place; beyond it a clear badger trail showed leading across the field to the sett. The young foxes copied their mother's caution towards their badger neighbours at an early age. She took care to leave well before their emergence and her return at intervals during the night was always a scent, sight and listening one before her silent approach. Such young fox cubs have little fear of humans, however – another reason for my remaining unseen – distrust of man comes later. I recalled a photographer who waited patiently one evening at a sett for badgers to emerge, only to find they had already gone. A very young fox cub appeared nearby and walked straight up to him lying there busily taking its picture. The fox sniffed the camera, the man and seemed so totally unafraid, that fearing the worst for its mother, he picked it up and took it home. It was some hours before he and his wife realized he had been mistaken and returned it. That type of incident regularly swamps the RSPCA and animal welfare centres with fox cubs in the spring, often picked up by well-meaning children who keep them some days, making it uncertain whether the vixens will accept them back or reject them.

This was a time of memorable sunsets and risings with Venus as always, the first of the stars to appear so brilliantly and the last to leave the night sky. Truly called the Morning and Evening Star and benignly feminine, she glittered a welcome to my watches from her position near the horizon as escort to her lord, the fiery sun. Each evening a red sky spread and intensified, green at its outmost limits and orange above. Darker it grew as the burning embers scattered and faded, before silvery Venus sparkled and the sun's last fire hid itself from the night. That first darkness is always the deepest of all. Later when the other constellations rode clear in the sky and the darkness lacked depth, Venus had already begun her journey beyond my ken to reappear in the east before dawning and herald in the sun. No small wonder the ancients worshipped her with the sun and the moon. As a child I thought her my watching star and the night walks of adulthood have but reinforced that impression.

The roe were beginning to moult; their long winter fur was coming away. I picked up a clump of such hairs by Hoolit and found it very soft. The bucks were fraying the sheath of skin and hair known as velvet from their antlers by rubbing them against the sitka trunks. The mature animals cleaned theirs first (those with six points), the velvet coming off easily leaving the exposed bone white, but by May even the single-point yearling bucks would be in hard antler. Usually the velvet was eaten by its late owner and since it contains skin, blood vessels and nerves that once fed the growing antler, it is probably nourishing. For the first time it struck me what a remarkable process this yearly growing of antlers was – quite unlike the horns of goats, sheep and bovines which are permanent structures increasing in size as the animal ages. With deer however, only the pedicle from which the antler grows, is permanent. It was a time of change in the roe community. Yearlings were fully independent now, soon to be driven away by their dams who in a few weeks would give birth again. Breeding does are said to often return to the same birth place and mindful of my first ever sighting of a kid being born, I wondered if I might be so fortunate this year. The young bucks had a poor chance of attracting mates, though the instinct to stake out their own territory and hold it was strong. A different fraying was noticeable now and was to continue until the August rut. Trees were rubbed and scraped, most especially saplings, the bark hanging in fine strips; the ground beneath cleared of vegetation leaving imprints of the front hooves in the bare earth.

Each sett showed great signs of badger activity. Fresh soil was dug out on massive spoil heaps with old bedding discarded from the winter, turned out amongst it. At the Clackmon sett for the first time I found sheep wool amongst it and again in the Burn Badgers' spoil. Worms were plentiful on the grazed pastures although there was really no need to walk across the burn to watch badgers – ours came to us! Sandy's wife found one snuffling in her garden one early morning turning over piles of empty flower pots to take the slugs beneath. Sandy himself met one 'wi n'lug, in a haver' on my doorstep and he swore ever after that Spike knocked me up each evening if I was late out!

This started us on badger facts and fables and I told him of Nicholas Cox, in his day regarded as very knowledgeable on such matters who wrote of the badger in 1677: 'He hath very sharp teeth and therefore is accounted a deep-biting beast; his back is broad and his legs are longer on the right side rather than the left and therefore he runneth best when he gets on the side of a hill. He fights on his back with teeth and nails and by blowing up his skin in a strange and wonderful manner.' This last about the inflation of the skin is interesting because it is an observation in the field that is inaccurate although not totally without foundation. The badger doesn't blow its skin up when attacked or threatened, but it does make itself appear larger. This is known as pilo-erection. It is capable of either raising the hair around the neck like a gigantic ruff or the entire coat can stand on end. (In Kent I found several dead RTAs like this, their massive skull fractures indicating they had faced the oncoming danger head-on and fur raised.) However, Nicholas Cox got it completely wrong when he explained to his readers how badgers managed to move so much earth onto their spoil heaps. 'One badger falleth on his back, another layeth earth on his belly, so taking the hinder feet in his mouth draweth the belly-laden badger out of the hole and having disburdened himself re-enters and doth the like until all be finished.' It is a common belief still amongst old countrymen that if a ferret is accidently introduced into a badger's home it will be killed by the badger rolling upon it. The stories of badger 'funerals' have never been substantiated, but recent observers agree they will sometimes move dead conspecifics such as road victims, though not bury them. Some of the later writers were more observant however. Sir Alfred Pease was a keen hunting and shooting man, as well as an enthusiastic badger watcher. When he was having a break from these pastimes, he was also a member of Parliament. In 1898 he wrote of the badger: 'He is, too, of all creatures, the most inquisitive. He wants to know the why and the wherefore of everything, and his persistence in pursuit of knowledge is remarkable. Not even bricks and cement can prevent him from indulging his curiosity about things that were much better left alone, and with his powerful claws he will work away for hours at an obstacle that would discourage anyone but a genius or an Irish member of Parliament.'

Whilst I cannot comment on Irish MPs, from my own experience I have witnessed brock's massive strength when moving heavy obstacles from his way and he is a determined animal when aroused.

But for the tardy ash, the trees of village and shelter belt were in tiny leaf. As I followed the Cley's twists and tumbles, a smell of garlic pervaded the air from the white, star-like ramsons crowding its banks. It was a pleasure to explore again the slopes of the Wild Way sett. The rhododendrons that allowed no growth beneath them, gave me easy access along the riverside. It had been a cold night as my breath smoked before me with beckoning stars netted in the tangled reflections of the brooding trees that lined the banks. Now that the sun had risen up above the Dark Hill, the leathery rhododendrons' leaves still drooping from the cold would soon rise. Their glossy green was misted dull, but from each cluster, a sturdy tight-closed bud promised the beauty to come. Warm sunlight was already touching some as I passed. Now the sett and holt were left far behind and the pace of the river grew slower. I waded along its margins, sometimes stopping in the sunshine for long periods to watch shoals of small fish. Stickle back abounded and once a long, green pike slipped from the weeds mouth agape in search of a meal. There were small, wild trout too, as well as the red-finned roach. This was a lovely haven, the water a series of natural runs and pools, often through leafy dells. Happily exploring that fine spring morning I noticed something from my position in the river that I must often have missed when walking its banks; it had been there many weeks, even months. Entwined amongst the overhanging branches it trailed in the water; the continually bobbing movement caught my eye. Wading over and close to the trees, I lost sight of it again, but forcing myself through the slimy trunks, walked into it and spent long, heart-breaking moments freeing the pathetic body from its watery grave. Once – and how I remembered my watches – it had been a young dog otter playing with its sister where the rhododendrons grew two miles away. Now it was a hideous mockery, all flesh gone from the wasted body, lips turned back in a perpetual grimace as the fine-wired snare had sawed into belly and back. The snare had not been set in the overhang, so its struggles must have pulled the wire up allowing it to escape – to this lingering death. I walked home and gave it to Sandy and Will knowing it was not their doing, but hoping that perhaps their anger might communicate itself to their neighbours and influence where I could not. If its death could convince just one farmer not to snare then that suffering might not be in vain.

CHAPTER EIGHT

Summer

I took to frequenting the lochanside beneath Dydor and enjoyed sitting watching the waters if the weather allowed. At night the play of wind and light gave a thousand different twists and turns to its surface. By day the sun glinting as the breeze ruffled and patterned, made pictures appear in each crest and trough. It would have seemed empty now that the geese were gone but for swallows hawking for insects over the waters and two strangers floating serenely below – a pair of mute swans, unusual here. Upended in the weedy margins in search of food, they came upon me unawares and immediately the cob raised his wings and hissed a warning. Hopefully they would stay and perhaps have cygnets. Now the bilberry's pink, lantern-shaped flowers covered their stubby bushes and I smiled to think of badger feasts to come. May heralded weeks of glorious sunshine and blue skies – the hottest and most settled weather I had yet experienced in Scotland. Perhaps flowering early because of the unaccustomed warmth, I found the year's first heath spotted orchids; within a week they seemed to crop up everywhere. Like the common spotted orchids of my native Kent, their colours were variable ranging from white through to pink and pale purple. The delicate spikes appeared in bogs, on heath, moor and any acid soil including that of the deciduous shelter belts that descended to the Cley. Bluebells waved beneath the trees and carpeted the lane verges a misty blue. Roe kids were being dropped. In spite of many long watches at last year's site, I failed to see a kid birth; but a chance long-eared owl watch (the male was bringing prey back for his mate and three young to their home in the old magpie's nest), happened to coincide with the birth of roe twins of which I had a grandstand view. It is perhaps ironic that both birth occasions were accidentals, yet such is life!

A visit to Kent and the remnants of my old badger clan, found Crisp was no more amongst them. Winters are harsh times for many wild animals, but a three-legged one has an added handicap. At my last sighting of her the previous autumn she had been six years old. This is a good age for a badger in our modern world, although without man's presence and the deathtraps of our roads, they are capable of living to twelve and even fifteen years. Dave planned to do some night watches outside Ashcroft Woods, the clan's territory, so we drove round the area as I pointed out concealed parking places used by past baiters and lampers. It was good to visit old friends and catch up on the lives and news of the farmers and farm managers. One man with his farm buildings close by another wood, recounted how he had a pair of rooks attempting to nest in his tractors kept in a Dutch barn. These birds made a great deal of mess with their droppings and seemed determined to peck the linings from the steering wheels. As the farmer remarked, it wasn't as if there were no suitable trees nearby!

I thought of this later in the year when an Essex friend had a rook dashing itself at her windows in the early morning and evening whilst its mate jumped up and down nearby on fluttering wings. We concluded it saw its reflection as a rival and was attempting to fight with it, for although they may nest in colonies and feed in flocks, rooks have a strong sense of territory and pairs may defend a small portion of their nest area driving off intruders. When the windows were netted, the attacks ceased, but in hot weather and for long periods it is difficult not to open windows and have them covered indefinitely. In mid-June with the netting removed the bombardment started again, but ceased abruptly when the rook injured itself, leaving blood upon the patio glass. The pair were seen after this in the garden so no fatality occurred. The feeling was that having 'lost' to its reflected image, the rook henceforth left its rival alone.

Whilst still in Kent I did some watches at Ninepenny Wood where I had lived in the caravan and found the sow Hattie taking down bedding one early morning. She had two cubs approximately three months old. Their mother busily collected bitten-off grass and blades of bluebell greenery. Tiny cubs not yet above ground must have their first introduction to the outside world from the smells contained in their bedding. Bundling it under her body and held carefully by her forepaws, she moved backwards into the sett as her offspring chased in and out of the trees. They had flattened the white, star-shaped stitchwort and bluebells in their play. It was good to see cubs again and to find these at least, were thriving and well.

It was on my return journey, covering as it did almost the length of England, that I was struck by the marked differences in the rural scene of both countries. You cannot travel far without a church spire above the English countryside where villages are profusely scattered. It is difficult to envisage a landscape with scarcely any villages, but this was so of Scotland until the second part of the eighteenth century and the early nineteenth. Then the lairds built villages to promote domestic industries, in an attempt to halt the mass emigration overseas caused by their Sheep Clearances, when people lost their homes and their hill grazings as the commercial breeds of Cheviot and Blackface – the sheep of the gentlemen – were moved onto the land. Scotland by our standards is still largely unpopulated. Where villages exist, you come across them quite suddenly as the landscape runs in, then out of them. Whilst there are Scottish spired churches, the oblong, unspired kirk is often encountered, a product of the Episcopal church and the move away from Catholicism. For me, rural England is a land of spires, patchwork fields dotted with numerous villages; Scotland a country of skyscapes, small, isolated communities and wide, still, wild spaces.

I returned to Hoolit cottage well into June on a cold, grey fret of a day with a slight haar. The weather soon changed, however, mist giving way to sun. I walked to the Wild Way again for with thoughts of Kentish badgers in mind, I had a longing to see the lone cub playing. He was well enough, but it was with Cudoun by day that my memories remain. Beyond the rhododendrons I would lie on my stomach in the sunshine looking down into the Cley. The sun burned into my consciousness and with Cudoun in midstream, I dozed. A solitary blackbird sung a short refrain, paused, tried again and was silent. The cool breeze touching my hair and made the yellow iris dance in the margins. Even the sheep in the far fields were silent. Only the water murmured on its ambling way to the Firth.

Many shoals of small fry darted back and forth, the warmth making them at their most agile. The play of light and shadow on water fascinated me as I lay watching the sparkle of the current over weed-green rocks. A large fish glided below me, the mearest turn of his tail fin speeding him forward. He was a roach about 34 cm long with pink-hued pelvic and anal fins and occasional gold glints to the upper scales of his body. He was joined by another identical roach and yet another. At that moment a female damselfly (*Argrion virgo*) chose to land on the hand that lay by my face. She took up most of my vision – the deep green of her body eclipsing the grasses and reeds of the bank. A sinuous brown shape below us twisted and dived as the damsel flew off in a blur of brown lacy wings. I lay looking down at Cudoun. A line of bubbles rose from each corner of his mouth to join those from his coat; each paused for a moment on the surface and burst in quick succession. I wondered at the time why there should be bubbles from his fur but concluded that they were probably air trapped between the otter's two layers of fur, his short, dense undercoat and the long guard hairs of his top or outer pelage.

Now he swum on his back near the bottom, legs tucked against his body, the broad tail propelling him as his turning head led the way. He wasn't hunting, merely swimming for the pleasure of space and movement. I plucked a long grass stem at my face and dangled it below the surface. In a moment his head broke out of the water, took the stem and dived below – so suddenly that I was caught unawares. A large, smooth pebble followed the grass and he dived and caught it before it touched the river bed. With it clasped between chest and paws, he rose again and I was showered with water drops as he lay on his back and pebble on chest, floated before me. I learnt much about otters like this, finding for instance, that they can drink with their heads completely submerged. Cudoun's sight wasn't very good on land, but it was excellent in clear water by day or night. His luxuriance of vibrissae, or whiskers, I was told, are used to detect the movements of fish in murky or muddy waters.

There was a grand array of foxgloves near the village with nettle-leaved bellflowers in glorious profusion at the water's edge and wild roses with entwining honeysuckle scenting the farmland hedges. The full moon appeared enormous on rising. That June it was still a great lemon disc at

11 p.m., yet by 1 a.m. it seemed its usual pale colour and size. The Burn Badgers were frisky, Millie and Spike even joining the terrible twins and the others in a romp. The dry needles scattered and tossed as Grace did a snout-dive amongst them. Moments later they were all running down the steep bank to the burn. At its side, their mad five minutes forgotten, each went its separate way in search of the important business of food. Only Spike loitered till the others had gone, then trotted briskly onto the rocks to stand, a small statue, near the far side. The moon rode high, picking all out in vivid black shadow or silvery illumination, the trees like spilt ink above gleaming waters with a tracery of dark bushes and lighter rocks below. Spike was fishing. Time passed. Abruptly the boar moved forward as something silvery flung up, flashed, twisted, missed the bank and flopped splashing into the shallows. On the instant, Spike was after it. He sprang onto nothing, a quick splash forward and held it securely this time. It was too far away to see whether trout or another, but I was content to lookout over the scene at the drifting clouds, quaintly suggestive of high-turreted battlements, the breeze-touched trees that stretched out crinoid arms and the badger feasting on his fish. Meal over, he disappeared into the seeding grasses and tangles of rushes on the further bank.

These summer evenings with the young long-eared owls learning to fly in front of Hoolit were entertaining, noisy affairs. It had been a regular breeding site for the birds as long as the Robertsons could remember and since the cottage had been built and named in the early 1800s, it is probable the association went back at least to that time. Swallows too had returned to their nest site, this time under the eaves of the cottage itself. Now the five youngsters lined up on the bedroom windowsill were small miniatures of their parents only lacking their long tails. They flew very short distances at about three weeks after hatching and were still fed by both parents. No food was visible in the adults' beaks, but the insects were carried in the throat which was then emptied well down into the fledglings' gaping beaks. The gape flanges were whitish and showed up clearly. Two youngsters were on the wing one evening flying carefully from wall to sill and back again. In the early morning and late evening the parents hawked around the steadings and hedgerows, but by day they followed the burn. They would probably raise another brood before migration. I was slightly uneasy about the close proximity of young swallows and hungry owls, but found my concern was unfounded.

These were mornings when swathes of mist trailed in the hollows and followed the line of lane and burn. With the sun well up before 5 a.m. there would come the distant call of the sheep and their well-grown lambs. Another hour and the high-pitched, creaky call-note of the grey partridge sounded from the depths of the corn on the far side of the lane. Together with the pheasant cock's regular cry from the garden and the woodpigeon's placid cooing, they seemed to welcome another fine day. The swans still occupied the lochan beneath Dydor and could often be seen with their five cygnets in tow. At times all the family would come out to preen, rest and peck about in the grass. One parent – usually the pen – would lead the way, the cob to the rear with their family between them. One early morning an otter appeared on its water; not Cudoun, his mate from the Wild Way or the bitch yearling. Was this another of his wives? The swans spotted it swimming the moment its head broke the surface. The pen ushered her youngsters from the area as her mate reared out of the water, hissing and snorting, wings held out wide and neck curved as he went into the attack. Whoever named this species mute, must have been stone deaf. It was the first and only time I saw an otter at odds with another creature, but the swan most certainly meant business. The other saw its danger and promptly dived, though the matter didn't end there. Round and round the swan rushed sometimes stabbing downwards and once in a flurry of water and wings it appeared to have hold of the otter. I think if it could have caught the invader of its territory it would have tried to hold the enemy under to drown. Eventually the cob lost his quarry, but continued for perhaps another ten minutes to swim vigorously back and forth on lookout. It was obvious from its attitude that the attack had been unsuccessful. Much later as I sat on the grassy bank with the tiny white and blue flowers of marsh bedstraw and common milkwort speckling the green, there was a movement in the sedges and an otter slipped by me unknowing, all smooth and gleaming from the lake. I was to know this otter bitch well before another winter passed and called her Dratsie, the Shetland word for otter which somehow suited her. She seemed born to go where other otters feared to tread!

The bark of the roe had been a common sound these past weeks and although both sexes do this, the 'challenge' bark is that of a buck patrolling his territory. The mature and stronger males drive away younger, older or weaker bucks as they establish a desirable territory ready for the rut in July and August. There was the sharp bark that I thought of as questioning or inquisitive, a gruff one used when frightened and in full flight and the harshly scolding bark of challenging males. The roe were splendid now in bright, foxy, summer coats, the kids growing fast and losing their spots. Twins will play endlessly, butting, jumping and chasing round and round trees – tiny, enchanting creatures. I found roe bucks very aggressive towards other males with fights amongst them commonplace and occasionally deadly. Their 'points' are daggers that inflict much damage, but it is their sharp little hooves when a rival is down that can kill. I came across one such mortality in a shelter belt; an old male who had been prepared to fight rather than give way and paid the ultimate price.

Karen and Harriet came to stay. My daughter had been working very hard and badly needed a rest. They arrived in Karen's car one beautiful evening and almost immediately, Jacko appeared to inspect the new arrivals, saw Harriet and stayed. He stood perhaps 25 cm high at the shoulder or two-thirds up the Rhodesian ridgeback's hind leg. In spite of having to stand on his hind legs to reach up and sniff, it was clearly a case of love at first sight. Harry was a trifle disconcerted at such a tiny suitor, but confidence was soon restored after much sniffing at the diminutive Jack Russell. In her adolescent way she began to play – much too roughly of course – so Jacko put her in her place by growling and then snapping at her.

Karen took her luggage to her room and unpacked having said goodbye to Jacko and firmly lifted him outside. Later we sat talking over mugs of coffee as Harriet stretched out, huge front paws dexterously gripping an equally large marrowbone as she cracked it in her great jaws. Of all the dogs we have kept or known, it is only Karen's that has this ability to use her front paws to such good effect, curling them round and splaying out the long toes in the manner of fingers. It was while dog and owner were out for a walk, with me busy in the kitchen, that I heard an odd noise as of something knocking on wood, bomp – bomp, bomp, bomp. I looked round the corner into the hall and there was Jacko, the back door slightly ajar. He had Harriet's marrowbone in his mouth held by one end whilst the other dragged on the ground. That marrowbone was a quarter of his size and there he was trying valiantly to sneak off with it! The gap left between door and frame was big enough for him to come in though not large enough to go back with his booty. Gently I took it from him and he wagged his docked tail. Fortunately Harriet never knew he had made the attempted kidnap and their friendship blossomed. In the late evening I took the ridgeback out on her flexi-lead and Jacko came too. He had never followed me on my walks before, nor would I have wanted him, but for the period of Karen's stay I enjoyed both dogs' company. That day we found another dead ewe on her side, the eyes being pecked out by three crows that flew away as we approached. All this was new to Harry of course, though commonplace to us. We returned at 10.50 p.m., still not dark with the low, moaning hoots of the owls coming from the shelter belt nearby.

July is a good month to holiday in Scotland with plenty of daylight hours – light at 2.45 a.m., now and the hills at their best. Walking Harriet accompanied by Jacko about 7 a.m., a curlew was calling as it circled low and many lapwings were on the land. We met Will complete with crook and collies, rounding up the first of the sheep to be sheared. Here this always seems late with the ground already littered with shedding wool. Driving through northern England and the Borders, Karen had noticed the sheep there already shorn. Harriet was happy enough on her long lead; these were her first encounters with sheep. The hares intrigued her. What were these strange rabbits watching us for as we passed by? She adored the burn, but poor Jacko stood on the edge watching her delighted swimming with utter bewilderment. Fortunately, she never insisted going beyond the length of the flexi-lead or I might have ended up swimming the burn myself! She was a big dog to sit on a rock midstream, but we found one and settled comfortably whilst the terrier wandered off till we chose to return. Harriet had never seen fish. If small ones like the stickleback and minnows attracted her, they were nothing to the effect of a big, fat trout that swam lazily by. For a dog of fifteen months old, she was remarkably quiet. Her large, floppy ears rising in amazement and the wrinkles of her long face deepening, were her only movements. A fish jumping clear of the water for crane flies was an added bonus as it landed back into the water with a loud smack. She never saw an otter in Scotland, but walking her early one Sunday morning in England some months later, she did – a surprise for both of us. Curiously, neither dog nor otter reacted as I would have expected.

It was a dull, grey day in Essex. The wide, grassy path meandered in company with the slow-flowing river nearby. I had Harriet on a shortened flexi in case she should try swimming. We were quietly standing looking at the placid waters when an otter's head appeared on the surface rounding the curve. Immediately the dog sat down, ears raised and forward as I knelt beside her. True I had seen an otter along this stretch before, but it had always been at night. The swimmer came ashore a few metres away, shook itself and saw us. It is an area where people walk their dogs so I expect at some time in its life it had been chased. Instead of retreating however, the otter stood up tall on hind legs and huffed! Harriet's ears and tail dropped as she tried to hide behind me. To my horror the otter chose to come on making an aggressive, rising, chittering noise as its tail lashed from side to side. It was the first time I had witnessed this, but the meaning was unmistakable Fearing the worst for the otter (I'm sure the dog would have retaliated if actually attacked), I stood up abruptly and shouted, whereupon it slid back into the water and continued swimming though not at any great speed. It didn't appear unduly frightened. Confidence regained, Harriet sat by my standing figure as it swam on, but she immediately appeared unhappy when at the next bend, the otter rose up again to look back at us, before disappearing from our sight. The dog's mistrust I think was not only due to the aggressiveness of the other, but also to its unexpected change of shape; that tall, thin, upright from a long, low-slung body. Why wasn't the otter afraid? A good question. It would have been used to people sitting fishing; it would surely be acquainted with dogs. Was it a bitch with cubs nearby? To this day, I do not know. We returned to Karen still in bed who would have given much to change places with her dog that morning.

With the car we could travel with ease to the far range of hills I had first visited that cold December night. Karen took Harry off for a walk leaving me to explore the old quarry sett more fully. At most entrances there was no earth to dig out, so no spoil heaps. Three clefts in the rock were shiny with use, the stone worn smooth with the rubbing of something passing, but were badgers still resident? At one such entrance a harsh, bicoloured hair rested on the polished surface and the narrow ledges that served as paths leading to each were littered with recently bitten-off fronds of bracken and sedge, already beginning to wilt in the day's warmth. Yes, this sett was surely occupied. I sat contentedly in the sunshine lower down waiting my daughter's return. A hardy rowan clung tenaciously to a fault in the strata, its berries well-formed and yellow. Glints of light on water revealed hidden pools on the quarry floor. Stretching below my ledge till it gave way to wet areas and the brightly red and green sphagnum moss, an area of bracken seemed to shimmer in the heat. I thought its movement a trick of the light until my eyes took in the shape of a neat head and large ears, another and another. It concealed a doe with two fawns ruminating in its shade. The humming of many insects filled the air with bees collecting nectar from the flowering heather. I could sit unnoticed against the quarry face as the oystercatchers' fluty calls of 'kileep-kileep' intermingled with their occasional piping cries warning others off their territory. The chicks of these pied waders were still very young and following the parents to be fed. High up on my craggy perch I spied Karen from afar, so was able to meet her and dog well beyond the quarry and its busy communities.

She found something of interest on her return journey and with Harry nothing loath at the prospect of an extra walk, we went to inspect it. I had expected to see a Larsen or other corvid trap from what had been said, but this cage or trap was something I had not come across before in a bleak and lonely area of windswept upland moor and sheep country. It was made of 2.54 cm wire mesh and stood 1 m × 64 cm. It had an inner wire mesh cage not fixed to the ground like the outer one. Wire mesh covered the top of the outer cage, but not the inner. A tunnel of corrugated tin was placed in one corner of the large enclosure. This was large enough to shelter a lamb or fox. There was a small container for water with an empty plastic bottle lying outside. Inside the large cage were the bones and wool of two very young lambs together with black feathers and a crow's beak. This would not have been intended to trap corvids for if one had flown into the uncovered top of the inner cage and pushed under the bottom wire to feed on the lamb, surely it could have returned the same way? I have seen foxes make a successful run up wire fencing so entry could easily be effected in this way, though not out for there would be no room to make a run back. Perhaps the crow remains were incidental or was a dead crow also used as bait? Hopefully, living, ailing young lambs were not used as bait and the water and shelter were humanely provided for trapped foxes until the shepherd arrived. I did wonder briefly if the bait was poisoned and the elaborate caging was to prevent others being poisoned along the food chain, but in these circumstances that is doubtful.

Karen's week seemed to go far too quickly. We enjoyed walking the purple hills with the heather coming full into bloom. It was good to follow the steep-sided ravines onto rolling fells and climb sharp-tipped Lytlaw to savour the view. Fleeting clouds gave light and shade to the braes and my old favourite Dydor echoed to the strident calls of the colourful grouse. If Jacko came and we went further than his small legs could manage, he would return of his own accord. Indeed, his master had said as much when Karen and Harriet first arrived. He most enjoyed our evening walks and was adept at timing his appearance to the opening of my back door. There he would be waiting, short tail waving as he stood on hind legs excidedly to say hello again to his holiday romance. Sometimes as the shadows lengthened, one of the farm cats would accompany us too. This the little dog disliked, but the feline was well in charge of the situation and had no hesitation in a hearty nose-dabbing if the terrier persisted. At first it would follow along the drystane dykes, but once on the moor would lead the way, tail upright like a banner. All this was an education to Harriet on her flexi who viewed the proceedings with absorbing interest and would probably have befriended the cat given the chance. However, she wasn't, Jacko saw to that; there was little doubt he was jealous. It was the terrier who found the young foxes' hideaway inside the wall of a ruined steading at some distance from the farm. He jumped up into a hole in the wall and shortly after, his muffled barking came from a spot higher up and some metres farther along. I called him several times, but a dog in pursuit of quarry is well nigh impossible to retrieve. Knowing him as a keen ratter, I concluded he had tracked one down. Cat, Harriet and I walked on and returning found Jacko's rump sticking out of the entry hole as he whined and pushed. Carefully I grasped his hindquarters and gently turning them sideways levered him out. None the worse for his adventure, he sniffed around at the base of the wall, urinated and set off for home. All this while the ridgeback was sitting quietly on her haunches gazing up. True to her breed she had used her nose to good effect and was watching four little foxes silently huddled together watching us from the top of the wall. I spoke to her gently stroking the smooth, long brown ears as she thrust her great muzzle into my hand. She often scented foxes in her home woods, though whether she had encountered cubs like this I had no way of knowing. Together we followed the others now well ahead, a comic sight along the track. There was the cat-that-walked-by-itself, tail up and leading with a not so much larger Jacko trotting behind. Once Harriet pulled back and I turned to look also. Four sharp little heads still remained in dark silhouette against the late evening sky, all red, mauve and yellow in the dying day.

The cottage seemed sadly empty with my company gone. A check of the wood pile found the den deserted; not unusual with vixens. The surrounding area was littered with prey remains; sheared-off woodpigeon wing feathers, a rabbit scut with part of a leg and well-gnawed bones. Doubtless, inside the den was badly fouled with several weeks of cub occupation and the answer was to move and start afresh elsewhere. I took to watching Jacko's hole in the wall and found this was indeed the same fox cubs with both parents fetching food for them, though leaving it at some distance to encourage the family to forage for themselves. Several times I found fresh otter spraints prominently displayed on the moor and with the strange otter in mind, wondered if they were hers or Cudoun's, though at that time I had no way of telling whether the newcomer was bitch or dog. Occasionally at the Five Springs area I smelt that unmistakable otter smell. A curious instinct said something was watching me once. If it was Cudoun, he would have revealed himself at my whistle. I stayed till the sky darkened and rain lashed down.

As I moved to go, a long, slender shape seemed to slip into the burn, but was it a trick of tired eyes, bad visibility or wishful imagination? I couldn't be sure. Dispirited, I returned to the shelter belt by the farm to be out of the worst of the storm. Strange how my most exciting 'roe' sightings have been accidental. Beneath the trees was a fine six-pointer buck coupled to his doe in the act of mating. Impossible to say how long they had been so. Forgotten, the fruitless search for the dratsie. Those magical moments will always remain etched on my mind; this pairing unheard above the thundering burn and the torrential rain lashing the tree tops. Dry enough on the conifer needles below; a picture suspended to wild, mad music. All too soon they finished and moved down the steep bank to the rushing stream. Two small shapes – her kids – crept out of the bracken and followed the adults out of my sight. Into the storm once more, buffeted by a head wind intent on pushing me off my feet, long plumes of rain were blowing across the stiff sitkas as I reached Hoolit's green door. Jacko no longer graced me with his presence (which was perhaps as well), but a soaking farm cat was waiting as I lifted the latch and together we went indoors.

It is hard not to notice a heron's nest. They tend to use the same one year after year, merely adding more material each time. Thus a nest say, in a Scots pine, may start as a flimsy structure and finish top-heavy until it finally falls to the ground. In coastal areas of Scotland herons nest on ledges which prevent them becoming too cumbersome. With the sea miles away however, it was the Scots pine that was popular here. Sticks and even small branches were brought that spring mainly by the male, but it was his mate who weaved them in with quivering bill movements, though she was in truth an untidy nest builder. The few heron nests here were solitary affairs, not the colonies of the south. Last year's bright orange acquisition (the workmen's plastic strip) was still there, but tucked about the projecting twigs. The parents had reared three nestlings this time. For the first few weeks the youngsters looked perpetually startled with bristle tips of down bolt upright on their crowns. As they grew and developed they would clamber all over the nest and nearest branches trying to balance on their awkwardly long legs and exercising their wings. The nickname 'branchers' for young herons probably derives from this period.

Herons will take many other kinds of food besides fish – moles, voles (including water voles), mice, rats, worms, beetles, lizards and young chicks. Frogs may be taken in great numbers when spawning just as Cudoun did; buzzards too are partial to them. Unlike the otter however, herons leave the oviducts. The lining of these oviducts swells into a whitish gelatinous substance when exposed to moisture. Sometimes it may contain eggs which can be very puzzling to someone seeing it for the first time. The country name is 'star slime.' When I see a heron in flight, another old country name comes to mind for once they were known as cranes. And that sad, wonderful poet John Clare who wrote:

While, far above, the solitary crane
Swings lonely to unfrozen dykes again,
Cranking a jarring melancholy cry
Through the wild journey of the cheerless sky.

I found this family great fun to watch and easy too, since herons seem to have little fear of humans if one is reasonably discreet. When the chicks were very young, one parent would stand guard at the nest whilst the other hunted, but once grown beyond this size, both would search for prey and return with it. The nestlings grasping the adult's bill in theirs to encourage them to regurgitate reminded me vividly of young foxes pulling at their parent's mouth for the same end. This noisy family party gave me endless pleasure, although standing directly under the nest at feeding time could be somewhat messy as when a piece of disgorged, pink flesh came sailing down onto my head. I like my trout first hand and preferably not in the hair!

I was still on the trail of the dratsie. It was a pleasant walk from Hoolit to the Five Springs whether I was fortunate to have another sighting or not. I crossed the farmland onto the further lane and where it ended, followed the side of a shelter belt to the high moor. Fragrant meadowsweet adorned the water courses here in creamy masses and the cotton grass of the hillside bogs had its 'cotton-wool' tufts. This shelter belt was edged with many wild roses. There was the field rose (*Rosa arvensis*), common enough in the south but only occasionally naturalized in Scotland, and the burnet (*Rosa pimpinellifolia*), another white rose with different leaflets and a multitude of bristling spines. The dog rose (*Rosa canina*) with its pink and white blooms is common throughout, but it was the first time I had seen *Rosa sherardii* with its bluish-green leaves and beautiful pink blooms for this is mainly confined to the north. Bell heath and ling bloomed abundantly with quantities of tiny sundews inviting insects on the bright sphagnum; everywhere vivid and colourful in the hot sun. Insects there were aplenty with shoals of shimmering blue male damselflies (*Enallagma cyathigerum*) searching for their grey-green females clinging to the stems of bogbean with those magnificent creatures the green lestes (*Lestes sponsa*) resplendent in cobalt blue, bronze and bottle green. There were clouds of midges too though Lothians' to my mind are easier to live with and not the agony of Galloway's when keeping a late evening watch.

I found the peaty pools of upland moor, cradled within a morass of sphagnum and covered by floating algae, held a surprising amount of fauna besides frogs and toads. There were crustaceans, dragon- and mayflies, beetles and water boatmen to name but a few. I would see the cast larval skins of dragonflies still adhering to the sedges and the dark bodies of the darters could usually be seen resting on sphagnum well away from water. At times the air above these pools would vibrate with the humming wings of many insects. Other small insects, butterflies and moths especially, unwary enough to fly close, would be seized by the larger dragonflies, particularly the common aeshna (*Aeshna junceum*) males, who would tear off their victims' wings before devouring their bodies. These were the pirates of the pools.

By now the evening shadows were lengthening with my own, infinitely long, tarrying far behind. Somewhere high above me was the source of the Five Springs. Below the hill top a shieling perched, roughly-hewn grey stone set against purple brae. The area looked poorly populated with sheep, but in truth, the owners of many shorn backs went unnoticed, hidden by rock, bracken and flowering ling. A sudden rumble and then a thunderclap caught me unawares. A wind blew up as from nowhere and the rain turned briefly to hail as I reached the shieling's door. All was muted within, the old, thick walls saw to that. Only the frozen white stones hitting the windows and bouncing off in a tinny clatter; then they were gone and so was the storm. A small, ragged square of blue became larger as the sun rode out from a drift of black cloud. Going outdoors, all was clear and distinct, still shining with the wet of the storm, the tremulous line of the nearest spring all picked out in white by the unmelted hailstones piled high along its course. As the sun's strength increased, the steam rose up from the water in silent white wisps – an incessant succession of wandering ghosts vanishing in the warm air. A movement drew my gaze from the water; something long and lithe, something richly brown and watchful. The dratsie that I sought had found me.

Now that I looked closer, four- sometimes five-toed spore were all about in the newly wet earth; earlier, they would not have shown. With tongue to the roof of my mouth I tried 'tuking' and her small ears turning forward listening intently. Moving ever so slowly I sat down on the wet grass and with arms round legs and chin on knees, left her to make the next move. Close to Dratsie was lovely. I who held Cudoun the most graceful of otters, found my allegiance shift shamelessly to this lithe creature, his second mate. She moved behind me and curious to see what, if anything, she would do, I was content to sit and wait. She reappeared on my other side so close her whiskers nearly touched my face. Suddenly a curlew was circling low between us and the shieling calling repeatedly as they will when trying to distract a predator from their young. Even as it did so, a stoat came from beneath the heather carrying a young curlew in its mouth. It was all the hunter could manage for the bird was well grown with long, thick legs, a plump body and a comparatively small head. The breast and belly were still down-covered with feathers growing on the large wings and a beak with the faintest suggestion of a downward curve. The stoat negotiated the thick-stemmed bushes with its burden, put it down the better to renew its grip and with the parent still circling and calling, continued past otter and I down the burnside. Why didn't it eat the meal in the heather's shelter? I suspect the stoat too was a mother carrying back food for her kits.

Dratsie bounded after and I followed too, though at a distance. So it was that I lost all trace of them and stood at the meeting point of the headwaters wondering which way they had gone. There was nothing to tell me, no movement nor sound; only the calls of well-grown lambs (distinguished at a glance by their woolly backs) and the raucous cries of carrion crows. A movement in the heather caught my eye, but it was merely a meadow pipit searching for insects. I had noticed that while skylarks were common on the grass moors, they appeared to be scarcer on the heather where the meadow pipit predominated. Turning to walk on I spied Dratsie finishing her curlew meal! A pair of long legs and a beak seemed to be all that remained and of the stoat there was no sign.

I was due to leave in a few days first for Dumfries and Galloway, then on to the Grampian region. One evening I set out for a farewell walk to Dydor. All was bathed in sunlight after a sudden shower and I reached his humped back at 10.15 p.m. as the sun was going down. A magnificent rainbow hung over the far hill range to the east. Water slipped gurgling down craggy ledges with thousands of minute white moths flitting about amongst the vegetation. The moon had risen when I eventually left the Dark Hill and bats were out hawking along the water margins. The lochan was a great bowl of silver now, its surface dotted and twisted with strange patternings. Something rose from beneath, breaking the shining into shivering, quivering wavelets. Swarms of insects mating above the surface were being snapped up by hungry fish patrolling below. Something else was hunting, biding his time. He too grasped his meal from below and the fish never saw or knew till too late. Cudoun rose to the surface with a large trout clasped to his chest. Once there, the otter took it up in his mouth to bring ashore and eat. It was here that I met him crunching up bones, merely leaving a few scales and fewer still of the teeth. It was good to see him once more before I left and to know he fared well.

CHAPTER NINE

A Trip to Galloway and Grampian

The train from Sanquhar ran through mile upon mile of meadowsweet and willowherb, especially along Nithsdale, the valley of the river Nith, and so to Dumfries. It was grand to walk in Dirl Wood once more with its heavily lichened trees that felt furry to the touch. Beech, wych-elm, alder, hazel, rowan, birch, oak all clad in shaggy coats. Hard to tell a tree by its bark in Galloway! There was no sign of badgers; Melanie felt they had moved well away. Earlier in the year she and a friend watched from the tree above the site for several evenings but with no success. I made four visits to Dirl Wood during this stay and photographed the slate quarry.

The tawny and barn owls seemed to have resolved their differences; at least, I saw no more signs of aggression between the two species. However, the white owls did not appear to have reared any young. The hedgerows were bright with ripe raspberries, harebells and weld, but the foxgloves were fast fading. This lush, milder southwestern corner of Scotland tends to be earlier than the central belt.

The bats were active again, but not this year in Melanie's home. The experience of watching them and the barn owl hunting as I sat in the churchyard under the full moon, will always remain with me. A fox lay crouching on a table tomb; he listened with ears forward to squeakings and rustlings in the grass below. Perhaps his possible meal found a safe haven under the stone for he lost interest after a while. Now he noticed the low-flying bats. His head followed one with a large moth in its mouth. It was taken to a stone high up on the church wall where the pipistrelle hung down from the rough surface and devoured its prey. Tree shadows cast their long fingers over the dead and a broad-topped yew, almost certainly older than the church itself, evoked memories of Walter de la Mare's words:

> The Yew alone burns lamps of peace
> For them that lie forlorn.

I thought of my first Kentish home and the village church that in common with so many others, was built on the site of an earlier one and an even earlier ritual place with its sacred tree. Yews figured widely in pagan worship and early Christian missionaries wisely continued the tradition by preaching beneath these already hallowed trees. Later, wooden churches were built nearby. This guaranteed a willing congregation and time would replace the old gods with a new. The ancient yews, far older than any man-built monument, were allowed to remain and new ones planted. To this day they are synonymous with our places of worship. Nor do many of us stop to think at Christmas, for instance, that the one we worship was born in a different month altogether, for those first missionaries took the old pagan festivals and superimposed their Christian holy days upon them.

A screech interrupted my reverie as the barn owl rose then dropped amongst the graves. The fox reared up on hind legs and snapped at the other as it flew easily out of range and perched on the strut holding the bell in the church tower. The owl watched as Reynard shook himself and with ears laid back in apprehension, jumped the low wall and was gone. The small figure above the bell turned its heart-shaped face this way and that as it listened intently to the slightest sound. Then down it flew on billowing wings to search out the living amongst the dead.

Moonshine was still tangled in the hedgerows as I walked slowly back along the lane. It stretched in phantom cobwebs from flower to flower. But light was overflowing and overtaking it with a faintness in the eastern sky. Dawn was coming, pale at first, then growing pink and warm. The sweet smell of ripe raspberries lingered at the field edges and the gentle burn tinkled quietly over the pebbles. First birds called and with them the plucked strings of the oystercatchers' cries – a distinctive and, somehow peculiarly Scottish, sound for me.

Otters are common in Galloway, but unrecorded in my own area. A husband and wife team working for the Vincent Wildlife Trust completed a two-year otter survey in Scotland in the late 1970s. Although I had no intention of revealing otter whereabouts to the general public, I did feel that 'my' animals should be recorded, not least because of their scarcity in the Lothians. The couple now had an otter sanctuary not far from Melanie's cottage and one fine day we drove there. It was good to speak to someone so experienced with otters, someone who had spent many years watching, studying and helping to build up their numbers in areas where they had declined. I was told that each location was checked twice in the survey for any otter signs and although spraints, spore, holts and prey remains, or some of these, will be recorded where otters are present, signs of the itinerant or occasional animal are less likely to be found. (This has explained how I have since come to find 'non-existent' otters in Essex.) My sightings were checked on the Ordnance Survey map and duly recorded. I was told that a dead otter road casualty had also been picked up on the far side of my range of hills. For me it was a tremendously rewarding conversation, rather like the correspondence that passed between myself and that great pioneer and expert on badgers Dr Ernest Neal so many years ago. He had patiently explained so much to me, a bumbling novice in the badger field. My theory that otters like badgers, spraint territorially was confirmed, though interestingly, it was suggested that where otters are scarce, they may not have the same compulsion to advertise and warn off intruders when none exist. (Another reason for not finding spraints prominently displayed when surveying.)

My last visit to Dirl Wood was on a typically Galwegian day – mild and mizzling with a faint suggestion of sun. Where the quarry walls were damp and shaded, the single-celled algae *Pleuroccus* formed a powdery, bright green growth. I sat amongst the slates with camera and notebook and saw that sapling birch, ash and sycamore had regenerated amongst the ferns and mosses. White stonecrop had helped to secure some of the more treacherous slopes of scree and in places the green effect was dotted with its tiny white flowers and pink fruits. It was remarkable how a once barren landscape blasted by man, was living and flourishing. Moss was the first colonizer, helping to fix the unstable slates. Gradually seeds had germinated in the moisture and nutrients produced by this living green carpet. Not only stonecrop, wood sage, enchanter's nightshade, tormentil, marsh cinquefoil and foxgloves, but acorn, mast and berry too, their roots thrusting through gaps and faults to flourish in the life-giving soil below. Now some of the trees – alder, hazel and best of all the oaks – had grown to their full height. At my feet dropped the quarry itself and over the far side and facing, were towering stacks of jagged rock. Through its vertical fissures, trailing bramble and briar had a tenuous hold. A faint wind sprang up, unveiling the sun's hazy face, whispering amongst the foliage and whimpering softly into the tunnels and entrances of the mine.

I had watched one night on the Cumbrian fells at such a place to see a badger appear briefly at a fissure, the white and black mask strikingly clear. Its owner crouched to slip through the entrance but once outside, stretched in the unrestricted freedom. It has been suggested that the reason for the badger's striped face is that others of the clan will see it in the dark confines of their underground sett, thus reducing the likelihood of collisions and subsequent aggression. Having explored underground mines and tunnels I know this cannot be, for once round the first corner, the darkness is absolute. No animal or bird can see in complete blackness; night is never wholly without light. I suspect that underground the badger relies on his excellent hearing, his vibrissae and sense of smell.

From my seat I could hear subdued birdsong – chaffinches, a wren's 'clink-clink' near at hand and in the distance, a pheasant's call. Flies were buzzing about my head in the welcoming warmth as I gazed down into the main area of the quarry. A movement amongst the tallest ferns below to my left revealed a family of roe feeding on the willowherbs. Absorbed in admiration of their beauty and the fawns' playfulness, it was some time before I took in the meaning of the twitterings close at hand. A family of four fledged wrens were asking to be fed as they fluttered their wings and gaped expectantly each time one of the parents approached. The adults came closer to inspect me sitting amongst them; such attractive, tiny birds with those barred side wings, sharp little beaks, bright eyes and upturned tails. Curiosity satisfied, on they went feeding their impatient and noisy family.

One parent disappeared into a barely visible crack in the nearby rock face only to reappear from another cranny some distance away with a bill full of insects. These were jammed into its offsprings' beaks and the search continued, this time amongst the overhanging vegetation. An ideal place to rear a hungry brood! Quite suddenly they were gone, slipping away into denser undergrowth. Turning my head very slowly so as not to betray any movement, I looked carefully around. The deer had gradually moved all this time and were nearly out of sight, but the wren family would not have seen them and in any case, surely they didn't fear distant roe? The shape of the vast jagged strata on the quarry's far side had altered slightly. Even as I puzzled, something moved its head and instantly my eyes focused onto the perfectly camouflaged buzzard perched there. What I had taken to be a symmetrical line of lichens below it was, I suspect, an accumulation of its droppings; buzzards keep to their perching sites from where they have a good view of a locality. Its talons clasping the rock were like crooked, yellow hands as it sat upright, keen eyes noting the slightest movement. Rabbits were out now that the roe had gone. The hawk leaned forward ever so slightly. They never saw it take off, but perhaps instinct or shadow caused one to squeal, high-pitched like a child's scream. It might even then have escaped into denser vegetation, but the long legs reached out, the grasping talons tore and the full weight of the hunter cut short the cry.

Walking back through the trees, I looked at a mossy trunk more closely. Galloway's damp climate makes for ideal growing conditions where mosses not only tend to grow larger but are far more common than in other regions. It was noticeable that in Dirl Wood they seemed to be particularly luxuriant on the north side of the trees and on those that were sheltered from the prevailing winds. Branches and leaning trunks had the shaggiest mosses, probably due to the fact that rain collects on horizontal surfaces better than on vertical. On the reclining trunk I was examining, its upper surface was covered in a deep, deep layer of moss on which grass and flower seeds had germinated, but the action of the water-absorbent moss had caused the trunk's under-surface to become quite dry. The foliage of my tree was moving. It swayed and waved as a juvenile red squirrel came into view and began playing all by itself, on the broad moss-covered branch above. Every young animal seems to love tail-chasing, be it another's or as in this case, its own. Round and round it dashed, then it turned somersaults. Now it hid from an invisible enemy, next it was out and boxing with a trailing stem. It was joined by another and together they dashed helter-skelter through the moss (almost hidden by its height), then sadly, they were gone from my sight. I knew by the commotion and waving leafage however, that their game had merely shifted to an upper storey. Few people came to this tiny, private wood and that was possibly its secret. It was lovelier and better populated than many far larger.

On my last day in Galloway we drove into the forest watching the red deer and feral goats. Most tourists go to the Highlands, bypassing this quiet corner so although this was a Sunday in the height of summer and the weather sunny and warm, there were few people even around the lochs where there is excellent fishing. We stopped to watch a female kestrel hunting along a drystane dyke. No other raptor hovers better than this species although I have seen a rough-legged buzzard come close to it. Hovering is best done when there is a wind; then the kestrel can make maximum use of the air currents and use up less energy. Watching the female that morning, its old country name of windhover came to mind. She flew into the wind at the same speed as it was blowing her back, so that with outstretched wings repeatedly quivering and tail fanned out, she remained stationary above the object of her hunt. Often this will be a small mammal such as a field vole or mouse but sometimes prey as tiny as a beetle. Coming back to the cottage in the evening light, the calves were chasing the sheep again in a nearby meadow. The first time the sheep were herded into a corner of the drystane dyke, I had thought the collie was busy, but this was a popular calf game, though I suspect, less appreciated by the flock.

The tawnies were calling after midnight as I went out to watch for the last time. It would appear that their secret of amicable survival with the barn owls was not to be in the same place at the same time, rather like urban foxes whose territories overlap. They will all hunt that space for food, but do so before or after the others. This must be particularly difficult for the night-loving tawnies in the summer when hours of darkness in Scotland are so brief. First light found me near a conifer plantation and I wandered on intending to pass by the steading tucked away in the far hollow and so reach the lochside road. The sky was suffused with delicate shades – wet watercolours running into one another applied by a careless artist. Even as I stood gazing, an owl floated, the whitest thistledown, its claws scratching on the stonework as it squeezed through an opening under the steading eves. Another dropped onto the roof with a not inconsiderable bump and began in the manner of barn owls to make that snoring, wheezing communication to its mate already inside. She – or he – poked its moon-face out and wheezed in answer. Then both owls gravely bobbed their white, gold-flecked heads to each other, before solemnly withdrawing into their roost.

That day I left for Lockerbie station to the calling of a swallow family perched on the telephone wires behind the cottage, the youngsters immediately recognizable by their short tail streamers. The train passed through Fife, Dundee, Montrose to Aberdeen. I had never been this far north before and found the farms curiously Kent-like with their market gardening and irrigation, wheat, barley, pigs, sheep and cows. In some areas the harvest had begun and even where hills and moors predominated, a network of arable fields below them prevailed. I was met at Aberdeen by Margaret, wife of Mike Harris the man who had helped draw up management guidelines on forestry operations over badger setts. Together we drove to their home not far from Fraserburgh on Scotland's most north-easterly coastline. Badgers have made a good recovery from earlier persecution and are flourishing in this Grampian Region, especially in the agricultural areas. As the growing season is short and the winters long and dark, I had not expected the Pick Your Own wayside signs here. (These were for soft fruit however, not orchard produce.) I suppose too, Grampian in my mind was synonymous with the mountains of the same name, whereas much of the area is relatively flat. This is a fertile, often bitterly windswept land of the northern lights – aurora borealis to the more scientifically minded, or the 'merry dancers' to the local people – flickering blue, green, yellow and red lights that stretch across the winter sky. I came at the wrong time to see them, but sometimes witnessed brief leapings of the dancers on the horizon when out on the hills above my village; tantalizing glimpses of a wonderful natural phenomenon.

Exploring Grampian's coastline was a fascinating adventure. Its beaches, quays and harbours with cottages perched above, often side-on to protect them from wind and harsh weather and the miles of cliffs and shoreline to walk along would take months not days to explore. A few villages no longer saw fishing fleets; the roads down to them were far too steep for lorries taking the catch to market, so some cottages were let out as holiday homes. Others were probably as busy as they had ever been and traditions like the Blessing of the Fleet, were quite as strong. It was on this long, rugged coastline that I saw my first lobster creels and that pretty blue rarity the oyster plant, growing from a pebbly beach. I never did see the Grampian mountains, nor indeed, the Highlands, but this magnificient coastline more than compensated. I was totally unprepared for its steep cliffs, conglomerate, weather-eroded 'stacks' along the shore and the sea birds. The flat farmland is often split by 'dens', some gentle, others deep: steep-sided chasms, rugged and usually tree-lined – popular places for badger homes. The bottom of most contain water; some have a burn running through them and many dens continue to the sea.

The day after my arrival we visited a cliff top, the termination of one such den and stood overlooking the opposite cliffs of near-vertical strata. Gorse and grass covered most of these walls that disappeared into deep folds to a rocky beach and the sea seventy metres below. Sheep and cows grazed the far cliff top and the air was filled with the cries of nesting birds. Where we stood on our cliff, wheat was soon to be harvested. I had been brought here not merely for the view, breathtaking as it was, or the birds, but to look through the binoculars at holes a few metres below the opposite cliff edge where badgers had dug out their home. I have seen setts in some strange places, but this seemed suicidal, all the more so since this clan regularly descended to the beach and back. We walked on and smelled the gannet colony well before reaching them. Here too were kittiwakes, puffins, fulmars, gulls (black-headed, great black-backed, common and herring), razorbills and guillemots perching on narrow ledges. Many of the gannets were gone now so the smell was strong but not overpowering. Here the cliffs were perpendicular in places with no vegetation. It was difficult to imagine how such large numbers of birds managed to nest on these thin rock shelves especially when considering how big some of these species are. The puffins were entertaining little birds. I was told they had suffered a decline a few years ago which was linked to human fishing for sand eels which make up much of their diet. When this was stopped, the puffins made a comeback. These had already nested so I did not see them emerging from holes in the ground (often old rabbit burrows) where they lay their single egg near the cliff's edge. The gannets were a thrill to watch as they soared and glided over the sea. They had a white body with black wing tips and a yellowy-buff head. A wingspan of slightly less than two metres and a dagger-like beak completed the picture of a highly successful predator. We watched them drop vertically from a great height with wings folded back to catch the next fish. There were a few of the smaller black guillemots floating on the sea with their distinctive white wing patches and a large colony of the ordinary, chocolate-coloured guillemots.

As with most of Scotland, there was no badger group in the Grampian Region, though for one man, Mike has achieved a great deal. There were now two others who help him, mainly to map setts. As in England, Wales and Ireland, the presence of such a sett is often only discovered when a road traffic accident (RTA) badger comes to light, though here was the first Scottish area I have known where this applies. Mike systematically checked for setts during the short winter days when vegetation dies back and holes are more easily detected, but with a good badger population and traffic increased with tourists, as many were found in the summer. Indeed, in the fortnight I stayed with the family, Mike was alerted to eight RTA badgers all dead. How many go unnoticed or are injured and stagger away to die is anyone's guess of course. RTAs here have been increasing yearly, but Mike suspected this was due to more public awareness of his interest, than an escalating death toll in real terms. Occasionally as I had found in my area of Kent, a badger might have injuries from which it duly recovered after treatment and rest. The area where it was found was checked for a sett and when recovered, it was returned and released in the near vicinity. Lawrence Brain, a local vet with a great interest in all wildlife, treated these badgers and performed postmortems free of charge. This was a tremendous bonus to Mike and a considerable achievement for the busy vet. (Lawrence later formed the Grampian Wildlife Rehabilitation Trust.)

The following day we drove to the site of one such reported RTA. Mike spoke to a man driving a tractor cutting the verges. It transpired that he was the farmer and husband of the lady who had found the unfortunate badger. The sett was not on his land and his neighbour had gone to the mart (market), but we were welcome to go to look and record it. This was my first experience of a grossly cattle-trampled sett. Regular trampling causes the entrances and spoil heaps to disappear into bare areas in the surrounding pasture. Thus the badgers have to dig themselves free each time they wish to emerge. Where the land is open and rolling with no hedges and few trees, setts are commonly dug like this one in fields. We returned, passing sections of discarded stob and wire fencing left along one field edge. Mike thanked the tractor driver and, leaving his card, suggested that should his neighbour agree to a fence round the sett area, he, Mike would be happy to assist. Quite apart from badger welfare of course, cattle – and horses – have been known to break their legs in entrances.

We continued on to another area where a dead badger had been found some weeks earlier. No sett was known in the locality; Mike had checked all along a nearby den. It could have travelled however, as the distance between setts of the same clan can be as much as 1–1$^{1}/_{2}$ kms. Alternatively, they may have only one sett in a large area. Grampian is like the Lothian region in this and totally dissimilar from the south. This was more hilly countryside and we parked the car near another and opposite a small cottage overlooking the den. Mike hasn't my southern reserve on the subject of badgers. A 'hello' and an enquiry led the other car driver, an elderly man to tell us that he and his friend in the cottage had only been discussing badgers the other day after the friend had seen an adult and cubs together on the lower road. Before he himself retired as a postman he had often seen badgers in the area. Did he know of a sett? Shaking his head slowly, he suggested the den below us, which of course Mike had already checked. I enquired as to the sitka wood next to the cottage, but the ex-postman again shook his head. Nevertheless, we decided it was worth the effort now we were here (and I love unknown woods at the best of times), so leaving the car we split up and began to check first the outside and then under the trees. Though predominately sitka it was a lovely site of perhaps six hectares and contained a possible sett now long-abandoned, a rabbit warren and several snuffle holes. Returning to the car with the sun hot on our backs after the dark trees, I took a photograph of the undulating landscape.

That afternoon we followed a quiet stretch of burn where Mike sometimes watched an otter. There was so much to see along its margins – willow and marsh warblers, skylarks and meadow pipits with yellow iris, bog asphodel and many more. An occasional mink as well as the otter sometimes frequented the area, but that day we saw neither. It began to rain heavily so we sheltered in a disused steading. It was near a house that was falling into decay. The small farms of a few hectares are uneconomic. Farmers buy up other farms but do not need the steadings and houses, so derelict buildings are commonplace. Sometimes incomers buy the farmhouses, renovate and live in them but many, many more become ruins open to the sky. This steading in which we sheltered had once been a habitation, though now the fireplaces in the ground floor room and upstairs were bricked up. The little stairway was in a good state and the stone walls had been repointed inside and out. The rafters too were recent and the roof good. It connected to another steading next door so had probably been the typical Scottish but-and-ben (one up, one down) with the animals adjoining for easy access in the long, bleak winters.

That night we watched the cliff-top badgers through telescope and binoculars: a great thrill. Their black and white heads showed up clearly in the good light without optical aid, but at such a distance it would have been impossible to see details. The telescope was ideal, showing the incredible steepness on which these badgers lived. An old boar leaned back scratching, his head raised chin-up like a dog in the ecstasy of an itch relieved! The yellow-brown area around the sub-caudal gland (with which it scents or musks) was very obvious beneath his tail. Mike pointed out the small white patch of fur on one leg. He had found several RTAs in widely-spaced areas with this marking and one with a neat white patch on each leg. As far as we know this has not been observed outside Grampian. If such an inherent characteristic is peculiar to one clan it would suggest that the family has spread and recolonized very successfully. A sow badger had emerged with the boar, but almost immediately disappeared again. Now she re-emerged and going upwards, dug out much bright, sandy soil from an entrance in the strata above (three holes lower down had grey spoil heaps). Growing on the near-vertical face in the wiry grass were many wild flowers and ferns amongst the rocky outcrops. A burn flowing through the further den entered the sea a few metres beyond our seat and an enormous distance below. I found it a mistake looking directly down as the drop made me giddy. Meanwhile a rabbit tried unsuccessfully to nibble grass at a point somewhere below the sow badger, but gave up rather wearily after the third cascade of sand dropped down over him. By now the boar had left by a round-about route to avoid a roe doe browsing on the harebells, devil's bit scabious, vetches and other flowering plants. I noticed with interest how the flowering heather was left by the feeding deer. The steepness of the incline often caused her to browse in a near-lying position (indeed, the rabbit had its feet splayed apart). At an area of heath she neatly took off the vivid Scottish 'bluebell' blooms growing through the springy shrub-like heather, but did not touch the bell-shaped pink blooms on that plant itself. On this cliff face she was spoilt for choice, but in other situations would probably have taken heather too.

The boar reached the runnel, an almost frightening perpendicular dip by which the clan descended to the beach seventy metres below and moved fast down it with brief pauses to scent-mark his returning route. Sometimes his form disappeared beneath the ferns and bracken growing along each side, but even with the naked eye, his striped face coming into view was easily discerned. Now he was far below us as we watched his progress from the opposite cliff till bracken at our feet hid him from our gaze. Time passed. The sea birds were quieter so that we could just hear the waves breaking on the distant beach. A figure showed briefly foraging amongst the flotsam and he was gone. Mike said that the boar might continue along the shoreline, though his experience had shown that more often the badgers came straight down via the runnel, crossed the beach and continued *up* the far side on our cliff (where a small empty sett also belonging to this clan was dug into its face) and so onto the fields on our side to forage. Strange when each cliff top had large areas of arable land, some grazed by sheep and cows, others now with baled straw left to dry. Surely this farmland was rich in foraging grounds? Even as we sat quietly talking, a foxy head popped out of a hole on the opposite cliff face, cautiously checked that his neighbours had dispersed and crept upwards to a patch of gorse. Even with telescope and binoculars we could not follow his path beneath its concealing thickets until at the very top he was momentarily etched against the sky. All this was seen in good light, the sun still well above the horizon. At 10.00 p.m. we began to pack up and move; only at 11.15 p.m. did dusk descend.

I was told these badgers and others in quiet situations are frequently seen during the day. Were badgers always nocturnal I wondered, or was it man and his activities that made them so? Once wolves and other predators roamed the British Isles, but they hunted by night as well as day so probably didn't influence the badgers' lifestyle. Whilst it is arguable that Lumbricus, which makes up much of their diet, is also nocturnal, it has been suggested that earthworms haven't always been a large proportion of their food. The earth taken in with worms is thought to wear down the teeth unduly and in hotter climates such as France and Spain the humble earthworm figures little in their eating habits. It was interesting to speculate.

I found this eastern Scottish stretch a great pleasure. The hills that I loved were not present, but these vast open vistas of land, sea and sky gave an exhilarating sense of space and freedom. Even the few villages did nothing to alter that impression, merely a handful of houses scattered here and there. As in the Lothians, the local Scots were friendly and interested. At no time in Scotland have I been made to feel an intruder; the term white settler was no more an offence than the Scots I met were dour. I remember meeting a young walker on the hills above my village. He was at university, taking a breather from his finals. He was lost; I was not. He was a native Lothian; I was not. Typically I teased him for not knowing his own hills and we walked together for the rest of that day, he recounting Scottish history from the Scottish viewpoint. I am not overproud of my country's record towards its northern neighbour, but was surprised to hear that Scots were used and exploited by their own wealthy class usually educated in England and showing more allegiance to that country than their own. This English education up to recent times explained why some people of my own generation I have thought to be white settlers like myself, only to find they are Scots born if not bred.

Most people in Grampian to whom Mike spoke showed an interest and enthusiasm in badgers although I suspect his years of work with police, Forestry Commission employees and vets on the animals' behalf had cemented that attitude. Here too had been a region of large estates where any wildlife that might threaten game-rearing was systematically exterminated with poisoned bait, traps and snares. The only remnants of these estates now are along the major roads planted as shady avenues with their successions of grey-trunked beeches like sentinels, some of considerable girth. Inland and further on in the mountains, estates still flourish and with the tourist revenue of paramount importance, snares usually intended for foxes are commonplace. (Poisoned bait and many traps are illegal now; decoy corvid traps catch magpies and crows alive.) The law requires that free-running snares only may be used and these must be checked every twenty-four hours. Many are not checked however, but are left for days even weeks until the gamekeeper has time to check the hundreds of snares he may have set. The Aberdeen Association for the Prevention of Cruelty to Animals had recently been alerted to a badger dying in such a snare and close by to it, the snared carcase of another. The debate over snares I find interesting. Many argue that the snaring of foxes is the only practical and cost-effective form of vermin control. Yet a large estate in Grampian does not share that view, but maintains excellent pheasant shoots. Nowadays only two keepers can be afforded and they are needed for all the other work. There isn't time to set the thousands of snares required, let alone regularly check them, so foxes are shot.

One morning we drove to a Forestry Commission plantation of many thousands of hectares in the hills. Once there, we walked the site of the first of the Commissions' implementations of their management guidelines on tree-felling over setts. Like others before me, I too had experienced the death of a badger when its sett was partly destroyed during logging operations (see *The Badgers of Ashcroft Woods*). This had been coppicing of overgrown sweet chestnut transported via heavy machinery on a steep, wet slope. There are several problems associated with felling over setts. The badgers, if not killed or injured, are disturbed and vacate the site due to the noise and associated burning of lopped branches and top wood. The sett may be destroyed or partly destroyed. Felling and coppicing is often done (with the best of intentions) in the winter when nesting birds are not present. However, the first half of the year is the most vulnerable time for pregnant sows and cubs and since implantation of blastocysts may occur as early as December, and stress is known to retard or curtail implanting, that is a vulnerable month too. As already noted, many Scottish badgers do not have alternative homes like their English counterparts – certainly not additional setts large enough to accommodate the entire clan.

The Forestry Commission guidelines forbade any work in a main sett vicinity from 1 December to 30 June inclusive. It is not practical to leave a tuft of trees over a sett as these are soon blown over with the subsequent uprooting destroying entrances and tunnels. The recommendation of cutting trunks to 1–1½ metres above the ground had been carried out. Hopefully these would reduce the loss of familiar surroundings and acting as sett 'markers' prevent any accidental damage to the sett by machinery during the operation. Broad leaved plants had been planted inbetween the sawn upright trunks and the foxgloves were already of a good height. Soon cover would return to the sett and no future trees would be harvested there. Forest operations are by their very nature noisy affairs and in this instance bad weather had protracted the work. Had this precipitated the clan's desertion? The badgers had moved to another, smaller home some distance off in the plantation, demonstrating the importance of secondary setts where they exist. Many Forestry Commission plantations are thirty years or more old and must be felled within the next few years, but hopefully if these guidelines are adhered to, the setts will remain though stress to the animals seems inevitable. We wondered how, if at all, these guidelines would be implemented in the private sector?*

The sun appeared to dry the earlier rain as together we walked on talking. The belief that badgers dig their homes on the fringes of conifer plantations so often doesn't hold true here. On the whole, this type of forest is sterile to their requirements, merely giving a protective canopy to the sett from whence they can emerge onto adjacent pasture or farmland to forage. Why is it then that some setts are deep amongst the trees necessitating long journeys to and fro? Perhaps these existed long before the planting and had not been destroyed by the machinery that prepared the drainage and put in these trees.

Wide grassy firebreaks led up the steep hillside strewn about with rocks where ferns raised delicate feathery arms and stately foxgloves grew in tiers. Here fluttered green-veined whites, ringlets and meadow browns and on the purple knapweed crowded six-spot burnet moths. Returning to the car, a sparrowhawk dashed by us in pursuit of a small songster that successfully evaded death as it dived into the trees' dense shade.

Rain running down the window panes was a good excuse – if we needed one – to sit indoors blethering about badgers next morning. By early afternoon we set out in warm sunshine to visit a nature reserve and explore its expanse of sand dunes. The man in charge grew native wild flowers and trees and Mike wanted some white campion, harebells, ragged robin and bogbean for his pond. At the reserve's entrance the large flowerbed crammed full of flowering corn marigold was a brilliant yellow blaze. During my stay in the north I was to see one or two of these blooming at the edge of harvested wheat, though it is rapidly declining in many parts of Great Britain. I was amazed to see great and dark mulleins growing happily at the centre; somehow I had thought of them as southern plants. The nursery trees ranged from holly and oak through to hazel and a great variety of willows, poplars and alders. Mike bought his plants and having put them in the car boot we continued on through the sand dunes to the sea cliffs beyond. Photographs of these dunes could never give a true impression of the place. Except for the grasses and other plants stablizing

* In 1994 problems still continued with felling over setts as contractors often subcontract. Forest Enterprise (formerly the Forestry Commission) and other organizations hope shortly to devise a system of compulsory licensing. In this way it should be simple to establish who is responsible, i.e., the holder of the licence, when the guidelines are ignored.

them (many rare or localized), the dunes would be forever shifting in the wind. Enormous holes were made by rabbits; no badgers here, indeed a sett would soon collapse. The path wound back and forth for perhaps 1 1/2 km. Most of the plants I didn't know. Only the tiny white, sometimes lilac flowers of Danish scurvy-grass, thrift, greater sand-spurrey and sea campion looking rather like a low, white bladder campion could I readily identify. Before the cliffs were reached we came upon an inland lochan on which gulls and coots were resting. Water avens, reeds and rushes were all outdone in splendour by a great bank of purple loosestrife. Further on came a grassy slope to the sea. On either side of the small rocky beach, tall cliffs stood guard on whose steep formations rested sea birds, their squabbling cries a continual gaggle that hid individual voices and the murmur of the waves. Some flew up calling at my approach, but soon settled once more. These granite towers were iron-stained and dwarf sea pink thrift grew from their highest ledges, the densely clustered flowers bowing to the breeze. This sunny afternoon they were the food plant of many insects and bees.

I returned to Mike sitting quietly up above and we began discussing the cliff-dwelling badgers watched a few evenings earlier. They had a small sett near the top of both cliff faces, only occupying one at a time. The clan had four members. Yet whichever sett was currently in use, the family made the nightly journey to the further cliff top to forage. My companion pointed out that it would be far less energy-consuming (to say nothing of being safer), to go round on the top of the cliffs as we had done. Either there was some reason unknown to us for this arduous journey or – dare we say it – their intelligence was low! This brought us to the other question. Why have clans chosen to live in these difficult situations when other, more accesible areas for setts are available? Could these cliff setts have their origin in past times of persecution when only those that remained were the clans clinging on (almost literally), to more inaccessible habitats, i.e. cliff faces, mines, screes and it was those that slowly recolonized the fertile areas when that persecution ceased? I thought of the wad mine badgers in Cumbria and the same question they posed me in 1981. Then the Wildlife and Countryside Act was going through its final stage in the Lords, but a Forestry Commission ranger in Keswick was doubtful how successfully it could be implemented especially regarding badger conservation. Here too was a long, relentless history of persecution and old habits die hard. Even though the 1973 Badgers Act had given a certain protection, nothing had altered in the Lake District he said. Children and their fathers regularly had a Saturday or Sunday afternoon with the terriers on these fells searching out the badger for sport. In more recent years these animals have increased in Cumbria, but except where people in the valleys were against the digging practice and looked after local setts there had been few occupied badger homes on lower ground. Now I thought of Mike's cliff badgers; fifty years ago had only those in remote, more inaccessible areas survived? And Melanie with her few Galwegian brocks that seemed forever on the move. Those that escaped the blocking/gassing/digging of their home would be stressed and the likelihood of reproduction poor.

Writers of the last century had reported few badgers left in Grampian with whole areas of Scotland devoid for many years. They had consulted local gamekeepers for their information who reported with pride of the last badger shot, trapped or snared in their area. I can understand a Victorian gentleman not knowing the true state of affairs, but gamekeepers in an age when it was considered right to exterminate – surely not? No, I feel we must take these records as the true state of affairs.

One afternoon I went with Mike to meet his vet Lawrence Brain; he had two more RTAs to take for postmortem. I expressed surprise at tawnies and kestrels recuperating together in an aviary and was told that provided they are of the same size and well fed there is no problem. However, this could not be done with peregrines or buzzards. A duck was keeping an ivory gull company. The latter is a resident of the high Arctic and a rare migrant. At present it was moulting and very dirty, due to its love of rolling in its meals of rotting fish, but the winter plumage would be all white with a yellow-tipped red bill and black legs. It had a vermilion orbital circle around each eye. It was the size of a kittiwake and was found with a sheared-off wing, possibly caused by flying into a power line. The otter cubs brought to him went to the couple with the sanctuary in Galloway and were not returned to the wild here in Grampian as he felt the area had its full complement of these animals. A dominant dog otter will be aggressive towards a young male and if it doesn't leave will attack it. (I recalled the sanctuary owner telling me of the bite marks found on some males brought to them.) The vet fed the cubs on goats' milk not cows (as one does badger cubs) weaning them on liquidized fish. At the sanctuary they were cared for in groups until old enough to be released. North Yorkshire has been the site of several group releases and regular monitoring has shown these to be successful.

The two postmortems revealed both badgers had sustained massive internal injuries apart from those to the skulls. The sow's stomach was full of pea-like objects; some sort of seed. The boar's contained some too, with many worms and grubs. An incisor tooth was extracted from both and would be sent away to determine age together with a few of the seeds and all relevant details. It is sad that RTAs occur, but at least valuable information can be discovered from them if a vet has the interest. Before returning home we checked the area where these badgers had been found, but could not trace the origin of the seeds. A stoat peered at us from a beech, ran back behind the thick trunk, but curiosity getting the better of it, popped out once more to see what we were doing – nothing as it happened, merely standing still trying hard not to laugh. His agile movements as he left one beech for the next and raced up it were a pleasure to watch.

It was in Grampian's northwest that I encountered my first wildcat, sadly a dead one, fallen victim to that most ruthless and indiscriminate of predators, the motor vehicle. Though only in part recognizable (for it had been run over several times), it was clearly not a large domestic tabby. Later I was to be shown the pelts of three more RTA wildcats collected over a period from the same region where they are not uncommon now they have legal protection. The taxidermist to whom the dead cats had been given, hoped to make two good specimens from the skins. The first thing that struck me on seeing such a cat was the very broad head with its extraordinary profusion of long, stiff, white whiskers extending far beyond the head width. The legs are longer in proportion to the body and combining with the head, give an immediate impression of strength and power. The body fur is longer and softer and to my mind, the legendary thick, untapering, bushy tail with its black rings and big blunt tip, is also longer than any domestic cat's. My immediate thought was that the tail is as much a contrast as the fox's is to a dog. The biggest of these pelts measured one metre from nose to tail tip and that I was told is not large. I would dearly love to see a live wildcat in its natural environment.

The loneliness of the landscape here is sometimes touched by the sight of great stones rearing out of the ground; stark fingers of time set in eternal silence. It was a breezy warm day when I went to view one of these recumbent stone circles. This was an impressive sight even in the sunshine, but how did it appear to its prehistoric builders in a low midwinter sunset or by night? These particular circles are peculiar to northeast Scotland, although their type of burial and architecture together with the artefacts often placed in them, strongly suggest a relationship with the Cork-Kerry recumbent stone circles 500 miles distant in southwest Ireland.

This one stood in a small clearing on a solitary hill top surrounded by a conifer plantation, so that pushing through the sombre trees I came upon it suddenly as I emerged into the light. Such circles consist of a ring of upright stones graded in height with the two tallest guarding or flanking each side of a huge prostrate block. This 'recumbent' is the megalith's focal point and although the weight of it varies from site to site, the average has been calculated at 24 tonnes. It is obvious that these early peoples desired an impressive stone; the placing of it and its flankers was of paramount importance to them. Not so the rest of the circle which was rarely geometrically so, but more of an ellipse or a rough oval. Within these circles the sun and moon were worshiped. Undoubtedly the recumbent's position was deliberately chosen, so consistently is it placed in the southwest quadrant of the standing stones and this siting provides the clue to its function. It was intended to catch or 'hold' the moon at its major risings and settings, that is, the moments when it appears to stand still.

In my quest for historical information on Scotland's fauna I had discovered the 1527 *History of Scotland* by Hector Boece and in it the first mention of these circles.

> In the times of King Mainus . . . huge stones were erected in a ring and the biggest of them was stretched out on the south side to serve for an altar, whereon were burned the victims in sacrifice to the gods. In proof of the fact

> to this day there stand these mighty stones gathered together into circles – the
> old temples of the gods they are called – and whoso sees them will assuredly
> marvel by what mechanical craft or by what bodily strength stones of such
> bulk have been collected to one spot.

At the time I had smiled at the historian's mention of human sacrifice, but
modern findings suggest his assumption may have been correct. Most of
these Grampian circles have been found to contain offerings of cremated
human bone. In the centre of the Loanhead of Daviot one for instance, as
many as 2.3 kg of fragments were found, more than fifty of them belonging
to the skulls of children whose ages had ranged from two to four years old.
The evidence of annual rites at these sites imply sacrifices rather than death
by famine or disease.

Although most stone circles are believed to have connections with
observing the sun, moon or bright celestial bodies such as Venus, it is
doubtful if that was their primary function. A line of stones (or even
a horseshoe of uprights to calculate a calendar) would have been a far
better shape for this. There is a great gulf between scientific observation
and primitive superstition, however, and circles had the magical properties
of holding and keeping in, and perhaps safety in its encirclement for those
intent on securing some of the supernatural power for themselves. Many
recumbents and some of their flankers bear 'cup-marks' – depressions about
75 mm across made by rasping the surface with a stone. The recumbent of
one such circle bears 119 of these cup-marks.

The Grampian megaliths were a far cry from the structures on the braes
I knew: three ranges of hills, from east to west, the Lammermuir (made
famous by Sir Walter Scott), the Moorfoot and the Pentland. East Lothian
has small ring-cairns set amongst its peat and heather high in the hills.
Further over is the impressive Kingside Hill with its thirty stones and central
mound brooding over the moor. Its purpose is uncertain though a cremation
cemetery has been suggested. Midlothian has Marchwell, a 12-metre oval
ring in which a food vessel was found and the large barrow at Newbridge
with its three surrounding stones where a fine bronze dagger was discovered
in 1830. All give the beholder a sense of history, of unanswered questions
and a feel of timelessness, but the recumbent stone circles of Grampian leave
one with a sense of awe.

It was my first experience too of peat cutting. I was told this was on a
small scale locally, but to me it seemed a vast area made worse by the
knowledge that it was destined for Swedish power stations for fuel. In part I
can sympathize with the farmer who has many hectares of wetland he cannot
use, but I grieved for the disappearing bog. First the ground was cleared
of its top layer of moss and plants to expose the peat and then channels
were dug to drain off the water. After cutting, the peat was stacked into
piles reminding me of coal slag heaps, then packed and transported across
the North Sea. Where cuttings bordered the still untouched bog, the sterile

landscape contrasted strongly with the living, so full of colour and insects, some of its plants already rarities though I suppose that is of small concern to the owners. A rural vandalism – so quick to effect, so long to evolve.

Now the hay was being turned and the barley soon to ripen. The latter, when good quality, is used for malt whisky, and when poor, for animal feed. In sheltered places the rowan berries were ripe; everywhere wild raspberries dropped from hedge and verge. Grey partridges had well-grown young and picking raspberries on a sunny bank, I found a lone, olive partridge egg – probably long-addled. Flowering heather coloured the landscape and the warm air was punctuated with the sharp reports of bursting gorse pods. I spent happy hours photographing derelict steadings within whose shelter grew wild flowers in profusion. I saw many swallows, though few swifts and no barn owls; the white owl is not common here as in Galloway. Splendid tiger moths were flying and the small pearl-bordered fritillary, such a fast-moving butterfly keeping close to the ground in its quest for flowers. A kestrel hunted a sunny field; the cows resting as they chewed the cud with the busy hunter above them in the clear air. Well inland a sand quarry had sandmartins nesting in neat holes high up in its walls, unbothered by the noise of workmen, machinery and heavy lorries trundling by. Grampian has this fascinating mix of soil and stone types from pure sand to the dramatically weathered outcrops of its coasts.

Mike had a telephone call from a head forester to say that two badgers had been found dead in snares. The local police had been informed; would he contact them and arrange an on-site visit? It was a gloriously sunny day, but our visibility was obscured as we drove up the steep, winding hill track through the plantation as the dust rose in clouds from the two police cars in front. The soil was poor and light here and the recent hot weather had evaporated any surface water. We left the cars at the end of the route and continued on foot to a point where the sitkas ended. Here was a wire and stob fence with a small burn outside and below it. Beyond this was a sheep farm with pasture meeting the slow-flowing water. In the middle distance stood a small steading with a van parked in its yard.

The mature sow was but recently dead in the wire snare attached to the fencing. Rabbit mesh was fixed from ground level to perhaps half a metre up the fence but this was broken and rusted with age in places with clear trails or paths made by fox and badger giving easy access through it. The stream we were told, not the fencing, marked the end of the Forestry Commission plantation; the Commission did not allow snaring on its properties in the region. Grass and vegetation grew profusely below the fence and beyond until the sitkas cast their shade obscuring the light. Typically, a circular area under and around the badger had been scraped into fresh earth devoid of any growing plant where the victim in her long, protracted agony had twisted and turned, clawing the ground in her futile efforts to get free. The snare had passed over the sow's head and fore limbs only to tighten on the lower abdomen. Unable to progress further it had bitten deeply above the pelvis and held the wretched badger ever tighter at each movement, cleaving through fur, skin, flesh until it reached the bone. We took photographs before the snare was carefully untied from the stob. In spite of the hot weather, the smell was not excessive and the stomach had not as is usual, begun to swell. We were to find the answer to this when the vet performed his postmortems.

Now we were taken some metres down the slope under the sitkas to another snared badger, although this had been dead weeks, perhaps months ago. Its flesh had long since decomposed leaving a dehydrated, shrunken husk of skeleton beneath fur and a faint, not unpleasant, musky smell. The snare was still upon it, but at some time had been cut. So the victim had been brought here, but where had the snare been set? Whilst the men examined it, I walked back to the fence and followed it downhill. A constable caught up with me and offered to help. 'Shouldn't be difficult to find,' I told him. 'Look out for another torn-up area of bare earth though it won't be fresh like the first.' Sure enough, there it was in the same type of situation – a trail leading from the pasture at the far side of the burn and through a broken section of stob and wire. But for the bare earth, however, we might have searched long for the secured end of the snare; old wire onto the rusting wire of an equally ancient fence. This time there was a small area of exposed earth the other side too as if in mounting the torn fence the badger had fallen back on being snared, scrabbled frantically for awhile before mounting the fence again and ending its life there. We knew it had indeed died *in situ* because a large quantity of its fur lay on the ground next to the fence. Again I took photos. As we rejoined the others under the trees I picked up something white – the badger's tail – and laid it with the body. Whoever had found this badger had deliberately cut it from the fence and thrown it here. The forester doubted that it was a member of the public. This was a lonely, isolated place too far off the beaten track with nothing much to see anyway. The only locals were the farmer and his family in the steading beyond.

I was asked about the animal trails; were they fox or badger? They had been both. I felt too that the target species had been fox in this sheep-rearing country. There was general agreement on this. No animal whether protected or not should legally be left in a snare for more than twenty-four hours. One body had been hidden and much later another victim had also been left to die. The snares were free-running so were legal, but the owner was on private property snaring without permission. The forester took us to view a small sett further into the plantation. It appeared to be empty. Had the snared animals been its last occupants or was there another? Now the men left Mike and I to continue checking the perimeter fence. We found nothing more except another (empty) snare although this time it was strengthened in its position with a peg. We did not find another sett but by now time was short for we had promised to rendez-vous at the police station. This we did, taking the third snare with us and each made a statement.

On our way home we found the vet just locking up his surgery and he did the two postmortems straight away. The sow had been dead not more than two days. Her stomach was quite empty, its walls fused together; technically death was from starvation. He estimated she had taken anything from seven to ten days to die so her body had been there less than a fortnight. The dehydrated boar could have died many, many weeks ago. Even from so thin a body, the vet could not remove the snare without dismembering the carcase. The insane – or merely ignorant – MP who had declared in Parliament that free-running snares were more humane than self-locking, should have been there with us. All snares have this potential to self-lock, whether due to a kink in the wire caused by the victim's struggles or caught on its fur. The vet promised to pass the results with the snares to the police.

It was a dismal end to my stay in Grampian, though not without hope. Mike was delighted that the police were thinking of prosecuting if it could be proved who had set the snares. These two made seven snared badgers brought to his attention that year. One had survived. After treatment and a period of convalescence, it had been released back into the wild. Only one snaring incident had been discovered the previous year. Again, as with RTAs, the increase probably indicated public awareness of Mike's concern especially as local radio and newspapers had been willing to cover the problem. Even so, these incidents were only the tip of a very large iceberg; in such vast, remote areas most snaring abuse must go undetected. Mike had been upset that in spite of excellent evidence of a farmer snaring on a similar occasion and the sergeant's desire to bring charges, his inspector had put a halt to proceedings. It is remarkable what media coverage can do, however, coupled with local people's concern. The sergeant we had spoken to that day was convinced the nearby sheep farmer was responsible and he knew the man well. He would leave matters for a fortnight or so in case the convoy of cars had been noted, then pay one of his regular visits to the steading for a friendly chat. True to his word he did this and in conversation asked if the farmer ever snared. Cheerfully came the answer. Yes, for foxes that might take his lambs and he fixed the snares to the Forestry Commission fence. With that, he was taken to the station and charged.

Mike's survey of badger setts had uncovered evidence of gassing at ten; others appeared to have chemicals illegally poured into them. Whilst the snaring of badgers was primarily through ignorance, the best way to combat this is through publicity, and a successful prosecution, as this one proved to be, helps to warn people who insist on snaring to check their snares regularly, or find themselves the subject of a court case. But what of Scottish regions where there are no concerned persons to care?

CHAPTER TEN

Autumn

I t was good to be home again even though for two days the rain was torrential. By 1 a.m. on the third, it had dwindled to a light patter and the waning moon shone through low, grey sheets of stratus cloud. The long-eared owls were ahunting near the loaning, their sighing calls coming faintly on the air. Now the moon shone out, riding clear in the sky as the rippling clouds dispersed, bathing the grassy stretch between the old buildings in its silvery light. A rabbit and then two more, stole out to feed and I leaned on the bedroom windowsill to watch. One sat up and began to wash; it held a long ear in its left paw as it washed with the other. The fox startled me as much as the rabbits and the grooming was never completed. Its victim was carried under the spread of a beech to be eaten. I didn't latch the back door in case it made its usual sharp lick; foxes have excellent hearing. Once outside it was easy to move silently nearer on the wet grass. The fox dragged over the body and there came the crunch of tooth on bone. Still the owls called as they worked their way along the tree line and *Vulpes vulpes* finished his meal. He dug a shallow hole and dropped in the remains for another time. With his nose he tupped over the earth and went on his way. He had made a poor job of burying his booty and part of a leg protruded from the dirt. That night I saw Millie and another badger taking worms from the pasture, slowly weaving their way as they did so, in and out of the sheep. The morning was breezy but sunny as I went down to the village. Before leaving I checked the buried rabbit and found it dug up and gone. Part of the fur was turned inside out and badger spore showed in the damp bare earth around it.

There were young willow warblers by Hoolit and white-throats by the farm track as I made my way to the lane. The parents of the former had nested on the ground as they usually do, though this seemed an unwise choice when there were so many small trees and bushes nearby. I was rather surprised that the eggs had survived, let alone the nestlings, especially as a white hedgehog was frequently seen in the vicinity. Albino urchins are said not to be uncommon, but this was the first I had ever come across. The sight of its pink nose and feet and those white spines still gave me a sense of surprise. Albino foxes have a problem hunting; white is so obvious in anything but snow. For a hedgehog, lack of pigment would probably make little difference to its success in finding slugs, worms, beetles, fly larvae, caterpillars and insects. They also enjoy eggs if they find them. True, an albino's sight is poor, but so is an urchin's; they rely heavily on their acute senses of hearing and smell to find food. I would miss the birds, most especially the willow warblers' sweet, wistful songs heard earlier in the year. They would soon be gathering to move nearer the coast in readiness for their long flight to tropical and southern Africa. Incredible to think of such small birds making these vast journeys. I reached the lane noting the changes in my absence. The wheat was gone and the rows of stubble curved gently up to the horizon. Long morning shadows from the hedgerow trees crept towards me across the tarmac. They seemed to wave gaily as branches tossed in the wind. At the field entrance a hare stood tall, his black-tipped ears turning as he watched me pass. Behind crouched Dydor brooding over the moor.

It was again raining slightly when I next went into the shelter belt to wait for the Burn Badgers to emerge. The first head to appear was Neddy's sticking out long-necked to smell the air. Everything glistened with fine moisture, and after a few minutes grooming and walking through the bracken near the field edge to use latrines there, so were the badgers. The water drops accentuated their grey backs making them look darker. Spike emerged and stood on hind legs against the wych-elm's trunk to scratch it with his long-clawed forepaws. His shaggy, grey body fur being longer by far than the short black fur of legs and belly, gave him in that position the appearance of a wrapped-round cloak. Grace and Disgrace began a mutual grooming session that quickly degenerated into a game, whilst C.Goon scrambled over the log pile in search of beetle titbits. The pure white stripes of those badger faces showed up so vividly in the deep shade of the sitka night, though they would soon become dirty as their owners nibbled beneath green lichened stones or snuffled the pasture outside. Millie came up to me as I sat quietly watching, backed onto and musked my boots. She gave herself a good, prolonged shake, standing square and solid as she did so, then lifted a lazy left hind leg to have a pleasurable scratch. This continued with great gusto for some audible moments. It was marvellous to be back with the clan again and to be accepted so completely after weeks away. Millie lay flat on her back in the grassy area, back legs spread wide in the 'everything abandoned' attitude which told she was wholly at ease. She lay the picture of contentment, then up rose her head and her hind legs as she began the serious business of nibbling at her fur, the long front claws parting as her tongue busily washed.

Grace, Disgrace and Neddy wandered away, snouts to ground along the trail under the wire, stopping every so often to squat and scent-mark their route. It had stopped raining; a faint wind was drying out the wetness. I moved very little until morning, so much seemed to be happening and the night was very mild and pleasant. Badgers came and went. The numerous fallen or rotting tree trunks were home to good numbers of centipedes, grubs and other creatures. Strongly clawed paws can prise up resisting wood or rocks where edible delicacies might be lurking unseen though not un smelled.

Once again I was reminded of the badger's wide gape. They have this ability to upturn that flexible, rubbery snout out of the way to take food from the ground or similar flat surface. At first light came a snuffling and heaving – a pause and it came again. A broad-beamed grey back presented itself to my interested gaze. C. Goon was carrying hay collected from the field outside, backwards to an entrance. Typically, he had far too much, some slipped away, the carrier paused and the whole pile that moments before had been neatly held under chin and against chest, slowly collapsed spreading over a radius of several times its owner's size. Greatly exasperated, the badger strove to re-collect his hay, clawing it up and snuffling about. Grace stood by and watched the proceedings as the other with his bundle much reduced, continued backwards and down into the hole. Once he was safely below, the young animal hastily scratched together the remainder and backed off with it into a further entrance!

I left them to walk down the lane as the morning star hung bright in the eastern sky and the tawnies called, answered and called again from below in the village. Now light diffused over the landscape and a blackbird sung its sweet refrain sounding strangely with the still-calling owls. Another half hour and the blackbirds were silent, busily feeding as the other birds began to call. A tight knot of spindly beeches darkened my path to the river. Nothing grew beneath their light-denying canopy, but a solitary stinkhorn pushing through the dead leaves and decaying bluebell stems that lay criss-cross upon each other. An apparently sterile world that would stay so now until spring awakened it once more. A short distance on there were acorns and lime seedcases – the limes' leaves were already beginning to fall. Amongst these I found tawny and partridge feathers. The hips, haws and rowan berries were a deep blush in the hedgerows and blackberries were plump and juicy from the plentiful rain.

A wild, wet night is not perhaps the best to choose for a walk, but who wants to be a fair-weather wanderer and miss the hills' many moods? I took the way through the pass to the distant reservoir and sat on its drystane dyke watching the towering clouds break and re-form over the dark ridge above me. A tiny steading nestled in the folding hillside sheltered by stately trees that swayed and tossed as the gale sought in vain to snap them. The sound of the tossing trees recalled the sea on a distant Grampian shore; the dark sky with its lighter flecks, waves on a rocky beach. I had no wish to retrace my steps and instead, continued on following the steep track to the top of the next law, now sheltered from the crying wind. Here was sudden quiet with only my steps noisy on the rough scree. Pausing to catch my breath and look over the sheer face to the next range, I heard sounds of someone descending. Three a.m. on such a night was surely a strange time for anyone else to be out in so isolated a place. Whoever it was must be big and heavy to make so much clatter. I stood flat against the rock face to allow the stranger to pass, wondering if I should call out to warn the other I was there, or if in the still dark night, they would indeed see me. There was after all a sheer drop on the other side. Even as I hesitated, round the corner came – half a dozen sheep! Rather an anti-climax really. I was already forming some sort of feeble explanation for my presence, although the same might reasonably have been expected of the newcomers had they been human. They stopped momentarily in their tracks, then the leading ewe passed, her nostrils flaring uneasily. I remembered another occasion in mist on Lytlaw and said nothing as the rest hesitated awhile longer before hurrying after. Once I heard swans distantly calling at the next headland where the wind weakening now, awaited me. The sun was rising as I reached my home loch.

I had no desire yet to return to Hoolit, preferring to linger there as the scudding clouds banished its struggling disc. The dark ripples reflected their contest on its distorting surface and the swans with their well-grown cygnets showed vividly in the poor light. The wind on my face was warm as I followed the Craiglaw burn into the further hills. Barely a kilometre on I found otter spraints deposited on a prominent rock. Here and there amongst the spruce on the lower slopes were clumps of birch and beneath these, telltale snuffle holes. Most of the soil here is too acid for worms to tolerate, but the leaf litter of birches is alkaline, reducing this acidity. A weasel appeared among the scarlet caps of the fly agaric toadstools, reared up on hind legs the better to see me and ran back into hiding across the grass. A splash of orange/red further off proved not to be more agarics but a patch of orange hawkweed springing up from the turf. With its flower heads starting off life in tight clusters it is easy to see from whence its country name of fox-and-cubs derived. Not so clear is the source of the hawkweed title for this family of perennials, but according to ancient writers, the hawk 'was wont to quicken his sight' by eating the plant and so obtaining its milky juice.

Country names for plants may alter or be local to a county or district, whereas its Latin style makes for easy recognition for botanists the world over. Many old herbal names have their roots in the 1500s and were a guide to its uses; many more are forceful descriptions with the emphasis on impression at first sight. Apart from a great fascination with old names and their derivations, I'm sure I would never remember *Hieracium aurianticum* for the orange hawkweed or many other Latin flower names either! For originality, however, its old name 'Grim the Collier' is hard to better. This hawkweed like so many other plants was introduced from Europe. Gerard's revised *Herball* (1633) tells us: 'The stalkes and cups of the flowres are all set thicke with a blackish downe or hairinesse as it were the duste of coles; whence the women who keep it in gardens for noveltie sake, have named it Grim the Colliar.'

Now the trees and meandering dykes were behind me as I reached the open moor. Skylarks, grouse and meadow pipits were feeding in the first of the day's warmth, but somewhere it was raining. To my left was a rainbow in a black sky. Soon the 'bow and the darkness sped away and for the first time since the previous day, the sky was clear of clouds except for some tiny while fluffs crowning the peaks. At last I could make out the roof of the old shieling nestling under the far hill where I had sheltered briefly earlier in the year. Here were otter signs in abundance, not only fresh spraints, but seals too, the five toes and sometimes the webbing between them, clear in the wet mud by the burn. In October, the owners of Hoolit would be back and needing their cottage. I was due to return to England. I would love to have a few winter months in this deserted shieling. I must find who the owner was and see if I could.

A red sun rose in the dawn sky the next morning – a great, red disk. By 8 a.m. it was breezy but warm and the swallows were gathering ready for their autumn migration. The cottage pair, plus their offspring with short tail streamers together with others from neighbouring buildings, flew racing over Hoolit, then high up in the clear sky, wheeling, twisting, swooping and turning, constantly changing direction; such graceful birds. Two alighted on the guttering above my window, at first to drink from the night's rain collected there and then to preen. I could see only their light underparts and long tails with those white bars as they preened, all the while keeping up a twittering warble, very pleasant to hear. An hour later I heard more avian flurry outside the window. Two young swallows were facing into the room, sitting together on the apex of the porch to my right. Their breasts and foreheads were a pale imitation of the parents' russet; I would imagine this was the third and latest of the season's brood. The mother flew towards them and marvel of marvels – first one then the other rose and was fed by her in midair at my level, she having carried insects to them in her throat! It is easy with modern knowledge to mock the old idea that swallows hibernated in the mud of ponds and streams, a belief probably encouraged by their habit of gathering by such places before migrating. Surely it is nearly as strange to contemplate the truth? Not only do they fly the remarkable distance to South Africa, but these youngsters would probably go later with other late broods having no previous experience to help them. Young cuckoos moreover, must always 'go it alone.' Their parents leave by July, but the youngsters fed by foster parents (which are usually meadow pipits here) leave during August and early September. Meadow pipits themselves rarely stay this far north in winter, but with the arrival of other birds from the north, move to milder parts of England. How birds navigate over long distances is still not fully understood, although night fliers are believed to do so by the stars, whilst others use the earth's magnetic field or polarized light. These swallows, like the swifts, would fly by day, feeding on insects in flight. I would miss them greatly.

It had been a misty evening so was well dark by 7 p.m. I left Hoolit as the long-eared owls hunted from the fir plantation nearby. A fox was searching the tumbledown ruins of one of the old farmhouse steadings by the loch. The occasional clink of claws on stone sounded loudly in the quietness mist brings. He crept into a wall, crouching low in the confining space between the stones and disappeared. Reynard must have found somewhere large enough to move round within the wall, for on his return he came out head first with a brown rat in his jaws. The mist cleared as I walked on and lights flickered low in the sky partly obscured by the soft shapes of the hills. At first I took them to be the merry dancers, but they were not in the north, nor the right colours. Now a strong wind blew, howling over the moor as it raced through the wiry heather. The storm burst suddenly overhead, lightning flashing simultaneously with a great rolling crash of thunder.

I had left unprepared for rain and in an instant was soaked. The storm was a sheet of water pouring from on high. The lightning's brilliance seared my eyes even with the lids closed against the water that flooded them. I stumbled against stones, whether dyke, steading or cairn, who could say and with soaked back flattened against this slight shelter, waited for the tempest to ease. With eyelids closed I could still see well as each flash lit and relit my surroundings in swift succession. Water rushed through the heather swirling loosened bushes away in its passing. Flood water from higher up in the hills soon swelled this. Now I was knee-deep in a fast rising spate – no choice but to climb the wall at my back. Exposed it might be, but better than the torrent beneath that threatened to engulf me. The elements were deafening – thunder, lightning, wind and water seeming to outbid one another in primeval fury. Below me something grey swept by, tried fleetingly to regain its footing and was gone. Another sheep followed – the brilliant flashes revealing its curved horns, wide yellow eyes and flecked muzzle before it too disappeared. A lingering thunderclap, a flash and a small rowan, the only tree in the near landscape, was ablaze. It shone brightly at the storm's departure, but the rain soon turned flame to steam. Now the tempest was moving eastwards with a dark wall of rain clouds running before through which the lightning twisted and forked. Each flash I saw wasn't single, but two or three rending gashes from clouds to ground in a fraction of a second. It is curious how well one can see through closed lids in such a storm. I had found this before many years ago, but forgotten the experience until now. Though lightning still played on the horizon, all was much quieter for the force of rain and wind had gone. I splashed homeward to be greeted by one of the farm cats on the cottage wall. Unlike me, she was almost dry so had probably hidden in the wood pile under the lean-to, one of her favoured spots. I lifted the latch and she raced me indoors, her tail upright as she led the way.

Then followed a week of rain accompanied by winds that blew the yellowing leaves off the beeches. I went out one afternoon when the weather had eased, collecting dead wood and some still green, brought down by the storms. The green could remain to wither in the outhouse, but the dead would soon dry in the hearth for kindling. The wee cottage was snug and cosy with a fire burning merrily inside. The farm cat had taken me over since it found my warm fire. She sat a respectful distance from its occasional spitting, front paws tucked beneath snow-white chest and purred her contentment, the golden eyes opening and closing as she dozed.

In early October we were granted a brief period of hot sunshine by day and deeply misty, chill nights as if a kindly deity was showing us our earlier summer before the long winter closed in. I enjoyed wandering these mysteriously enveloped hills and moors at night, though with caution for this wasn't the gentle landscape of my birth. The cat declined to accompany me; she preferred hunting the broken walls of the old buildings, the shelter belt or even the wood pile rather than soak her coat in the open. 'You're no wildcat,' I told her and she purred her agreement. I loved these nights. Sometimes it wasn't a fog, but a ground mist with the sky and stars clear above so that climbing to higher ground I could suddenly look down to a thick sheet of white below, similar to the effect of walking cloud-covered hills. By first light, a myriad spider webs adorned heather, bilberry bushes and drystane dykes, each orb daintily clad in delicate water drops like jewels on a fairy necklace. As I crossed the pasture on my return, the grass was pearl-translucent from the wet. My boots crushed the moisture underfoot, sending splashes of water flying forwards at each step. Turning, I saw the 'bruise-trail' of my passing that left the water-freed grass a brighter green.

My view from the cottage window revealed a hazy sun slowly climbing a pale sky through a dip in the dark hills and below that a filmy moor in silhouette. To my left, the beeches were all adrip, their thin skeletal fingers pushing through the last of the fading year's leaves. Then the cat would come and sit on the windowsill over the sink and lookout too. Probably she was watching for a moving meal, though it was pleasant to believe it was my company that put her there.

The time had come to leave Hoolit and Scotland. My sadness was tempered with the promise of winter accommodation in the deserted hill shieling after Christmas. I was lucky for in the meantime I was moving to beautiful lodgings in Essex until I could find a permanent home of my own. I returned to the south to find another slow autumn awaiting me with trees still well foliaged and roses all abloom. Already I had forgotten that winter comes later here. Field maples flamed the hedgerows, each dainty leaf delicately lobed on its pink stem. There was a small private wood near my lodgings where I often walked. Each time the wind blew, the trees seemed to gather in groups, tall tops bowing confidentially together as if conversing. In sunshine their leaves made fleeting shadows patterning the year's ripe seed heads – foxgloves, campions, bluebells, primrose and catching the bramble leaves changing colour far below. Crab apples lay in golden heaps in many a ditch, each channel full of water for there had been heavy rains. A slow river that wound through the large garden had overflowed its banks and a mute swan family sometimes glided by taking advantage of the flooded lawns to spend several nights on the submerged grass.

Badgers were more frequently seen than in the Lothians, but were not plentiful. Earlier that year members of the local badger group had surprised two men one Sunday morning, digging into an occupied sett. The police were alerted and the offenders caught; one of their dogs had gone to ground. A case was brought against the terrier-men, but had been adjourned until the New Year. I enjoyed the tawnies that called around my new lodgings. There were barn owls and little owls as well as roe and muntjac deer in the area too. Though I missed the hills especially Dydor, this countryside had its own particular beauty and the view from my room was one of sheep on green fields stretching up to the skyline with a farmhouse on the horizon, the only dwelling. Even on a dull day the acacia's yellowy foliage amid the varied greens of the stately trees in nearly two hectares of garden, were wonderfully accentuated by a dark, grey sky while perfect pink roses scrambled over the old stone wall. Rabbits, stoats and weasels were present and a hunting fox often passed through at dawn and dusk.

Autumn was nearly gone and winter not far behind. The wood was alive with the fey pattering of a multitude of feet as deep frosts forced the last lingering leaves to abandon their hosts in gentle drifts. So many and so varied, revealing high up in the bare branches the rooks' twiggy nests and lower, the neater structures of tit, wren and robin. The rustling wood sighed at each faint breath of wind, grieving for its leafy beauty lying earthbound far below. Now the chill nights stiffened the short-cropped grass and the sheep moved into the lea of the farm and its buildings away from the worst of the frost. The kingfisher that haunted this stretch of river became increasingly bold. I could stand on the wooden bridge to watch him leave an ash tree's overhang and dart, an iridescent blue-green flash, under the planking to catch a fish. Certainly this jewel of a bird wasn't nervous of human company. The garden's owner and I were clearing the lawn of debris left by the retreating flood. Logs, driftwood and small trees together with slime-covered weed and rushes lay in long muddy heaps on the saturated grass revealing the high-water mark. These we loaded onto wheelbarrows and pushed to the fire site below the stables. We made many such journeys before the lawn took on its normal look but it was well worth the effort. Now came the trees. The nearest were willow, larch, birch and conifer; the foliage of this last was ground-hugging and fouled by the evil-smelling debris. The rake wouldn't go far enough beneath and in any case, so entangled was the tree by its sodden grave clothes that I feared I might tear the branches more if I was not very careful. Gently the silt-encrusted rushes were untangled from trunk and branches and lifted, still oozing into the barrow. The muddied green foliage rose slowly, relieved of its crippling burden. It is curious how trees have a vulnerability. None of them now in this garden were really old for the Great Storm of 1987 had seen to that, but the trees here were loved and cared for, each having space, air and light to grow freely, unlike many woodland species so they had taken on their natural, undistorted shapes. It seems right too that trees should be revered; many here would in their normal life span, far outlive any man. I felt I was privileged to help repair the ravages of the flood water. In a sense, I was repaying in very small

measure, the great pleasure I had from looking at them. Some people put
animals before their own kind, something I would not do, but I could think
of some humans, I would happily put such trees before! While we worked by
the river in the dappled sunlight, the kingfisher ignored us as he flew to the
willow's lower boughs and darted down for a fish. This he returned with to
his perch, deftly turned and swallowed it head first, then sat preening there.
He – or – she had no cause to fear in this garden.

Christmas I spent with Karen before journeying on to the Scottish shieling.
It was a pleasure to walk the Wrinkly (as I had long ago christened poor
Harriet), although the Yorkshire days and nights were laden with heavy
fog. Frost glittered mica-like on wall, copings and pavement as we went
by to the local woods. Continutal frost on frost would have made the
going treacherous, but for the ice-chains I wore over my shoes. These at
first intrigued the dog whose one aim in life was to play with everything.
The riveted chains set in their rubber surround, stretched over the soles, are
immensely useful in icy conditions and were going to Scotland with me. We
found no sun in the sky and no birds singing, even the rabbits were tucked
away in their burrows. The hoar-laden gorse looked like snow. Nonetheless
we enjoyed ourselves under the trees' bare canopy where a magic, mystic
wonderland reigned supreme.

CHAPTER ELEVEN

Snow at the Shieling

The fog never lifted as the train to Scotland moved slowly through the thick wet blanket on its journey north. It was good to see the Robertsons again and catch up on their news, before the leisurely ride into the hills to meet their furthest neighbours Robbie and Eileen. Robbie driving me up to the shieling that first afternoon was an education in itself. It was perhaps excusable that I put his erratic progress down to drink for in two days it was New Year's Eve after all and by now I had some experience of the Scottish tradition of hogmanay which like the English Christmas seems to cover best part of a week. No, this was Robbie's normal driving and at least he managed to avoid the outcrops of rock – usually – and there were no other vehicles on the hills. I was yet to experience his navigation amongst traffic. The view from the seat of the big wheeled Argocat was exhilarating, rekindling past memories of the place; my only sorrow was that I couldn't see the further view of Dydor. I had left South Yorkshire in mist which seemed to have followed me, so visibility was poor. From each dead seed head of grass and evergreen leaf on the stubby heather hung a tiny bauble of water. A grouse flew up abruptly at our passing, the movement making me start as his chattering complaint exploded almost beneath the 'cat. There was no track as such from the steading to the shieling, just old impressions of a vehicle's progress in the grass for the 5 km. Stone walls loomed up suddenly; we had reached the place that was to be my new home for the next few months.

It was agreed I should walk down to the steading the next morning and Robbie and his wife would take me shopping in the village. When he had gone, there came the moment I had been waiting for – time to explore before it got really dark. This was a one-roomed dwelling, the old sod roof replaced with tiles some time in the last century; its southern end had a woodshed built into the steep sloping hillside. There were deeply recessed windows on its three other sides. Apart from the door by which we had entered, there was another leading to the lean-to shed and this housed (in its darkest corner) a privy behind a low wall. The woodshed contained everything I might need during that winter (and some that I didn't!) wood, coal, hay bales and various implements including spades, shovels and two shepherd's crooks. The lean-to continued all round the shieling's southern side turning smartly at the corner and a few metres west. Its outside door hung from broken hinges and just beyond in a dip ran the burn, my source of water.

The shieling's rough walls were nearly a metre thick and on the woodshed side stood a little black stove with a fire thoughtfully lit and burning merrily. Nearby were a wooden chair and scrub-topped table and in the corner, two wooden pallets set side by side on which I laid my sleeping bag and pillow. I had brought a store of candles and three small butane canisters for my wick burner. The last-named was a luxury for when I should be writing; a candle would suffice for this evening with the added light of the open stove door. With its four uncurtained windows it was never truly dark inside my new home and most of the candles remained unused. That evening I made do with the remains of my sandwiches and hot tea from a flask. The stove could be kept burning low all night and whenever I was out. I had only to come in, however wet or cold that winter, and open its creaky black door. That evening I lay in the sleeping bag very content. What would tomorrow bring?

The mist was still on the hills as I set out the next morning, retracing our route of the previous day. Except for an occasional call of grouse or crow, all was silent in the enveloping grey. I reached the first drystane dyke enclosing the flock that had been brought down from the hills weeks earlier out of the worst of the weather. They would remain here till lambing was over in late spring before going back to their summer pastures on the heather-clad slopes. Shopping for Robbie and Eileen was a leisurely affair as well as a day for visiting relatives. Once my provisions were loaded we parted for a few hours, I to walk along the river bank, Eileen to take tea with her sister and Robbie for something stronger in the village pub. Most of these fields were autumn-sown, but where one had been freshly ploughed, lapwings and gulls were feeding in the fresh earth. Gulls are notorious thieves; a peewit was being harassed by one and abandoned its find to the more aggressive scavenger. The sun stole from behind a cloud as a dipper gave its sweet warbling song from a stone midstream and the Cley's clear waters sparkled and tumbled in its radiance. As from nowhere swarming insects danced beneath the beeches' bare brances and I wondered if the woodpeckers would nest here again in the New Year. Before returning I checked the Mound and found it empty except for rabbits on its lower clinker slopes.

Once at the farm we transferred my shopping to the 'cat and so back to the shieling in glorious sunshine. For the first time I had a good view of my new home and Craiglee at its back – blue skies with Lytlaw and Dydor in the distance, the former still white-peaked from earlier snow. That afternoon the urge to explore took precedence over what should have been a badly needed cleaning of the 'wee hoose' – after all, that could be left for a bad weather day. Camera in hand I resolved to cross the burn in search of otter signs. It was scrambling on the rocks midstream that I slipped and fell, smashing the camera; not an expensive one, but damaged now beyond repair. In unsuccessfully trying to save it, I took the worst of the fall on my left arm and wrist. A stupid thing to do I told myself furiously (if only I had worn the ice chains) and returned home to get dry.

There was sleet the next morning with the midday sun like a leprous moon in the grey sky. From elbow to wrist my left arm was bruised and black, but as I could move the fingers, hopefully nothing was broken. I would rest it as much as possible for the next few days. Whoever had used the shieling in the past had certainly seen its potential. On the north-facing side in the far corner opposite the sheep pen, was a larder set into the wall. Not only was it spacious but I imagine even in summer would have been the coldest place. In spite of the earlier sleet, the next few days were spring-like and sunny and the nights mild. The view from the top of Craiglee was breathtaking. The shieling scarcely showed from this distance, its mossy tiles blending with the green heather and its stone walls part of the rock-strewn landscape. No other dwellings protruded onto this vista of hills, burn and moor, not even the steading far beneath the steep slopes to my left. Except for the birds I was completely alone and the feeling was great!

My purpose in coming to this place was to hopefully study otter(s) in a bad winter. I had taken the chance of finding Dratsie here as in the summer, but if she didn't materalize I would spend most of the time travelling down to Cudoun's main feeding places. Once off Craiglee, it was a matter of checking for any otter signs and I made a start that day by looking over the Five Springs area. There were indeed, spraints aplenty though none very fresh. By the time I returned tired, hungry but well pleased with my day it was nearly 4 p.m. The setting sun had dropped below the hills leaving a palette of red, green and indigo seeping through the sky. It bathed the landscape in a ruddy glow turning the rough grey walls of my home to the softest pink.

Everything took twice as long one-armed, but really that scarcely mattered. Time was of no consequence with only myself to care for. Already I had become used to going indoors via the old woodshed door partly because one didn't need to open it to enter and partly to collect the bucket of coal filled in the morning to replenish the stove. Bending to grasp its handle with my good hand I stopped, puzzled. Something was different – but what? Straightening up and a careful look round revealed only the usual wood stack and coal, the usual untidiness of a shed given over to odds and ends and things that might come in handy. There was an unaccountable yet strangely familiar smell, though it was subdued by the stronger ones of hay, fuel and old possessions left to the ravages of time. That evening I sat by my little open fire, its rosy light dancing on the table's old legs and patterning the low ceiling. I thought I heard a noise of something dropping coming from the woodshed behind the wall and immediately thought of the odd smell. I knew from recent experience that once through the door and round the corner, the woodshed would be in pitch blackness, so I dipped a candle onto a burning coal to light it and took it in my good hand to investigate. It really wasn't a great help for finding what I imagined was a rat for my candle was a tiny tongue of flame that kept the shadows perpetually shifting and stirring. Twice I heard a movement and directed the little streaming flame in its direction, but nothing was there. I turned with the thought that I was wasting a valuable candle. If rats were present I had best protect my food in the larder. Tomorrow I would do so and search for the rats too. As I turned, the mystery smell assailed me strong and clear and was a mystery no more. That distinctive but indescribable smell of otter. Had Dratsie or Cudoun even, found me? The remainder of that evening and night were a disappointment for I heard and smelled no more. That did not matter however, the main thing was to avoid investigating again for fear of disturbing my visitor. The thought that I hadn't a rat problem after all was a relief. What had the loch fisherman said about otters? In the north where they are common, they may lie up in sheds and outhouses. Could the woodshed be Dratsie's winter holt? It was a possibility. When I filled the bucket that morning, the first thing I noticed were otter seals in the coal dust! With elation I brought the bucket in with me so not to use the shed more than strictly necessary.

I didn't actually see the owner of the spore until two days later on my return from searching the burn almost down to the steading and back. Something came bounding towards the water at my approach and entered it even as I whistled. A sleek, shining head broke the surface and a bewhiskered muzzle turned my way – Dratsie indeed. She seemed content to stay where she was and watch me, so I continued indoors – the front way this time, leaving her to her own devices. That evening the sounds of a busy otter on the far side of my wall made me smile in spite of the pain from my left wrist and fingers that had begun to swell. I had never actually met Robbie and Eileen before my arrival at the shieling and wasn't due to meet them again until next Wednesday for the weekly shopping. Now was the weekend and I hesitated to bother strangers. Best put the arm in a sling and leave matters till then.

That weekend deteriorated armwise, but was hugely enlivened by Dratsie's insatiable curiosity. I was in my sleeping bag dozing between bouts of pain some time after midnight on Sunday when instinct told me I was not alone. The stove was dampened down for the night, but something was sitting in front of its closed door busily washing itself. Since I lay almost at floor level she took up most of my vision. First she cleaned her neat white front and then her flanks, nibbling into the fur occasionally and finishing with a vigorous shake that settled her fur leaving it even and tidy. Now she began to investigate the floor. I had eaten toast and honey for supper and a piece must have dropped. The otter's whiskers quivered as their owner checked its credentials, then wolfed it down. In doing so, she knocked over my toasting fork with a great clatter that sent her fleeing back to the woodshed. (The fork had come with me; I had an open fire at home and found it invaluable.) Whiskers preceded their owner as she checked the ensuing quiet. Yes, all was well for a safe return. She sniffed the offending fork and putting a paw on its long brass handle to hold it down more firmly, licked the three prongs thoroughly. However, her whiskers may have touched the warm metal stove, for she stopped and looked at it hard, the dog-like nose quivering before backing a little away. My stay was probably the first occasion she had found it to have heat.

The shieling had never been used in winter and these days, only occasionally in the summer and early autumn after the Glorious Twelfth for the grouse shoot. Perhaps I would ask Robbie about it some time. I had read that otters live solely on fish (including eels) with infrequently, small mammals, amphibians and birds according to availability, but did not eat carrion. Inland otters moved to coastal areas where possible when burns and lochs froze. Many that could not, died from starvation. I suspected otters did eat carrion rather than starve if it was there and Dratsie's liking for toast and honey (however small the amounts), suggested she wasn't too fussy. I longed for a hard, snow-bound period to find out more; last winter had been too mild. This was the main reason for my stay in the shieling, though the solitude and beauty of the hills was a strong inducement too.

It was a mild and blustery Wednesday that I left Robbie and Eileen with their respective friends whilst I continued on to Casualty. It had been difficult to persuade them not to take me, but I found the farmer's driving hair-raising enough along the lanes where traffic was minimal, but to the city . . . oh no! To my surprise, the wrist was merely badly sprained and the bone chipped; it was the arm itself that was broken in two places. This was duly set and plastered and I was kept in the infirmary overnight. Being in a large ward full of other patients, I found far more traumatic than a mere broken arm – which shows how ungrateful I must have appeared to the really kind hospital staff. It was with enormous relief that I met Robbie at his favourite pub the next day and returned to my home under the hill.

Dratsie had made good use of my absence, coming and going from the woodshed to the shieling through a large rotten portion at the bottom of the communicating door. If it had a hole before I left, it certainly had a much larger one now. She seemed to have brought in many wisps of hay but whether this was accidental, i.e. caught up in her fur, or deliberate, was difficult to judge. The sound of the 'cat's engine had scarcely died away before the otter herself put in an appearance. Acting on the theory that if she came into my house I should be able to go into hers, I walked into the woodshed on the pretence of shovelling up coal and looked around. There were several hay bales stacked against the walls, but Dratsie, wise creature, had chosen those directly behind my stove in which to dig out a holt. Much later I discovered she had made two entrances to this home – the other emerged further along between the wall itself and some planks and a ladder leaning against it. I respected her privacy and tried to leave her to it though continuing to use the shed as quietly as possible. It was clear she had investigated my 'holt' however, to her heart's content in my absence and in future I must put anything breakable – or dangerous to her – out of harm's way. An unopened tin of baked beans had been rolled about the floor and wedged in a corner of the sheep pen. The tin that held my half-used loaf lay unended and empty. I never did find the loaf so concluded it eaten – more scientific data blasted! That evening as with many more to come, I didn't bother with a candle but sat with the stove door wide open and worked by the light of its fiery heart. The wind was rising outside and rain beat loud on the windows. It was good to have a snug, warm home in such weather; a far, far cry from the previous night in the infirmary ward.

Hours later the wind strengthened to gale force and I woke to a surprising lightness though it was long before dawn. A blizzard was raging outside my snug retreat causing snow to build up on the north and west windows, leaving those facing east and my front door clear. My only regret was the broken camera, but never mind, I had been granted my desire for snow. There was everything necessary inside the shieling and if the burn froze denying me water, well I had melted snow before, two winters ago in Kent.

By mid-afternoon the snow ceased and I went in search of the burn. This was a raw, bone-biting, windy day and very cold. It was essential to keep one's bearings. Since my home had virtually disappeared in the drifts, the one stable marker was Craiglee towering to the south. I had left from the shieling's east side and needed to walk round to the west to find water, if the burn was still running. With one arm in plaster and the other clutching the pail, I must have made a comic picture as I tried to avoid the drifts in a strange white world. How beautiful it was, this unblemished blanket smothering all in its white embrace. The grey sky had a flicker of pink from the dying sun in the west and the freezing wind sent tiny particles of ice to sear my face. I had almost given the burn up when suddenly I was in it! Only a trickle now with most of the once rushing water concealed under ice and snow. With the plastic cup I had brought, the pail was slowly filled. This would probably be the last time for some days that I would come here; soon even this dribble would be stilled. In the dip of the burn where I was sheltered and away from the wind there could be heard the soft tinkling of water under the ice. Returning was easy as I had only to walk in my tracks already created, but halfway I met someone making use of them too. Lithe and brown she was humping along and with scarcely a pause to allow me to stand aside, she hurried over my boots and disappeared, her thick rudder floundering after. The snow each side made towering banks to little Dratsie, though no more than knee-deep to me. If I had been able to use both hands, I would happily have dug her a better path, but that being impossible, she would have to make do with my tracks.

The full moon was beautiful over the frozen landscape that night, its radiance touching all with a glittering sheen. Then a wind sent snow clouds to cover its face till a blizzard screamed outside. It was wonderful within my four walls, so very light and warm. Something came in uninvited that evening and continued to do so throughout much of my stay. She must have been hungry I reasoned and I opened a tin of stewing steak, putting a small amount in a dish. I couldn't chance wasting it if she wasn't interested for there was no way of knowing how long we would be snowbound. I noticed with a wry smile that already my thinking was in the plural! She merely moved the meat about, spilling some onto the floor and went to look at the open door of the stove. A little tongue of flame flickered round the largest coal, licking and caressing as it consumed. Dratsie settled down in front with myself in the chair nearby. The fire's heat sang a soft song in its orange, glowing depths as the wind wandered in the chimney sometimes bursting the glow into a thousand minute sparks. Slowly the big coal was eaten, lighter cracks appeared in its base from which tiny flames spurted in twos and threes. They reached up into the deep, black carbon of millennium's dead forests and lovingly twined themselves around. Their light reflected into our faces, its leapings sometimes bright and sometimes low. Around the walls my crouching shape and the otter's dark head seemed forever moving to the singing flames of the demi-furnace.

Out on the hills the blizzard raged for a further three days and nights. When I was able to walk down again to the steading ten days later, Robbie told me the wind had at times exceeded 100 mph, but without a radio I had no way of knowing at the time – certainly, it had been impossible to stand up in safety for fear of being blown off my feet. There was no danger of damage to the shieling; that had stood for centuries and would do so for more. Often the wind blew straight over Craiglee and down into the valley, missing my home that it had half buried in drifts. Its voice changed from bloodcurdling banshee wailing, to long-drawn laments of unutterable loss or the sullen roar of some atavistic beast. In a distant age when omens and ghosts were beyond denying, I wondered what man attributed to the wind? Once in a while the voice would be stilled and in the gaunt silences the world held its breath. The snow still fell, great fluffy flake upon flake and all was hueless and lacking identity – no points of the compass, no colour, no beginning nor end. Only eternity shrouded in white.

Dratsie came and went to the burn now completely frozen beneath the thick snow. From there she travelled down the hillside protected from the worst of the blizzard. I knew she was finding food and it was not fish. Not only were they no longer available, but her spraints gave her secret away; they hadn't that smell nor tar-like appearance indicative of fresh fish. Watching her of an evening I noticed that however wet her coat might be on her return through the snow, when she came to sit by the stove (by now her favourite grooming spot), as she parted the long, wet guard hairs, the dense, short undercoat was still dry and soft. Neither did she ever give the appearance of being cold – her love of the stove was purely 'I am on to a good thing here' – certainly not necessity. One evening when she had successfully ousted me from its direct warmth, I shivered involuntarily and unthinking, extended my right hand past her to its warmth. She turned regarding me quizzically with those small, dark eyes (so like that other member of the musteline family, the badger, in some ways), then sniffed my hand. That action decided me not to consider her too carefully in future. If I was cold I merely came to warm myself at the stove whether she was there or no.

I never knew her to move right away, so concluded she had accepted my presence as a condition of its comfort. As I came to know her well, other badger attributes revealed themselves in curious ways. Brock's love of taking sticks down into the sett seemed an act also beloved of Dratsie for her holt. When the snow eventually melted, she brought several of these from the steading area one at a time. They were neither heavy nor large, but it was after all a distance of some 4¹/2 km from the nearest trees in the shelter belt to the woodshed. In they would be taken, sometimes to be stuck in the tunnel before she seized an end and successfully retreated into her sanctuary, deep inside the hay.

Water was no problem, though a large bucket of melted snow makes only a few cupfuls. Never mind, snow was clean and plentiful and I had the wherewithal to make it liquid. (My problem in Kent had been lack of heat, not just water.) When the wind eased on that third day I ventured out and picked up my old trail (kept open by a resourceful otter) as far as the burn. In the distance, the pure white hump of Dydor beckoned, deceptively close. The rawness of the air took my breath away. The full force of the gale was gone, but a message was borne on the cold wind, one that I knew well from winters past. From its faintest stirrings the calls came nearer and louder. A great exultation surged within me as a formation of pink-feet cleared Craiglee's rugged summit; surely these are the most musical and thrilling of geese. They were low in the air as I stood on the steep slope, so low that individual voices came to me clear. Their V-formation ebbed and flowed, sometimes one bird taking the lead, then briefly in a straight line before another headed away with the rest trailing after across the grey sky. Now the dark heads and pale bodies blended to specks, their constant calls a distant murmur tossed by the wind. Like a wonderful dream on waking, I was left with an aching sense of loss, earthbound on that white moor.

The blizzards returned and intensified, but whenever I could I struggled out as far as the burn. Unlike myself, Dratsie left the shieling by way of the woodshed, linking up with our combined path to the west. She had dug and burrowed beneath the deep drift from the broken door that side; no mean feat since the piled snow reached the roof. Her excursions were not geared to night or day, but were rather like mine – whenever the gale eased. Dearly would I have loved to follow and trace her source of food, but the physical effort of moving through deep snow, of fighting the wind and being one-armed made this unwise, at least until the winds eased. As she groomed by the open stove after one such foray, Dratsie reached up to my face as I knelt there repairing a tear in my anorak; from her mouth came the faint but unmistakable halitosis of blood. What *was* that otter eating?

Dratsie's insatiable curiosity gave me some headaches since apart from the larder, the shieling had no cupboards or drawers. Clothes I had to keep in my two suitcases and everything else, in cardboard boxes. The otter loved boxes in which to explore. Nothing was overlooked and everything had to be thoroughly examined . . . and tested, generally with her teeth. An empty box or one with a few expendables especially for her wasn't nearly as interesting. Ones with my papers, crockery or anything else, however, were fascinating. Grooming over, she would go in search of something to do. There were small boxes that she could lean in and sort their contents and really large ones that had to be swarmed up and dropped into. Otters are poorly equipped to jump, but Dratsie excelled at swarming. She would reach up, scrabble furiously with her hind feet, and tail waving, disappear from my view. Once she did this with a near-empty one which promptly fell on top of her, but details such as this do not deter an enterprising otter, far from it; they seemed to spur her on to greater feats. Once inside a tall box, there would come sounds of pounding. Sometimes she would chatter and whicker almost talking to herself and again I would be reminded of badger vocalization; some sounds are similar. Several times so energetic were her 'in-house' activities that the box unfolded outwards and lay flat with its contents around her, still busy trying to open an object of interest with her teeth. Again like the badger, an otter's jaw and its bite are very strong, easily denting metal. Her thick, heavy rudder interested me; it left a wide, clear trail in dust or snow. True the shieling wasn't spotlessly clean to start with, but Dratsie had a knack of producing chaos out of relative order. I suspect too, that even had I had the necessary drawers and cupboards, she would still have found ways of forcing their secrets out. The larder was too high for her to reach, though certainly she was aware it held edibles and would stand on hind legs beneath its door, her whiskers twitching and her nose aquiver. I wondered if her Shetland name meant anything – after all, Cudoun literally means burn dog. If it didn't perhaps the Shetlanders had experienced an otter's curiosity in their homes. The old cast-iron saucepan that stood on the stove bubbling with stew was of no interest until empty, clean and put away. It was very large and exceedingly heavy and the otter loved nothing better than scrambling inside, curling round and going to sleep! Why it should hold such attraction is difficult to say since metal is cold to the touch.

   The snow and gales continued for a week, but on the eighth day the snow briefly turned to rain. Immediately it seemed, the high carpet of white was reduced some centimetres, only to freeze again as it returned to snow. In the rain however, I followed Dratsie's trail along the still hidden line of the burn. Here was a slope made shiny with use where she slid down to the lower level and a disturbed area at its side showing the upward scramble of her return. At its top was a sprainting site with her paw marks already blurred by the wet. She had cut across the fields at the tree edge where sheltered from the blizzard's worst efforts, the otter had dug out a sheep's carcase. Earlier frosts may well have frozen it, but beneath the snow's blanket it was far from rock hard. She had torn into the underbelly and exposed the ribs, and I was afraid that like this, crows would find her source of food. If I could loan a rope from Robbie surely I might drag it back to the woodshed where it would be safe at least from avian scavengers.

The farmer and his wife would have none of it however, Eileen exclaiming that her man would take it up! I was so fussed over that I felt sheepish myself; one would have thought I had crossed Antarctica on foot rather than walked down the hillside. I was sat at the table and an enormous plate of dinner put before me. The regional news was shown on their television so for the first time I saw central Scotland's traffic battling and abandoned in snowdrifts as the police begged motorists not to venture out. There were pictures too of the oil tanker *Braer* off the Shetlands, aground in the Minch. More snow was predicted with even stronger gales; by now I was anxious to return. At the door Eileen hugged me and I warmed to her kindness, sensing she was not normally demonstrative. As Robbie went in front dragging the carcase I appreciated that never could I have done so myself. Already the snow had returned, the rising wind twisting that lying into grotesque shapes. Eddies funnelled the falling flakes into whirlwinds that spun madly round in a frenzied dance. At the shieling door we parted – Robbie would need to get back before the blizzard set in. I dragged the sheep through to the very end of the woodshed and the start of Dratsie's snow tunnel. Scarcely had I finished before she appeared from the hay holt, pulled at the body and gnawed a protruding rib. I was glad to leave her to it whilst I took off my wet clothes. Altogether it had been a good day.

One morning I was cracking eggs to make an omelette when I wondered what Dratsie would make of one still in its shell. She carried it carefully off to her holt so I didn't see her eat it, but it was obvious from her efforts to reach up to the pan on her return, that she knew all about eggs and enjoyed them! I always shared my drinking water with her. Melted snow has a smell rather like that of wet carpet but is pleasant enough to drink. There was also an excellent supply of skimmed milk in cartons which, understandably, my friendly otter preferred. Once when she obviously wanted milk and I plonked down water instead, she grasped the bowl in her powerful jaws and turned it upside down with a resounding clunk. I got the message loud and clear.

Now came an unbelievable day when the snow ceased and the still strong wind drove the grey clouds away revealing a pale, wan sun. I left the shieling to flounder through the deep snow, eventually reaching the summit of Craiglee. The effort had made me sweat so I took off my wax jacket and sat on it in the snow whilst I got back my breath. My arm scarcely bothered me now though I found the plaster heavy and cumbersome. The view was sublime with the sun low in a now blue sky and nothing but white hills continuing on to eternity whichever way I turned. Something came humping along my track. I might have known it – an otter called Dratsie. I was beginning to shiver in the raw wind, so put on the jacket again as my companion began purposefully digging nearby. Her big webbed front paws might not have claws as long as those of a badger, but she made good progress nonetheless, shovelling the snow under her body, kicking it backwards with powerful movements of her hind legs. The side of a rock came into view as she jumped down into the hole and continued. Now she was tugging at something her efforts had uncovered. It was large and feathered – a pink-footed goose. My thoughts returned to the flock and their musical progress as they cleared Craiglee in the wind. It is easy to think of these beautiful birds in flight as ethereal, but they too are mortal like us. The otter's sense of smell must have been superb; she had dug down almost a metre. Whoever wrote that otters don't take carrion should have seen Dratsie with her goose. A welcome change from mutton I suppose. I stood awhile watching her, then decided it was time to return. The sun was gone from the lonely sky and the wind blew flurries of snow into our faces. I picked up the goose by one wing as an indignant otter huffed and growled showing her teeth. Determined not to leave it to another predator, I insisted on taking it back. Having shown her mettle she persisted no more, seeming to accept that it was coming back with us. A well-grown goose is a fair weight to carry. Once I slipped and still clasping it, slid past her whereupon she came scampering after in agitation – not at my falling I might add, but at her dinner disappearing round the steep corner made by our outgoing tracks. Thus the goose ended up with the ewe. Find a cow I told her and we'll open a butcher's, but Dratsie was too preoccupied with her latest acquisition to heed.

Her curiosity made me realize how easy it is for otters to become trapped and drown in fyke nets. Fishermen use these long, tubular nets to catch eels and I would imagine that even with no eel caught in its bag or cod end to entice it, an inquisitive otter would still investigate one. Fyke nets are about two metres long or more with a hoop holding open the mouth of the net and other hoops inside the body. Each hoop supports a cone-shaped funnel ensuring that whilst entry is easy, the exit takes too long to accomplish for otters before drowning occurs. These freshwater traps with their multiple wide-entranced funnels are particularly popular in East Anglia where I now live and where otters have been reintroduced successfully. The ratio of males and female otters drowned in fykes nationally seems equal, together with family parties of bitch and young where the cubs have followed their mother. The problem of otters drowning in fyke nets is not a difficult one to solve. I wrote in December 1991 to Don Jefferies of the Joint Nature Conservation Committee who, with his colleagues, worked on producing a guard that allowed eels to pass through the entrance, but not the larger otter. He answered: 'The Vincent Wildlife Trust have now made stainless steel guards . . . which are now issued free with fyke net licences. Some, but not all, authorities have byelaws insisting on their use, but not unfortunately the Anglian as yet.' (East Anglia is one of the major eel-fishing areas of Britain.)

I saw and photographed lobster creels on Grampian's coast and these too were the focus of experiments to make them otter safe. Don Jefferies wrote of these; 'I feel that the best approach is either the flattened oval entrance or indeed, doubling the entrance size. It may need research to show such creels will still provide "reasonable" catches of lobsters before any commercial people will make and sell them.' Bitches and cubs rather than males tend to get trapped in creels since adult dog otters are larger and the traps' 12 cm diameter round entrances are too narrow to permit them to pass through.

I often saw red grouse round the shieling. The barred red-brown bodies were a welcome sight against the all white background and their white leg feathers extended to the feet leaving only the toenails bare. Dratsie's body colour showed up well too and the birds were well aware of her interest. The worst of the gales were over, allowing for deep, frosty nights. One morning I walked down to the steading and was given a lift to the Robertsons' farm. Whilst the men went inside for a blether, I wandered off to examine the Burn Sett and found, by the beautifully clear badger spore around its entrances, that the occupants had been out and about. The shelter belt around the sett seemed in a haze not unlike fog at a glance. Each frail twig and branch clothed in white gave force to this illusion. Even the sitkas' bright green was now subdued, covered in the all-embracing hoar. Strange to find the burn quite silent. The ice chains on my boots allowed me a safe crossing on the glassy rocks and frozen water. Above the pool hung a petrified waterfall. Neither bird, beast nor man broke the silence as if time stood still waiting for some magic word. A shaft of sun touched the rocks near me, the weak light unable to unlock the iron frost. One or two trees at the shelter belt edge had been snapped, but that seemed to be the extent of the damage caused by the continuous storm-force winds. At the loch, the wind had turned its rippling surface to ice. I was watching a dejected greylag trying to stand upright on its glassy face when Sandy and Robbie appeared. They had driven up in the van to find me; typically, I had forgotten the time. Majestic Dydor seemed taller in white; for once the broad, smooth hump seemed to stand rather than crouch. Will had seen three badgers I was told, one early evening by his cottage. No one had seen Cudoun, but then none of the Robertsons ever had and if Dratsie could get by on carrion, especially sheep, I was confident that her mate would do so too.

The thaw set in a few days later when it began to rain. Slowly the tops of heather and rocks showed more and more as the white shroud shrunk and dwindled and soon everything had that flattened, drab look typical of vegetation released from snow. Now the burn began to sing, to shout and then to roar and the continuing rain uplifted all growing things in its path and our once freezing white world, became mild and balmy. Only the swollen burns told of the snow that had been. These rushing torrents were not only dangerous to humans, but to otters as well. They moved overland now rather than battle in the murderous waters and found fish in the shallows and quieter pools. On several nights I returned to the Burn Badgers and twice saw Cudoun catch fish. He left a neat pike skeleton on the loch bank – head, spine and tail all attached with many fish scales in the surrounding grass. I had forgotten how large the dog otter was. Dratsie's slim body was growing heavier which at first I had put down to the good

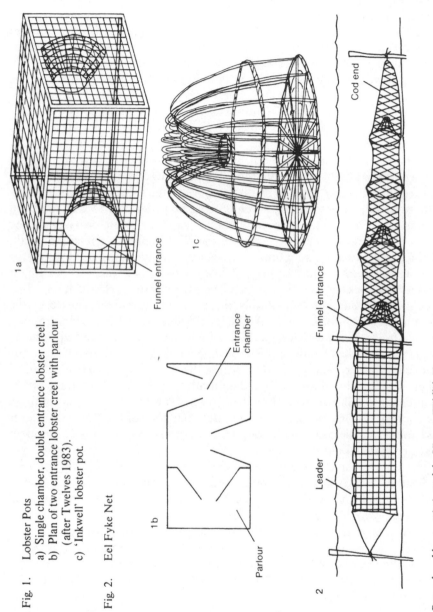

Fig. 1.　Lobster Pots
a) Single chamber, double entrance lobster creel.
b) Plan of two entrance lobster creel with parlour
　　(after Twelves 1983).
c) 'Inkwell' lobster pot.

Fig. 2.　Eel Fyke Net

1a

1c

Funnel entrance

1b

Entrance
chamber

Parlour

2

Leader

Funnel entrance

Cod end

The four fyke net otter guards and the Line device tested for fishing efficiency (all dimensions in mm).

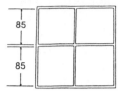

a. Square guard (rigid).

b. Ring guard (rigid).

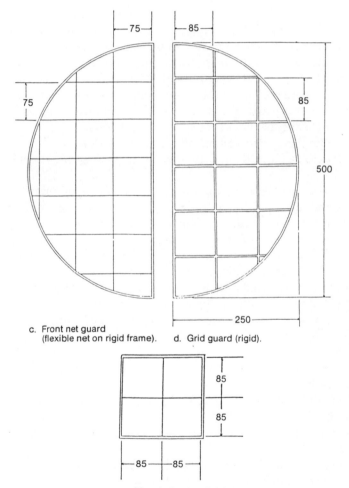

c. Front net guard
   (flexible net on rigid frame).   d. Grid guard (rigid).

e. Line device (semi-rigid line on rigid frame).

life, but could it be that she was in cub? The bitch was coming in to the shieling less frequently, preferring to keep to her holt in the woodshed behind the stove.

We were well into February now and a lovely mild period. The primroses sheltered at the burnside were all in bud and near the village the hazel catkins would soon be opening in showers of golden pollen. Will Robertson left a message for me at the steading. The shepherd had found a badger wandering in daylight round Hoolit cottage; it seemed dazed and lacked co-ordination. Between them the brothers got it to a vet who believed it to be concussed. He would take X-rays and keep it for a few days. By the time I met up with Will, the vet had already contacted him with the results. The sow was badly bruised but had no bones broken and may have been hit by a vehicle. She was very traumatized however, and needed somewhere quiet where she could recover before being returned to the sett. Housed at the surgery with dogs and cats was not the best environment for a badger. Would I have her at the shieling, the shepherd asked? Will was convinced that she had returned to where she had known me when I lived at Hoolit, but though a pleasant thought, I personally doubted this. Something the vet said made me think it was Millie; he was sure the sow was pregnant. Will drove me back to the steading and I left Robbie and himself to work out how to convert the sheep pen, as I already had an otter in the woodshed who must not be disturbed.

At least the weather was good for getting the necessary materials via the 'cat up to the shieling. Left to Robbie, planks and netting would have been taken from the woodshed, but Will had far more understanding of wild animals and agreed that Dratsie should be left in peace. Normally I would have been happy to have the convalescent badger; this rehabilitation was something I had been involved with in Kent. Inevitably the men working made a noise and I would be more than sorry if the otter moved away. I had suggested that the sow be housed at the farm, but Will for some reason, perhaps because of the dogs, had not liked the idea. However, my fears were groundless. Possibly Dratsie was away hunting for the few hours of labour that it took them to produce a really first-rate badger 'den' in the further corner of my home. Mugs of tea and biscuits all round whilst Robbie lit his umpteenth cigarette. The farmer was inclined to reminisce the afternoon away, but Will understood my mixed feelings and purposefully steered the other to the door. Quickly I brought hay in from the woodshed filling the den and making sure all was secure. Will would bring the badger up in the morning.

That evening Dratsie herself came investigating, climbing on top of the enclosure and scratching at its door. She was becoming too cumbersome to perform her old trick with the tall boxes. I took pity on her and laid the biggest on its side. However, forbidden fruits are far more inviting than the ones you are given. She merely regarded me with those round, dark eyes and came to sit companionably at the open stove. There was no doubt about it, she was pregnant. An otter's gestation is nine weeks, but I had no way of judging how long she had to go to the birth.

I heard the van long before Will came into view. He was driving slowly and carefully, avoiding the rough places to make the journey less stressful for his passenger in the back. He left the open cage inside the pen. The badger could leave it for her new home when she chose. It was Millie and she looked far from well. Will had also brought up my shopping and a stock of tinned dog food for when the invalid was inclined to eat. It was Dratsie's curiosity that finally caused Millie to move into her new quarters from the carrying cage. I wondered about that peace and quiet the vet had recommended. The dog food I had stacked in a corner got 'the treatment' when the otter pushed her muzzle under the lowest tin and all came thundering to the ground. Even Dratsie seemed a trifle startled at the commotion she had caused. Millie took herself off into the darkness of her den leaving the otter to whicker softly at her retreating back.

These unusually fine, mild days and nights were a welcome foretaste of spring. Fresh young grass, wild arum shoots, bluebell greenery and nettles were pushing through the clinker-based Mound in the shelter belt. Often I would leave the shieling halfway through the night to watch the badgers and linger near the Cley's side to hear the birds at dawn. Much as I loved the moors and hills, I missed the thrushes, blackbirds, robins, wrens, tits and dippers here. A heron might be stalking in the shallows or standing like a sentinel on one stilt, patiently waiting in the early morning light. The waters were still unusually high; Will had mentioned that Perth and Tayside areas had suffered their worst floods ever known. Walking home one morning I spied a snipe perching on a low tree stump on the marsh. I marvelled at that long bill that must have been a third its body length. Every so often it called a persistent 'chip-per, chip-per' as it turned this way and that. Another month and their courtship displays would begin again near the loch and over the moor. How quickly yet reassuringly the seasons fulfill themselves and the cycle continues for another year.

At home Millie's condition improved and at last she was eating, if only very small amounts. Next time we went shopping I rang the vet from the village (Robbie and Eileen had no phone). Although I felt it advisable to keep her until she was eating properly and showing some desire to return to her own, I didn't want her to give birth in the shieling with all the complications that would entail. The vet was a cheery soul who seemed confident that she wouldn't give birth until the spring – only to confound me by asking how long their gestation period was. As it happened, a badger's is only seven weeks after implantation, that is two weeks shorter than an otter's. Privately I didn't share the vet's confidence especially when on mention of Dratsie's condition he seemed to think the 'maternity ward' a great joke. Will and Sandy swore by the man with farm animals; I just hoped he was as accurate with those from the wild. No, the vet concluded, I should keep Millie for at least two to three weeks or until she was eating well and showing an interest in her surroundings.

Millie continued very slowly to improve and our past familiarity with each other helped this I am sure. There was no fear of her biting me when I cleaned her run – she defecated very neatly in one corner – or removed her bowls. The sow, however, seemed to have little desire to leave. Often of an evening she would be out in the run watching me writing by the stove. One night I blocked up the door into the woodshed (in case Dratsie should take an interest) and left the run open. Millie ventured out for perhaps an hour, snuffling around my feet as if we were both by the burn and squatting to scent-mark various objects in her path. One of these happened to be my writing pad; there were tiny drops of yellow musk sinking into its open pages. Gradually this limited freedom seemed to stimulate a desire for more which greatly relieved me. (I had visions of cubs and Millie as permanent fixtures in the place by mid-March.) Will had offered to return her to the sett, but I shied away from another bumpy ride however well intended.

One mild and starry night Millie and I left the shieling. Cats and dogs have a good homing instinct and I had discovered from a Suffolk lady that badgers do too. Millie was (and is) the dominant sow of the only clan for many miles. Whilst I doubt if she had ever had cause to venture this far up a hillside barren of badger interests, she must surely retain an instinct for the direction in which her life-long home lay. In any case I was armed with a large tin of her favourite dog food (and a tin opener) should her sense of direction fail her! I need not have worried. I followed her as a slow yet sure progress was made by the matronly sow back to the home of her birth, where she in turn would bear cubs. There was no hurry. We had all the long hours of darkness to shield us from inquisitive eyes, if there had been any to note our going.

Above the steading she cut across the pasture following the line of shelter belt and drystane dyke. Millie stayed here finding beetles in the sheep droppings and picking out small slugs from amongst the damp rushes. A crescent moon shone over the loch when we finally reached its shores. Here the Scots pines slow moved their dark stately heads and the damp air was pervaded by their deep resinous scent. Far out on the water someone was hunting; his long sinuous shape rose and dived once more. Slowly we followed the margins and disturbed a drake mallard who flew off deeper into the loch. A hare feeding amongst the old dead cones and wiry grass, loped away at our passing. Unexpectedly we came upon C. Goon and after an initial cautious approach, he whickered and musked her. Millie returned the compliment whilst I stood by in relief. There is always that uneasy feeling when you have convalescent badgers that they might not be accepted back. In this case it was unlikely, but could not be guaranteed. However, Millie now had one of the clan's scent upon her and she seemed raring to go! From a stately waddle, she produced a steady trot. She had come a fair distance already, but was on the home stretch. Millie took the route by the steep-sided burn so I left her to follow the easy way to the sett. With my arm only recently out of its plaster, I preferred to keep it that way.

Close to first light, the sky had become overcast, but through the flocculent grey of the heaped clouds, a brilliant star sparkled to welcome the sun. At the sett I remembered the tin and why I carried it, so sat down on the rock and proceeded to open it, tipping the contents by the entrance that I last recalled Millie clearing out. Unfortunately Spike appeared at that moment under the impression that this was his lucky morning which I suppose it was. After the first few mouthfuls he slowed; it would seem he had already eaten well. A big, shaggy form came over the brow of the slope, her mouth still wet from a drink in the burn. Millie stood stock still as her mate approached. Then Spike began to purr low and guttural as she whickered a greeting. I left them, glad and relieved at the same time that all was well. Light was seeping over the fields as I walked through the flock, some still lying, some up and grazing and so to the farm. One of the collies barked and the other joined it as Will came out to see who was there. A mug of hot tea was very welcome; it seemed to have been a long night.

Will was concerned that Millie might not have stayed with me, that she could have run off. 'But where to?' I asked. 'She couldn't have gone up much higher and would have found her way down without my help.' Then I told him of Margaret Grimwade and her experience with a 'homing' sow in Suffolk. Margaret is involved with relocating monitored releases and this particular animal was one of a small group of badgers that had been kept together after being taken into RSPCA care. The group consisted of two sows and two boars and, unlike an earlier release, were not brought up as cubs. Indeed, the sow in question was 'an aged animal' that had bred. Each badger was fitted with a radio collar transmitting a different channel; they had been TB tested and vaccinated against parvo-virus. The release took place like the previous ones with full agreement from the landowner and after consultation with neighbours. The badgers were put into an empty sett in June 1987, fed and contained there in the usual way with electric rabbit netting for some time, after which the netting was removed. This was in an area where there were no other known badgers. By the following January, the sow was found to have moved 18.5 km from the release site. She had enlarged old rabbit holes for herself in the bank of a keeper's pheasant release pen. This was an unfortunate choice of sett, so she was cage-trapped on 8 March 1988, fitted with a new radio collar and relocated to another empty sett to the east and 21.2 km away. Here the same procedure was followed; she was confined there and fed until 3 April when the netting was removed. Within a short time this sow returned to her chosen sett above the release pen.

It should be borne in mind that Suffolk was a county entirely unknown to the badger. In approximately twenty-five hours she travelled 9.5 km but could not move directly back to her favoured site because a large town (with a population of 120,000) and a wide river estuary were in the way. Her radio signals were lost near the town so it is not known for sure whether she eventually travelled all the way round. It is likely however, that a branch railway was her more direct route through it in which case her journey back was one of 23 km.

I think the impression that will remain with me always of life in winter at the shieling was the lack of avian calls, for apart from the grouse and an occasional carrion crow, there is no bird life on the high moors. Rarely, a flock of geese would come sailing over Craiglee on their way to and from feeding grounds, but this event was unusual enough for me to record and only happened three times to my knowledge from December to the end of February. The burn here was too small to be heard unless close by so it was the wind – crying, moaning, roaring, whispering according to mood – that dominated my life. Basically I had everything I needed although if someone had offered me one luxury I would have opted for some sort of outside clothesline, however primitive. Washed garments had to either drip inside or hang from the eves out of doors. There was no tree, bush or post to fix the other end of a line and under the eaves washing trailed against the rough stonework. Hardly a day passed without a wind; my washing would have blown dry in no time, if it didn't blow away! But that was a small criticism of a simple and very happy lifestyle.

Dratsie spent much of her time grooming; scratching vigorously at her chin and face where vestiges of a sticky meal remained, nibbling through her thick coat with her front incisor teeth and licking the fur clean. There could be no doubt now that she was soon to cub; her belly was swollen and tight. I wondered where she was defecating for there were no fresh spraints at her usual sites. Then one morning watching her idly swimming the burn, I saw her defecate in its waters. This surprised me until I considered. Her time was very near. Was this the bitch's way of hiding her presence from unwelcome eyes, especially perhaps, the dog otter's? For two days and nights I didn't see Dratsie even though I could hear her at times moving about in the woodshed holt. Then one morning standing quietly in its dimness, soft twitterings and chirps came to me – she was nursing her cubs!

CHAPTER TWELVE

The Otter and Badger Families

I had agreed to return briefly to England for the trial of the men caught interfering with the sett in an Essex wood almost a year earlier. So far removed from the south now with its badger persecution, my English roots seemed in another world – a lifetime away. It was Will who offered to drive me to the station. For the first time as we waited for the train, the shepherd told me of his love of the hills and something of his work. A few weeks and it would be his busiest time of the year as the new lambs were born. Though he had often watched the Burn Badgers, Will had never seen an otter and would dearly like to do so. I was determined we would remedy that before I finally left Scotland later in the year.

Spring was there before me with daffodils and primroses nodding from the banks and the hedgerows white with blackthorn blossom. All nature bears manifold witness to its Creator, but never more so than in this first season of promise.

The local wildlife police officer, Sgt. Tony Kiff, and I met the Crown Prosecution Service (CPS) solicitor who would be acting for the police and we discussed the forthcoming case before visiting the sett in question. It had been decided to charge the men with 'causing a dog to enter a badger sett' as well as 'damaging a badger sett or any part of it'. The men had run away on being approached by the police and later discovered with their dogs hiding in a barn. When searched at the police station a 'locating' dog collar together with its batteries, was found in the owner's pocket. In court this would tend to confirm the man's statement that his terrier had run off and had not been put deliberately into the sett entrance by him. Alternatively of course, he could have removed it before arrest for this very purpose. Such collars together with the 'bleeper' box that is small enough to fit comfortably in the palm of the hand were invented to trace a dog's progress underground and enable digging down to it successfully if lost. They are also used to trace a dog confronting a badger. As a vet had pronounced the dog's injuries to have been made by a dog, fox or badger, the men could not be charged with 'cruelly ill-treating a badger'. Thus it was highly probable that the only successful charge the CPS could bring was that of damaging the badger sett which had occurred when the owner had attempted to dig down to his terrier. (The dog had found its own way out soon afterwards.) For this charge to be proved however, it would need to be shown that the sett displayed 'signs indicating current use by a badger' at the time of the offence as defined in the Act. From the excellent photos taken a few hours after the incident by the Scenes of Crime Officer and the sett records regularly kept by members of the local badger group, that should not, in theory at least, be a problem. However, we would have to wait and see.

It was a particularly interesting case for me as it was the first I had attended since the 1991 Act protecting the badger's home and its immediate environs. It should be borne in mind that the digger rarely makes holes at sett entrances; the animal is underground somewhere in the labyrinth of tunnelling below his feet or in a sleeping chamber. Thus the crowning-down hole may be at some distance from any entrance. In this instance, a hole had been dug near an entrance, but another much larger, was also made further off. No tunnelling had been exposed because the terrier-men had run off when approached, but the Act allows for this. The men were not being accused of digging for a badger which would have been difficult to prove. Even more these days than in the past, money governs which cases come to court; those brought must have a good chance of a successful outcome. The longer a case continues, the greater the costs and this one had already been adjourned several times. Whatever the private thoughts a wildlife officer or for that matter, a CPS solicitor may have on badger abuse, however strongly one feels about wildlife conservation, such cases cannot be given top priority especially when money is limited. The Essex CPS had already that year lost a case of interference to a sett by hunt employees; to lose another might adversely affect the chances of the next.

My court experience over the years has taught me a very hard lesson; trials often have little to do with justice. When people state that the British legal system is the best, I shudder for the rest of the world though I am not a cynic, far from it. The one bright spot on the horizon that day as I saw it, was the leader and older of the two men who was a compulsive talker. He couldn't help showing off his knowledge, even in his statement. Nowadays all such statements must be recorded on tape and may be played back in court, although as it happened, this proved unnecessary. Yes, he had told the wildlife officer he knew all about foxes, rabbits and badgers, indeed, before the first Badger Act 1973, he had put badgers into this very sett. He denied the sett was badger-occupied at the time of the offence, but here both the group's careful records, the police photos and the badger hairs picked up and retained from a nearby spoil heap amongst the freshly turned-out earth and bedding, proved otherwise. Soon after the case started, both men were advised by their solicitors to change their plea to one of 'guilty' and the charge of causing a dog to enter the sett would be dropped. This they agreed to do and the court resumed the hearing. So determined was the voluble man to put his case (one could almost hear his solicitor sigh), that unusually, he was granted his demand to go into the witness box to do so. This man had previous convictions for burglary and theft; he was a registered drug addict too, awaiting trial on a drugs-related charge. (His friend had a history of illegal hare coursing, drink-driving and assault.) As the law stood at that time, however, none of this could be disclosed to the magistrates. Only related offences might be read out to influence the sentencing and this was the first time either man had been detected committing any breach of the Badger Acts.

Why when warned that day by two members of the badger group that this was an active badger sett had he and his companion returned and dug into it? Oh, he knew he should have requested a licence from MAFF to dig into the sett and retrieve his dog that had accidentally gone into it, but he wasn't waiting around. He had applied heaps of times for licences in the past and never had a reply. Earlier, the CPS solicitor had contacted the Ministry who referred him to ADAS, their department dealing with licences. He was told that when a licence is requested (and only one in Essex had been asked for since the Act), the ADAS representative immediately went on site with the dog owner to make sure a dog was still underground and the circumstances were not suspicious. If the latter, he must inform the police and the RSPCA although the dog's welfare was still important. In any case, it was his job to monitor the sett and decide if badgers were present. If he was certain there were no badgers involved, the sett could be dug to retrieve the dog, but if he was in any doubt at all about sett occupation he would leave the sett untouched for 24–48 hours. Then with himself and an RSPCA official present the sett would be carefully opened. On a change of tactics the terrier-man went on to say he was an ardent conservationist and loved nothing better than walking in the countryside with his dogs. What, with two spades, a fork, nets, locators, penicillin, disinfectant and ligature for stitching his dog's wounds? (The bag containing these had been discovered by yet another member of the badger group concealed inside a hollow tree some way from the sett.) Oh, you never knew if you might come across a fox on a walk and the dogs run it to ground. Perhaps it was not surprising that the chairman of the bench stated: 'We take this matter extremely seriously. The bench feel you were deliberately out to find or locate a badger.' The case was adjourned for a month for the magistrates to confer with the Probation Service and consider a custodial sentance. Thank heavens for a garrulous defendant and a concerned CPS solicitor, or the outcome might have been very different.*

Before leaving for Scotland, I enjoyed an owl watch near my village home. The previous October I had seen a barn owl harassed by a number of black-headed gulls one morning at first light. It was flying low following the hedge that bordered the road in an effort to evade its tormentors. This owl was one of a pair that roosted in an old barn belonging to a farmhouse nearby. They

* The younger, less involved man was ordered to do 150 hours community service and pay £300 prosecution costs. The ringleader was told: 'You went equipped, you are well acquainted with the area, you knew it was a badger sett and you know the law, therefore we have no recourse but to sentence you to three months in prison.' He was also banned from owning any dog for three years. This last would affect him considerably as he owned twenty-eight dogs and bred working terriers which he sold at shows. It was at such a show, the court had been told, that he met his companion. All the equipment seized was forfeited.

hunted over the fields and a clearing in a wood created by open-cast mining. This last was on several levels surrounded by trees and a fascinating place in its own right; the barn owls were an added bonus. The levels had been worked for the extraction of clay used in the making of bricks and part was still dug. Most however, was in process of reclamation by sallow, alder and cherry – a wet woodland containing a pond, foxes and many small birds. Those loveliest of catkins, the male goat willow, were gently opening in a yellow, pollen-filled haze. Each multi-stemmed, shrubby tree would soon be smothered in gold, providing the bees with pollen and nectar when flowers were still scarce. More recently excavated levels had grown a covering of grasses, foxglove, mullein and campion, a site ideal for the watchful owls in their quest for voles and other small mammals. With their long, sweeping glides and deceptively slow, silent wing beats, these ghostly hunters of the night fared well and gave me great pleasure. I picked up a roe deer antler on my way home that morning; it was nearly perfect. So often cast antlers are chewed down almost to nothing by rabbits and the deer themselves, it is believed as a source of calcium. Later that year I was to watch young fox cubs on the levels, fed not only by their parents, but by another young vixen too. She was possibly a daughter from the previous year's litter, her breeding ability suppressed by the socially dominant mother.

I returned to the north on a gloriously sunny day to find the first flush of lambs already born in the home pastures and curlews, meadow pipits, wheatears, a stonechat and sweetest of all, the skylarks' bubbling songs calling over the shieling. The hills were a living exultation. Even the wind seemed muted as if listening to the avian band and their vibrant promise. A pair of grey wagtails traced the course of the fast-flowing burn as oystercatchers called on their way to the loch. Entering the woodshed I disturbed a stock dove investigating the rafters with speculative intent. Not so Dratsie and her cubs however, whose utter disregard for my presence gave me great joy.

That first time I actually saw one of her offspring, the mother was away. I had gone to the woodshed to fetch coal only to forget my errand at the sight of a tiny, grey, silky-furred creature crawling at the holt entrance. Its progress was slow and undetermined, the prominent eyes still closed and the muzzle short and square. It moved in a 'flattened-out' way lacking ability to rise up on its legs or lift its head as it uttered tiny twittering sounds. I had heard these often enough coming from the holt when Dratsie was home. Now tiring of this, the wee creature yawned prodigiously showing a bright pink tongue and toothless gums, then slowly keeled over revealing equally pink pads. At this moment the reason for its exploration returned and grasped unceremoniously by the scruff, it was bundled inside.

Dratsie had greatly improved on the holt during my absence in England. She had dug and burrowed until the old stacked bales must have been as complex as a small badger sett. Her complete acceptance of my living so near her family dared me to put up two mirrors loaned by Will when she was next out hunting. I climbed the ancient ladder left permanently against the wall and found a place where hay had fallen away to reveal part of the nursery chamber. It was probably the warmth of the stove beyond the wall and the general gloom of the shed that had caused her to leave the hole and not reseal it. By positioning one mirror above and the other at an angle much nearer the floor, I could actually see inside the chamber, yet remain well away and out of sight. The first time a few days later she moved her cubs, I was convinced that in some way, instinctively perhaps, she had sensed there was a watcher. It took me a while to realize she was constantly moving her charges back and forth, from one room as it were to another. Nonetheless, they repeatedly returned to the 'mirrored' nursery and I was able to monitor their progress. I have wondered since whether in a less restricted landscape where there is plenty of scope beneath rocks, in hollows and amongst tree roots, a nursing bitch might have several individual holts within a short distance to which she would move her young for safety's sake? Certainly the moves were not due to fear or cleanliness, for like badger, fox, dog and cat mothers, she first licked their tummies and anal regions after a feed to stimulate defecation then ate the resulting faeces. She would hold them firmly down on their backs to do this and even at such an early age their little tails would wave as they obliged!

My first surprise was that Dratsie had three cubs as two is far more common. One was large; it was this stronger one I had seen crawling and later on I discovered it was the only male. At this tender age, the family was still being suckled with no solid food. Working back from the date when I had first heard cub sounds, they were now three weeks old. (That their eyes would not open until four to five weeks reinforced this.) Left to themselves the cubs were silent and I saw from their mirror reflections that they slept the hours away. Dratsie's return heralded a bird-like chirping as they searched blindly through her belly fur for a nipple. Once found and secured, each suckled lustily, tails wagging as vigorously as the lambs drinking from their dams in the valley below. I have watched nursing fox cubs paw-kneading their mother's belly to stimulate the milk flow and these little otters did the same, though Dratsie never became bald and sore around her teats as vixens so often do. Sometimes one would fall asleep still anchored firmly to her belly only to be rudely awakened with much plaintive 'piping', rolled over and thoroughly washed. With all her family full and sleeping she would curl herself around them and sleep herself. In those early weeks she never left them for long, only to satisfy her hunger further down the burn. It wasn't only fish that fed her.

One morning by chance as I approached the steading, there was Dratsie finishing off nestling rabbits dug up from their nursery hole. Will came to watch the cubs fresh from the sheep with the sweet smell of lambing all about him. Already the otters' fur was beginning to darken and it was comic to notice one eye opening whilst the other was still shut! He was amused to find what I had done with his mirrors (surely Will hadn't thought I wished to see myself – never a pleasant sight at the best of times!) Two days later he fetched another and by a clever adjustment we now had a finer, more detailed view inside the holt.

It was good to watch at the Burn Sett again with its background of tumbling waters and rising spray. Spring had arrived here and caught me unawares, primroses opening on its craggy walls and pink purslane brightening the boggy places. Everywhere were signs of badger activity and it was scarcely dark before the clan themselves appeared. Millie's wickering greeting, prolonged and loud, was flattery itself, until I guessed from her snuffling of my hands and pockets that she recalled a certain tin of dog food of a past encounter! With an easy heave she was on my lap reminding me of happier times with Kentish badgers before their demise. A large rough, hairy back pressed against my face as its owner turned and settled herself more comfortably; a warm cloying smell of milk told me she was lactating too. Spike, Grace, Disgrace, Neddy and C. Goon were all present, though Spike seemed suddenly to have aged, shuffling and shrunken. Neddy and C. Goon I saw were well aware of this from their aggressive and assertive attitude towards the old boar. How much longer would Spike remain dominant?

Once the clan went off on its separate ways to forage, I left the shelter belt to walk Dydor's dark hump. Already many geese had departed for their breeding grounds on Europe's moors and tundra. Soon all would be gone. A love-lorn wind sighed as it ruffled the sprouting heather, touching my face with faint, warm breath. There was a special companionship impossible to describe on the Dark Hill. Content to stay and watch the lower braes I sat on its shaggy slopes unaware of a leveret below me in its form. Only as the first straying fingers of day lightened the sky, did the approach of its mother to suckle it, cause me to see the tiny figure, so well camouflaged in its resting place amongst the grass. Her stay was brief as she crouched over her hungry offspring before a leisurely move away where I believe another leveret was waiting concealed. A slow skein of calling geese flew slanting across the delicate sunrise, punctuating my downward way to the lochan hidden below.

It was on my next visit to the sett one early morning that I saw Cudoun in the pool. Although Will had made me promise to wake him whatever the time when I next saw the burn dog in the steading area, I did so with some hesitation knowing how busy this season was for the shepherd. I need not have worried. Will was out and following me down the rocky slope in a matter of minutes and once above the stretch of open water, we both had the greatest surprise. I had left one otter industriously fishing; now there were two though neither had thoughts of food. They dived – there was a pause as the water above them churned a sea of white foam – then surfaced locked together in a writhing, twisting mass. We might have been forgiven for believing they were fighting, so turbulent their movements, but this was no display of agression, it was play. The smaller figure shallow dived and emerged onto the far bank whickering an excited invitation and I saw it was Dratsie. Cudoun chased her up and down the bare slope beneath the trees and when his lumbering gallop tired, she was there to nip him into chasing her once more. Puffing and calling, pounding and wriggling, their ungainly humped figures came and went amongst the tall straight trunks. Back in the water, the element they best suited, the streamlined bodies tossed, turned, dived and rose high in unison above the frothing surface. Will was asking had I seen this before – no need for silence now – and I could only shake my head in wonder. Suddenly it was over. Cudoun came out and groomed himself as if by some unseen signal and Dratsie humped along the bank following the burn upstream, probably homeward bent.

Back in Will's kitchen we discussed the otters' playfulness in the light of what we had both read, that is, except as a prelude to mating adults are solitary creatures and tend to avoid rather than play together. All I could say with certainty was the female had been Dratsie; I knew her so well now. And she would not be mating, unlike her relative the badger who mates soon after the birth of cubs, but through the process of delayed implantation will not give birth again until the following year. As otter cubs can be born at any time however, do bitches ovulate monthly? If so, this play could perhaps be sexual in origin, though not consummated. The only other meeting I had witnessed between otters had been Cudoun and the Wild Way bitch with her cubs. Then there had been no play.*

A snipe was displaying over the shieling; his resonant, quavering hum filled the air. There were many very young rabbits on the lower slopes and shelter belts. Possibly the mild weather had encouraged this. It was common to find a rabbit nursery dug into, contents gone and fur scattered here and there. Badgers tend to dig directly down, whilst foxes usually follow the line of the tunnel. Those young rabbits newly above ground suffered the attentions of predators also, including the owls, due to the newly emerged nestling's instinct to crouch down rather than run to earth.

Perhaps it was fortunate that neither Robbie nor Eileen had the faintest interest in the otter family for too many strange visitors might have disturbed Dratsie. Robbie did confirm, however, that the shieling hay bales in the past had been dug into by a large animal, though never before in their present position. It would seem from this that the hay stacked against the adjoining wall had been chosen for the warmth from the stove. The cubs continued to grow although as they grew older so the difference in their size became more marked. As is usual with litter mates, the larger was the most dominant. They could lift their heads now and with eyes well open and better co-ordinated movements, came the first signs of play. No longer did they merely eat and sleep and the bird-like chirrups were changing to a high-pitched piping, forerunner of the adult 'whistle.' It was not uncommon when their mother was gone, to see one (often the larger male), tentatively exploring the tunnels and they could be quite noisy. This demonstrated how

* Since writing this, Bridget and Don MacCaskill have published their excellent book *On the Swirl of the Tide* describing similar play situations.

vulnerable small cubs can be in their natural environment. I'm not sure when Dratsie began to return with fish for them to try, but I saw her take one in when they were eight weeks old. All this time they had become more and more active, their soft silky coats changing to a dense woolly chocolate and even the timorous smallest one had stuck her ridiculous, chunky muzzle out into the big, gloomy world of the woodshed, though she hastily changed her mind and retreated. What would she make of the wide, open moor?

I finished the washing one morning, hanging it up to drip inside the shieling near the badger pen and well out of the way of my living quarters, lest I make them wet too. Although I could now use my left arm, I had been warned not to carry anything heavy with it. At present there was little strength in the hand either which meant that I still could not wring out wet clothes. Emptying the last of the rinsing water into the privy as usual, I heard the cubs playing from the depths of their home in the bales and wondered not for the first time, whether all Dratsie's previous litters had survived. If so, one would expect a higher otter density surely? Apart from natural accidents and those on roads and in snares, I imagine people's dogs off lead would pose the greatest threat to young growing otters in the summer months. I suspected too that Dratsie of necessity would journey down to live on the lower slopes with her family soon to hunt in the well-stocked waters there. This part of the hills was isolated, but that above the village was popular not only with residents, but with tourists and weekenders from the city. I recalled the factor's words and the roe deer that suffered predation from walkers' dogs.

Housework over I walked up to Craiglee and stood awhile enjoying the vista of wispy clouds in a blue sky and the procession of hill tops, some gently undulating, some rugged or cone-like. The old stone cottage nestling deep into the heather below me was bathed in soft sunlight, mellowing its rough walls. I walked the ridge – no paths or tracks in this landscape – to the sound of the meadow pipits' 'pheet-pheet' flight calls so reminiscent of the little otters back home. This was the 'go-baks' noisiest season, already some hen grouse were incubating their eggs; another fortnight and all would be doing so. At a distance a cock leapt into the air, spreading his wings as he descended steeply, challenging a rival intruder with his barking call. Often those that fail to establish a good heather-clad territory will be killed by predators or disease.

The hillside dropped to scree and great boulders with a wide verdant carpet winding through. That green was too vivid, too inviting to be grass, so the scree way it would have to be, avoiding the bog. The going was slow across the broken rocks where glacial orange and grey lichened boulders were littered as if by a giant's hand. Old bones lay here, some with the wool still attached and high above black shapes flapped and warned, birds of ill omen. Now the ground rose up ever higher into heather-clad slopes so that briefly I turned round to trace my route far below in the sunlight before I found myself in cloud as thick and wetting as any mist. Not even a crow cawed here, no sound nor sight, only the clinging grey. I must continue up to the summit, then descend into the next valley and hopefully, visibility again. And so it was. Halfway down the traverse the cloud thinned allowing the faintest warmth to my soaked hair and clothes. A few more metres, a shaft of light to pierce the grey and the last wisps of cloud drifted, laggards consumed by a golden sun.

A map was spread out below me, light sparkled on the end of the loch that I knew so well, green pasture and grey ruined steading until descending further, I beheld tiny white dots strewn daisy-like on the green; the first of the ewes with their lambs driven to the foothills and the spring pasture. Bathed in steam that rose up in the welcome warmth to ease my involuntary shivering, the birdsong was a joyous echo of myself as I beheld the scene below, my clothes drying as I walked. The first family groups I reached were playing in the sun, bouncy and skipping, frisky as any young creatures, but always at this age, close to the heavy, reassuring bodies of their dams. Sandpipers staked their claims to the gravel edges of loch and burn, their musical 'twi-wi-wi-wees' punctuated by bleats and the oystercatchers' piping calls. It was pleasant to linger at the margins as the birds asserted their rights to their respective breeding grounds and the day slowly ebbed from the sky. A haze of insects, mainly midges, swarmed over the water and a sharp little wind sprang up diffusing the last of the warmth. It lifted the pines' stately branches and my hair as I past. A rabbit thumped a warning and was gone in a flash of white scut, but its cousin the hare merely stood tall, long ears a-turning, wild amber eyes ever watchful. A fine, thin moon proceeded me, seeming to hang on the topmost tree as I bent to enter the deeper darkness beneath the sitka belt.

Three grey shapes were already leaving as I reached their sett. I couldn't have said with certainty which badgers they were. My concern was growing for Spike's welfare so I was cross with myself for not coming earlier, if indeed, he was still denning here. A cock pheasant called stridently against the subdued background of baas and continually tumbling waters. I had nearly begun to move convinced I was too late to see more, when something white flickered and was gone at a further entrance. Minutes went by and it came again. A soft, gently-rounded face peeped out, to be jostled protesting by another. Millie's cubs were taking a look at the world outside whilst mum was away! They were about eight weeks old judging by their slow, unsteady movements over the earth of the spoil heap and their myopic gaze. Though the grey baby fur was still fluffy and would remain so for a week or two longer, there was no mistaking those beautifully striped faces for anything other than badgers; even to the white-tipped ears they were faithful replicas of their kind. One bumped into the other uttering a whickering twitter, so like the young otters' contact call of a few weeks earlier. Indeed, seeing badger cubs again, the similarities of the two species were most marked especially as very young brockies tend to have tails rather out of proportion to their body size, though in a month's time this would be less noticeable as the body grows at a faster rate.

Full of thoughts and pleasure at seeing Millie's offspring and with memories of her successful convalescence at the shieling, I didn't at first notice the vixen also watching her young neighbours. It was the movement as she crouched lower to the needle-strewn floor that caught my eye. This was a reversal of that scene so many years ago when an old boar badger ate a vixen's litter. There was no mistaking the fox's intent as she crept forward, eyes and senses fixed on the prey that would feed her and her cubs. Normally I would never intervene. Nature survives on catch-as-catch-can; one death is another's life however it may seem to us. But Millie's cubs! One could almost feel sorry for that vixen, for as I sprang up shouting, so she bounded up too with shock and fear in a flurry of debris and brush streaming after disappeared down the slope to the burn. I sat on until their mother returned, her snout and white mask muddied from worming. The sudden charge of fear emitted from the fox's scent glands was gone to my sense of smell, but it seemed from the anxious way she picked up and briefly followed the vixen's trail that Millie's nose had told her the story. Now she hastened below, her family's eager trilling for milk at their mother's appearance, a reassurance that all was well. It occurred to me that this sound made by the very young cub is peculiar to the badger only and has considerable carrying power. If the nursing sow is killed as often happens on our roads, hungry cubs may come above ground uttering this cry, surprisingly loud for such a tiny creature, intended as it is to guide the mother to her distressed infant.

Night passed away and I was still at the Burn sett, but although I waited well into the morning, no Spike returned home. The others were all present. Neddy was nervous of C. Goon and by the bites on his rump above the tail, it would appear they had been fighting. A subdued, dishevelled Neddy went to earth, probably to lick his wounds, whilst C. Goon came to me whickering, then backed onto and musked my boots. The pale sun rose like a full moon, striving to banish the early mist. Two cock pheasants quarrelled on the pasture. The victor chased the other through the cropped grass. Heads jerking, long tails flowing, the two gaudy birds rushed by on leaping legs till the vanquished gained a safe haven in the shelter belt, leaving the conqueror to strut like some gorgeous farmyard cock, to and fro, to and fro, proclaiming herself lord of his territory. The ewes and lambs took scant notice; neither did the rabbits. The sun too had won its battle with the mist as golden beams sought out the last grey still lingering in the sunken places and glittered on the iridescent beauty of the big bird displaying there. Suddenly to my amusement, that pheasant was chasing the rabbits. First one was pursued to the fence, then back came the pheasant to rout another. Once he caught up with a fleeing coney, pecking it repeatedly so that it squealed and with a last, frantic burst of speed, disappeared into the safety of the nettles. Now the sheep were watching and alert, one ewe leaving her companions to investigate this interesting spectacle, her little bleating lamb trailing after. The pheasant who was standing chest out and triumphantly calling received a rude shock as the big, woolly figure stood over him. With a loud whirr of wings and flash of colour he flew up into the trees to continue his proclamation from there!

One of the collies came up for a fuss as I entered the yard. Lambing was over now with a few of the late-born still with their dams in the home pasture. Tomorrow would begin the slow drive up into the hills with both sheepdogs and shepherd away long hours. Will called me to see the hens housed in an outbuilding. They weren't many but all were good layers, although for the last few days the egg yield had unaccountably dropped and the hens themselves seemed very nervous. Sandy's dog Jacko had flushed a stoat ten minutes earlier and the brothers were debating whether this was the culprit. The number of missing eggs seemed large so I wondered if the stoat had hidden any. I began moving oddments nearby but it was Jacko himself who nosed out five tucked under a stone lintel! When we looked closely (aided again by the terrier's nose) we saw there were fragments of shell here and there, although the hidden eggs were unbroken – indeed, they were unmarked. Stoats and weasels may pierce eggs with their teeth and carry them that way but seem to prefer rolling them along with their nose where possible. Careful investigation revealed a small tunnel dug under the run; either musteline could have used it. Sight of those eggs reminded my stomach it had not eaten for nearly twenty-four hours, so as we remedied that in the kitchen I brought Will up to date with the badgers. He was sorry about Spike having known and watched him as a cub, nine or ten years ago. Was the old boar dead or banished to the Mound? I would try watching there and let the shepherd know.

We came out of the cottage to find a pair of robins on the drystane dyke loudly scolding a farm cat who was standing with lashing tail to face us. Just in time we saw the tiny fluttering at our feet, the feline was grasped without ceremony and shut indoors. It was early here for fledgling robins, but this tiny speckled one was fully feathered except for its lack of tail. Driving off, we saw the parents now on the ground feeding their offspring who gaped and fluttered. Hopefully, they would lead it well out of harm's way before the other cats found it. Will dropped me at the hill steading where I had a further surprise – a cuckoo was calling. It was only the second one I had heard in all my time in Scotland. Eileen assured me it (or its descendants) returned year after year; only when they heard the call did the couple feel spring really had come to these hills. I stayed awhile with them out of courtesy – I saw so little of Eileen and Robbie normally – but in truth, was very tired by now. Walking home some time later I found to my annoyance that I was falling asleep as I went along in the warmth of a lovely morning; the 5 km uphill stretch seemed so much further today. At long last Craiglee loomed ahead and nearly at my door, I came across six olive-green, mottled eggs beautifully camouflaged amongst the heather and stole inside smiling – the grouse were busy too!

For three days and nights it poured. The fierce wind blew grey drifts of rain across the hills crying mournfully round the eaves and howling down the ravines like some creature in dreadful torment. It mattered little to the frolicsome cubs within my woodshed who scampered back and forth, in and out of the bales, knocking over and cannoning into the paraphernalia gathering dust there, squabbling and squeaking as they went. The favoured play area was my diminishing coal heap. Fortunately for them, all the fuel I had left now was the porous grey boiler nuggets or their coats would have been a permanent sooty black. It never ceased to amaze me how much they took my presence for granted. In pursuit of a sibling, my feet would be scrambled over as they chased, pounced, rolled, nipped and whickered. I was anxious that they should not become friendly towards me, so only entered the old lean-to when driven by necessity. It seemed wise to keep the privy covered since it appeared to be positioned over a pit of unfathomable depth. An inquisitive cub that fell in would never get out.

The noise of romping cubs was nothing compared to Dratsie bringing home a meal. The larger male would grab the nearest part of the fish dragging it away with growls and huffs, whilst his smaller sisters clung grimly on to fin or tail. Something would generally give with cubs tumbling over and over only to return and pull off a portion too. Dratsie would leave them to it as she sat a little apart scratching vigorously at her face and chin to rid the fur of sticky scales. Then outside she would roll to rub herself on the tussocky grass, first one side, then the other and finally squirming on her back with legs flailing the air; a last long shake would set her coat smooth. Back in the shed the only sounds now were of teeth on flesh and bone with occasionally, the comic hiccuping of a too greedy diner with a piece that had 'gone down the wrong way'! The overwhelming smell now was of fish from the remains of scales, skin, bones and the occasional head left where the prey had been squabbled over with the choicer parts eaten. These I could gently take away when the coast was clear and assign to the heart of the fiery stove. The cubs' spraints were another matter. Now they defecated outside the holt and Dratsie in common with other mammal mothers, no longer ate them. Somehow it seemed wrong to remove these too for surely this was also a marking of the family home? I made the most of the otters for shortly I knew, they would be gone.

Spike was living at the Mound. Early one morning his shuffling shape appeared above the fresh greenery of nettles, bedstraw and shepherd's purse. I spoke softly as the small, rheumy eyes looked my way. He came to snuffle my hair as I sat, arms around knees, back against the broken, rotting trunk of an old birch. It seemed from his unmarked head and body that he had voluntarily left his clan perhaps sensing his time was past, rather than defending his status within the group. There was no shortage of good foraging here. From his muddied snout it was evident that the old boar had returned from worming in the horses' fields over the way. Hopefully, he would live out his last days in peace. I scratched behind his ears, first the left then the spiky torn right, speaking gently all the while. He sat down heavily (on my foot!) and with much satisfied grunting, began to scratch.

Once Spike must have ousted the dominant boar to take its place as head of the clan. The wheel had turned full circle; now his time was come.

I returned home myself via the Burn sett for the sheer pleasure of watching the thundering waters swollen by the recent rains. They had opened the dainty pink bell-shaped bilberry blooms half smothered in bright green leaves. The moor was a living carpet of birds and plants with moisture glistening in a bright sun. Tiny flowers speckled my way with here and there the common butterwort's sticky leaves like pale green starfish, each waiting to curl round and trap any insect foolish enough to rest on its inviting surface. Some metres still from the shieling I came in sight of the slide on the bank that Dratsie had made during the snow to gain easy access to the burn. Three small figures and a larger one were there before me; the sounds of their play came loud on the clear air. Already the family was creating its own trails winding in and out of the grass and heath; the slide was muddy from recent use. This hadn't been so when I left home in the night so their mother was probably giving her youngsters their first experience of water.

It was an excellent place, neither deep nor wide. How they enjoyed themselves with Dratsie joining in too. I'm sure the bitch knew exactly what she was doing for even as I stood there she led the game farther into the burn. From paddling on the bottom, without fully realizing it they were out of their depth, their little legs dog paddling up and down. The air trapped in their still fluffy coats kept them bobbing about like apples in a bowl of water, each vying to reach mother's broad back in a wet, king-of-the-castle romp. How I regretted that broken camera; it was such a perfect scene. The male cub gained the high spot and tipped his sister off with a splash whereupon she found herself out of her depth, crying with sudden fright as her legs instinctively pumped up and down. Made fearful in turn by her sister's cries, the smallest began piping too as she clung on to mother's fur. Big brother growled and nipped her to release her hold – he was in possession. So Dratsie rolled over sending him in head first and little'un scrambled onto her stomach! I stole away home and left them to it. Although I heard them later that day in the woodshed, by the next they had gone, almost certainly under cover of darkness. How empty the place was without them, yet how fortunate and privileged I had been to have Dratsie and family so close. Only a hunch last autumn made me rent the shieling. Intuition had told me the bitch would overwinter nearby, but I might so easily have been wrong. Never could I have guessed in my wildest dreams that she would have cubs in my shed!

My own time here was drawing to a close. Though I hoped I might see the otter family once more before leaving, for their own good I had no intention of seeking them out. What I was most determined to do was check Spike and his well-being. Since he seemed so pleased to see me each time, musking my shoes and using me as an inanimate object against which to groom, grunting and snuffling as he did so like the old man he was, this gave me great pleasure. I duly relayed his progress, together with that of the

Burn Badgers and cubs, to Will and Sandy. Cudoun came and went, Millie's boisterous two regarding the big dog at first nervously, until interest and curiosity got the better of them. Both were sows, much too large to be taken by any prospecting fox now – that brief time was long past.

One night there was no Spike though I waited until the sun was high in the sky, hoping to see the greenery waving as he passed through. I stood on the highest point of the nettle-clad Mound idly looking out for some sign of my old friend; was he sick, perhaps dead somewhere below my feet? The boar had become so slow and ponderous of late – this could well have been so. A young woman arrived to feed and water her horse in the far field, but none came to her calling. Like her I became aware of all four horses grouped together nearer my end of the meadow, all looking down; one pawed at something in the grass. I dropped off the Mound and ducked under the wire with a sudden premonition. Whether Spike had simply died while foraging or been kicked, there was no way of telling for he bore no mark. He looked so peaceful lying there and somehow younger, as if he had merely lain down to sleep. I stroked a velvety muzzle and another slobbered over the back of my neck. Together the woman and I carried him to the back of the sett away from the horses' attentions. Will was out on the hills when I arrived at the steading, but Sandy drove the truck down to bring the old warrior home.

He told me a stoat had been trapped in the chickens' run so the egg thief was confirmed. The farmer queried why the hens themselves had not been attacked and I recalled how years ago in our back garden something similar had occurred with a weasel. My children kept guinea pigs and rabbits housed in two large wire runs on the lawn. One late afternoon we watched a weasel run through the wire of a run and out the other side in pursuit of . . . our dog's fresh, large marrow bone left on the grass! It tore at the bone (several times its own size) causing it to rock whilst the occupants of the runs stood paralysed with fear. For perhaps ten minutes the weasel tore pieces off and ate them, then returned the way it had come like a small brown dart straight through both sides of the wire mesh. Undoubtedly it was aware of the animals crouched there but wasn't interested, although a neighbour's pet rabbit wasn't so fortunate. It would seem that the smell of the bone was more stimulating, just as the eggs were to the stoat.

Will appeared and stood looking down at the old badger. My main reason for moving Spike had been to get the body away from prying eyes as well as the horses; it would soon begin to smell too in this warm, sunny weather. Nevertheless I was glad the shepherd seemed to take burying it for granted, but I had overlooked the fact that digging is largely impossible here; a short distance down and one strikes rock. The brothers conferred and agreed on a site by Hoolit cottage where the earth was deep. So Spike was laid to rest in the place he knew so well, close to his old home. Sandy reminded me how the boar had come to Hoolit when I lived there. He was still convinced Spike visited me. I had to smile at the improbability of the thought, although the farmer was sincere enough.

I would be leaving Scotland at the end of the week. There were notes to finish, especially on the otters and packing to do, but the rest of the time was my own. By day I walked the hills and saw that the grouse chicks were able to flutter and even fly at a very early age with wings developed well before the rest of their feathers. The moor's many predators made this vital if any were going to survive. The lambs in their chunky wool coats were growing fast. Like high-spirited school children they gathered in groups to play, chasing, butting, with a convenient rock as king-of-the castle, that universal game. Their dams grazed, stolid and comfortable. It was hard to imagine some ewes had ever been so frivolous as to play. Without warning a lamb would detach itself from the group and bending slightly, drink lustily from its mother. The action transmitted to the rest, sending them scurrying home thirstily too. Dydor still cast his spell. It seemed impossible to walk in any other direction. Clouds touched his smooth back and slid off to allow others to follow. The sight was a reassurance and a promise; the hills would always endure. How many times had I looked and seen him – I will lift up mine eyes unto the hills.

By night I followed the burn from its source, sometimes to the Robertsons' land, occasionally the further journey to the Cley. C. Goon had become the clan's dominant boar so completely, Spike might never have been. Yet he had passed his genes to these his sons and daughters; he had fulfilled himself. The king is dead; long live the king. The badger cubs spent much of their time in play, two little sows that seemed as inseparable as shadows chased in and out of the trunks, or greatly daring, ventured down to the great tumbling waters whose noise dominated their life. Splashing in the shallows quickly graduated to splashing each other. King-of-the-castle is even more fun it would seem on a wet rock from which you can give your sister a ducking! I returned from the river one morning at first light to find the sows playing and stood behind a tree to watch. A slight mist reluctantly lingered; the thundering backcloth of water hid any sound. I was puzzled. Surely there were more than two? One on the rock – three in the margins and the one silhouetted above the others had a long rudder-like tail!

It was apparent that Dratsie's offspring had played with the badgers before. There was no sign of nervousness, though the otters were older and larger. Now they were out of the water chasing up through the ferns to a great clump of red campion, the deeply pink flowers still lightly encased in the bud. They were very near me and away from the torrent I could hear their noise, whickering and growling, squeaking and pounding as they rolled and pounced in a whirl of bodies, too fast for my eyes to mark an individual. Sometimes an otter tail would detach itself waving, at others a black and white face might show an instant and be gone. Suddenly the game ceased; one sow beneath an otter, another with paw raised to clout – all frozen and silent. A rustle and Millie was there. Reassured the five relaxed, the otters to wash or search about for titbits under a stone in the boggy places amongst the pink purslane, the sows to go their mother who whickered gently as she sniffed them. The dog otter cub approached her with nose raised, then retreated and approached again. Her cubs looked towards him and jostled her jealously. Millie watched the other quietly above their heads and whickered. I thought again how alike both species are with this 'friendly' call. Greatly daring, the young otter came forward and the twins, I could tell, were a trifle put out as a small bewhiskered muzzle raised up within centimetres of Millie's broad snout. This really was too much for the sisters who pounced on their erstwhile playmate, bundling him for his liberty. Their mother now found herself the focal point for a game of chase as round and round and under her they went, the combined weight and energy of the three nearly sending her flying. Hastily she made off home up the steep bank and left the hooligans to it.

Badger cubs not infrequently will play with young foxes until a certain stage in their development, when each species goes its own way. Foxes develop a very pungent odour which I suspect has a lot to do with this termination. How long would the twins retain their friendship with Dratsie's litter? Probably any such mingling between young creatures is a tenuous association that fades with time and the need to learn the basics of survival.

The otters had heard something. Either my ears had missed it or it was a call too high for human hearing. They stopped in mid-act and calling loudly, bounded upstream, their humped shapes ungainly over the rough ground. Dratsie would not bring a fish to them when badgers were nearby. The goldcrest called its high-pitched song. He and his mate had built a nest of fine moss, tiny feathers and cobwebs and slung it from handles like a fairy basket below a sitka branch. A sunbeam stole into the morning as I took the path through the trees and a squirrel scolded me soundly for surprising him at his meal. Nearly out of the shelter belt something caused me to pause, peering through the sitka dimness to the light of the ravine where the burn raced. Someone sprainted amongst the needles, tail up and waving. Three small brown shapes imitated her to perfection and at once I guessed where the family had their new home. Now I took the long way round to the far bank dropping silently down to the water's edge where two years ago I had seen my first Scottish badgers, Millie and her offspring nervously crossing the burn. A movement above and beyond the stream caught my eye; that mysterious cleft high up in the rocks was Dratsie's new holt.

The mist was quite gone as I finally turned homeward. Dew sparkled on every grass blade and the bluebells' opening flowers. I tarried awhile enjoying the scene, the loch's depths reflected blue from the sky above, the calls of birds and sheep and Dydor like some great sentinel keeping guard over all. How I would miss this place, the people and its wildlife, but above all I would miss these hills. What the future held there was no way of knowing, yet one thing was sure. Gazing at the Dark Hill that morning, I vowed to return.